the JOY
of
MEDJUGORJE

A Collection of My Greatest Medjugorje Stories,
Moments, Memories and More

WAYNE WEIBLE

Author of Internationally Best-selling Books
on the Apparitions of the Blessed Virgin Mary at Medjugorje

The Joy of Medjugorje

First Printing: October 2017
Copyright 2017 by Wayne Weible
ISBN 978-0-9969616-2-2
Library of Congress Control Number: 2017916602

Printed by:
New Hope Press
Hiawassee, Georgia

Website: www.newhopepresspub.com
Email: judith@newhopepresspub.com
Published in the United States of America

Edited by Judith Weible
Typesetting and Cover Design by Janice Stallings
Front Cover photo: Dani Photography and Cinematography
Back Cover photo: Brooke Swanson

OTHER BOOKS BY WAYNE WEIBLE

Medjugorje: The Message (Paraclete Press, 1989)
Letters from Medjugorje (Paraclete Press, 1991)
Medjugorje: The Mission (Paraclete Press, 1993)
The Final Harvest (Paraclete Press, 1999)
Final Harvest Revised (CMJ Marian Publications, 2003)
A Child Shall Lead Them (Paraclete Press, 2005)
Medjugorje: The Message (Hard cover edition Paraclete Press, 2006)
The Medjugorje Prayer Book (Paraclete Press, 2007)
Are the Medjugorje Apparitions Authentic?
Co-authored with Dr. Mark Miravalle (New Hope Press, 2008)
The Medjugorje Fasting Book (New Hope Press, 2010)
Medjugorje: The Last Apparition (New Hope Press, 2013)
Medjugorje and the Eucharist (New Hope Press, 2014)
Intimate Messages From Heaven (New Hope Press, 2016)

ACKNOWLEDGEMENTS

I've learned over the years as an author that you don't write a book by yourself. It takes help, especially by those closest to you who will tell you the truth and not worry about your ego. I'm fortunate in that my wife and best friend is also my editor. And a very good one at that. Judith meticulously goes over the manuscript numerous times to assure not only the grammar and structure are correct but that the book is worthy of publication and reading. The last point is vitally important; I never have nor want to write for reasons other than inspiration from Heaven. Judith assures that I stick to that measure. I am forever grateful for her assistance and sometimes-necessary brutal honesty.

One other very valuable person who brings the books to life is my graphics designer, Janice Stallings. She manages to give every book just the right look from the covers to the content. I first met Janice in Medjugorje and she kindly offered to help me with the graphics of my books. I immediately said yes, sensing the Blessed Virgin Mary meant for us to work together. She has been terrific.

Of course, without you, the readers and your support, my writing would be a useless exercise in futility. From the bottom of my heart, thank you!

All scriptural references are from the New Revised Standard Version Catholic Edition (NRSV-CE) of the bible.

A SPECIAL MESSAGE...

Dear children, I am calling you to a complete surrender to God. Pray, little children that Satan does not sway you like branches in the wind. Be strong in God. I desire that through you the whole world may get to know the God of joy.

Neither be anxious nor worried. God will help you and show you the way. I want you to love all men with my love, both the good and the bad. Only that way will love conquer the world.

Little children, you are mine. I love you and I want you to surrender to me so I can lead you to God. Pray without ceasing so that Satan cannot take advantage of you. Pray so that you realize that you are mine. I bless you with the blessing of joy. Thank you for responding to my call.

—Message given to visionary Marija on May 25, 1988

May the God of hope fill you with all joy and peace in believing, so that by the power of the Holy Spirit you may abound in hope.
—Romans 15:13

DEDICATION

I dedicate this book in memory of my greatest supporter, Odette Platz, who departed this world as a living saint. May she rest in peace.

I also dedicate this book to Ronald Courtney who has assisted us in many ways by living Our Lady's messages.

CONTENTS

PROLOGUE

how it really began

You are my son and I am asking you to do my Son's will . . .

To say that I was shocked to receive such an undeniable message from the Blessed Virgin Mary is obvious understatement. Why would the Virgin Mary, whom I had never given a moment's thought, suddenly speak to me—an extremely lukewarm Protestant by faith and a journalist by profession?

In hindsight, it became clear that this crowning moment could not have become a part of the miracle of Medjugorje without first having a free will change of heart. Lukewarm wouldn't cut it; it does not adequately describe my state of faith at the time. There was an urgent need for deep soul cleansing before I could possibly be asked to take on a mission of spreading the messages of Medjugorje. It would literally entail giving up a lucrative business, which afforded me an abundant life style, and replacing it with a religious mission.

The beginning of the mission really had nothing directly to do with the supernatural apparitions in the little hamlet. It had everything to do with my worldly attitude, lack of real faith and practices as a successful, hard-charging businessman.

I was intensely competitive and did not mind shortcutting ethical standards if necessary to make money. I did not think of myself as unscrupulous or dishonest. Faith was for Sundays but when Monday came, it was about making money and all that it entailed. If it required an occasional little "fudging" on ethics, then so be it.

It was such an occasion that summer that led me to take one of those ethical shortcuts. We had started a new tabloid newspaper filled with beach-related advertising aimed at the growing tourist market in Myrtle Beach, South Carolina. The problem was another publishing firm was doing the same thing. Throughout the summer season we had battled for the customers, sniping at each other. The end result was neither of us reaching the goal of huge profits and dominance of the market we desired. As we neared the end of the season, it was time for drastic measures.

I called a meeting of our sales staff and informed them that our next beach guide issue would be cut to only five thousand copies. However, they were to tell the advertising customers that it was the usual ten thousand. By doing this, we would be guaranteed not to lose money. I dismissed the staff and all of them left—except one lady, Betty. I knew immediately that she was not going to cooperate and I prepared myself for the confrontation, determined to fire her if she did not comply with my orders.

Betty was a relatively new hire and was known for constantly talking about her Baptist faith. But she was a good sales person and therefore I put up with the religious chatter. We settled in and she began: "Wayne, I can't do this. I can't lie to the customers because it's just not right. It goes completely against my religious beliefs."

"Listen Betty, it's just this one time," I said while fuming inside. I knew she was right; that just made me more upset.

"I can't do it," she said as tears formed in her eyes. "If you want to fire me, I'll understand but I can't go against my faith."

At that moment, I suddenly became calm. *She's right,* I thought; *this is wrong.* It wasn't worth losing what little faith I had. I didn't know it at the time but that was the tiny spark, which ignited the true beginning of my spiritual conversion.

I sat very still for several moments and then slowly smiled at Betty. "I'm not going to fire you, Betty. In fact, you're right and I want to thank you for bringing me to my senses. This whole project has been nothing but endless worry and trouble."

Within seconds, Betty was around the desk and hugging me. "Oh, thank you, praise God! I prayed that you would see the truth and not make this mistake!"

"Yeah, yeah," I said in mock sternness, "Now get out of here and go sell!"

As soon as Betty left my office, I leaned back, looked up and said out loud: "God, please forgive me. From now on this business is yours."

Moments later, I called the manager of our competing beach guide tabloid and told him we were stopping production of our product and that I would be glad to give him a list of all of our customers. If there was anything more I could do to help him to please let me know. It was not until I literally walked into his office and delivered the list of customers that he actually believed me.

About a month later, the Blessed Virgin spoke to my heart asking me to make the spreading of her Medjugorje messages my life mission. For the first time in my life I knew God was real and that this is what I was supposed to do.

One evening shortly after having received the message from the Blessed Virgin, I received a telephone call from the man who owned the competing publishing company I had been at war with over the beach guide. He told me he owned 30 more small newspapers and wanted to buy my four newspapers; would I be interested in selling to him?

The rest, as they say, is history.

I've come to understand over the years that when Mary is sent to earth in apparition, it is always to lead us to her Son. I can only thank her for asking me to be part of the most incredible and important apparitions in the history of the world.

That moment of moral change was the *real* beginning of my mission. Making money was no longer the main motivation of life. The focus was now on Jesus and the reality of His life, death and resurrection. The driving force of it all was the Blessed Virgin Mary.

The opening words of the message the Blessed Virgin Mary spoke to me that fateful evening in October 1985 are burned into my soul: ***You are my son; I am asking you now to do my Son's will . . .***

—Wayne Weible

INTRODUCTION

the joy of medjugorje

The daily apparition of the Blessed Virgin Mary in the village of Medjugorje is special beyond the obvious. Each day of apparition is filled with sensationalism, wonderment, startling revelations, incredible miracles of body and spirit—and joy!

An apt description of joy is as follows: The emotion of great delight or happiness caused by something exceptionally good or satisfying; keen pleasure; elation.

This description of joy describes Medjugorje to the fullest. However, there is another interpretation of joy, which from a different perspective includes all of the descriptive elements of the definition above, along with deep suffering that may come with conversion. No matter the crosses, the purest form of joy is in total surrender and becoming a child of God.

The compilation of this book has been an incredible joy. Many of the stories contained here were originally published in my earlier books. They compose a collection of my greatest stories, but with additions, commentary and in some cases, updates. Interspersed among them are a variety of quotes from individuals involved in the apparitions as well as from saints and other religious figures. Added to that are many of the Blessed Virgin's messages and pertinent verses of Holy Scripture.

I also share extremely personal moments and events, all of which are related to spreading the messages of Medjugorje. In fact, it is a semi-autobiography in that it includes writing for the first time about the full, traumatic story of my childhood and life before Medjugorje. I do so at the perceived urging of the Blessed Virgin Mary as a stark illustration of how a soul besieged with near-impossible crosses manages to find joy in unconditional surrender to the will of God.

The book is titled *The Joy of Medjugorje* because joy comes from true conversion of the heart and soul. Joy fills us when we accept and then bask in the love that God has for us, regardless of the crosses that come with it. Therefore, even when we go through terrible sufferings as I relate in the story of my childhood, joy abounds when life converts to the teachings and love of God.

I want the content of this book to bring you to the same level of joy that the visionaries of Medjugorje experience each time the Mother of Jesus appears to them. She has made it known that she desires that same sense to envelope all of us who seek to be the children of God.

Our Lady has said many times in her messages over the years that *all suffering is redemptive* in aiding lost and struggling souls to find the love of God. That means all of our suffering is tied to the very same cross of Jesus that has redeemed all who accept it. And of course, all suffering ends in joy when the victim soul reaches the doors of Heaven.

What a joy it is to share these incredible stories and special moments with you!

—Wayne Weible

PART ONE:

the personal

Dear children, today I invite you to decide for God once again and to choose Him before everything, so that He may work miracles in your life, and that day by day your life may become joy with Him...

—From message of January 25, 1990

lessons of the cross

Clearly, the primary lesson of the Cross of Jesus is our salvation through His redemptive suffering. No one among us would willingly want to experience the actual physical sufferings of Jesus on the cross. Yet, when Jesus tells us in Holy Scripture to "Take up your cross and follow me," He means it quite literally.

The cross is a symbol of suffering. Paradoxically, it is also a catalyst of joy in that it is our way to redemption, which comes when we comprehend the ultimate joy of true conversion to the teachings of Jesus. The Catholic crucifix with the body of Jesus on the cross is a constant reminder of His gift of salvation gained through the most unimaginable human suffering.

Jesus died a horrible death in complete humanity; there was no divinity in Him as He was insulted, humiliated, kicked, slapped, spit upon, beaten and scourged with many blows and forced to carry His cross to the place where He would die for us. There were more than 5,000 wounds inflicted on his holy body. He accepted all of this cruelty so as to give the *purest gift of salvation* for all who would acknowledge it.

The only-begotten Son consented to it all in humility and obedience to God the Father.

All of us are given crosses in our lives. There are sicknesses, diseases, conditions, broken marriages, estranged families, grief, despair, addictions and far too many more. Our crosses vary in size and in the degree of suffering. Yet, from the smallest to the largest and most difficult, all are redemptive for the salvation of others; all are tied to the Redemptive Cross of Jesus.

In the beginning days of my discovery of the Catholic faith I was overwhelmed by the actual act of the Crucifixion of Jesus. How could He have suffered so much for us? In contrast, as a Protestant I had never given it a thought other than during Easter.

The cross of Jesus in Protestant churches is bare. There is no corpus, no sign of the suffering He endured. It is presented that way to emphasize that He suffered, died and was then resurrected. Thus, for Protestants the cross is empty to indicate the end of the Passion, His resurrection and His ascension into Heaven.

I find an empty cross teaches no lesson. It does not visually reflect the incomprehensible suffering necessary for our salvation. Rather, it becomes an ever-present reminder of the schism that divides the Church Jesus established on earth. It symbolizes the failure of God's creation to learn the true lesson of the cross.

Through discovery of the apparitions of the Blessed Virgin Mary at Medjugorje, I was introduced to the Catholic crucifix. It immediately had incredible meaning. I thought about it a lot. Then I learned to pray the rosary and it underlined the reason I was so fixated on the crucifix; the lessons became real, especially through the Sorrowful Mysteries.

I wondered if I would have had the courage of a Simeon to carry the cross for Jesus even though he was forced to do so. Would I be amongst the small crowd of devout followers, mostly women, who thought nothing of their personal danger for admittedly being followers of this man who claimed to be the long-awaited Messiah? Or, would I run away, like many of the disciples, filled with fear of suffering the same fate? The Sorrowful Mysteries of the rosary brought all of this to life and to constant thought.

I soon developed a habit of praying the rosary as I went on long runs. I was an avid runner and praying the rosary as I ran was becoming a favorite thing to do. Once, I remember finishing a grueling run on a cold, miserable rainy day as I prayed the last Sorrowful Mystery, the Crucifixion. I was so deeply into it that as I finished the run, I stretched out my arms in imitation of Jesus nailed to the cross. I stood there with arms outstretched, face lifted to the chilling rain, praying with intensity and brimming with emotion. I was exhausted from the run but I wanted to feel what it was like for my beaten and humiliated Jesus to have to carry His cross up that terrible hill and then die on it.

I wept uncontrollably in the moment.

I was now a child of God.

I am the vine, you are the branches. He who abides in me, and I in him, he it is that bears much fruit, for apart from me you can do nothing.

—John 15:5.

You are my son and I am now asking you to do my Son's will. Write about this event and if you accept, the spreading of my messages will become your life's mission.
—The Blessed Virgin Mary's first message to me.

2

life before medjugorje

What I am about to share with you is done with much difficulty as I relate my traumatic childhood years and include it here. The most painful part was having to mentally relive it as I wrote about it in great detail for the first time. It took much anguish and chilling remembrance to begin; I would write—I would cry. I would write some more—and cry some more. It is not a story of evident joy; yet in retrospect, it is.

The first seven years of life were filled with dark horrors of deeply engrained traumatic experiences. They remain with me to this day. No one, much less a child, should have to go through such pain, rejection and lack of love.

As stated earlier, during talks in the early days of the mission I would feel that inner nudge from Our Lady gently asking me to talk about the experience for the sake of others who shared similar stories of harrowing childhoods. I didn't want to do it. However, in obedience to the Mother of God I slowly began talking about it and now include it here for the first time in detail. It begins with the earliest memory and concludes with the life-changing day she first spoke to my heart.

My earliest memory as a child came when I was between two or three years old. It was a frightening moment of suffocation and subsequent hysterical crying as my mother tried to force the tight-fitting top part of a child's sailor suit she had purchased on impulse from a nearby store. My father was coming home on leave from the Navy where he was serving in the Pacific. She thought it would please him if I were wearing the little suit when he arrived. She finally succeeded and then realizing my fear, picked me up and soothed me as I was still in hysterical tears. It was the first and only memory of her sincerely caring for me.

Other than that singular moment, I remember very little about my birth mother. Sometimes I wonder if that one incident of claustrophobic fear was a portent of what terror was to come during my childhood years.

the traumatic years

Dark memories stirred within me as my flight began its decent to the Los Angeles, California airport. I would be giving a series of talks on the apparitions of Medjugorje for the first time in the state of my birth and my home for the first seven years of life.

The memories within me became distinct and clear as the plane taxied on the runway. Life had been a living hell for me, my younger sister and brother, a time I wanted to blot out forever. As the plane landed, I was surprised at the intensity of discomfort I felt.

My mother suffered a history of social ills that began in her early twenties. I guess in today's medical terms she was probably bipolar. Filled with insecurity and an obsessive need to be loved, my mother was unable to cope with my father's long periods of absence due to his service as a career Naval officer in the Pacific during World War II. She became an alcoholic and a drug addict; the responsibility of motherhood was forgotten or ignored. In truth, she didn't have the maturity and instinct to be a mother.

My mother had been previously married, divorced and had a son named Jimmy. She met my father, who after joining the Navy as a seaman apprentice was stationed at the Long Beach Naval station near Los Angeles. Coming straight off the family farm in Oshkosh, Nebraska, he was naïve and shy and knew little about the outside world. Due to the heavy workload of farming he only completed school to the fifth grade.

My father was completely swept off his feet upon meeting my mother who was beautiful and charming. Within a few months, she became pregnant with me. They were hastily married, and in the next three years my sister Lola and brother Jackie were born. I have no memories of their births—only daily crisis and fright. The only normalcy of life was when my father was able to come home from the war for a few days of rest.

The addition of two more children was too much for my mother to handle. With no husband around to help, escape was found in wild partying with equally irresponsible acquaintances. She would be gone for days, leaving her four children to fend for themselves. Jimmy, my half-brother who was four years older than I, would also disappear for days; leaving me at the age of six to care for the three of us. Lola was three and a half years old and my baby brother Jackie was just under one. I was often at a loss as to what to do and we went hungry far too many times.

I slowly learned to feed us by stealing small food items at the local grocery store and telling the milkman and other food delivery services that my mother instructed me to have them leave an order at the doorstep. Another tactic I used was to tell all of the neighborhood children to go home and get food so we could all have a picnic in the small playground area. It worked quite well.

By the time I was seven, I could lie and steal with proficiency, having swiftly grown up the wrong way out of a need for survival. I didn't know the love of a mother or the love of a father since my father was away for long periods of time. I felt I would die of a broken heart and I lived in constant fear. My only defense was to go into what I called "survival mode", which was to be tough on the outside, never cry and do whatever was necessary to stay alive.

Then came the wild night that would abruptly change our lives.

One early morning our little apartment was filled with people, yelling and cursing and screaming, all of them drunk. A large man came into the room where Jackie was sleeping in his crib. Lola came to investigate what was happening and he grabbed her and shoved her into the crib with Jackie and told her to stay there. I ran to my special place of hiding under the couch when these confrontations occurred. Unfortunately, they happened too often.

On this fateful night, I heard my mother arguing with the hefty man. Then she let out a painful scream as she tumbled down the stairs, having been pushed down by the man who kept screaming curse words at her.

It wasn't long before the police arrived, along with an ambulance. My mother had a broken arm. Several of our neighbors who had called the police when they heard the commotion were there to comfort us and arrange care for us until the authorities could sort things out. They watched over us until the following evening when the police came to our apartment to take us away. It was a living nightmare. I screamed and tried to hang on to my brother Jimmy where we were hiding under the sofa. An officer grabbed my leg and pulled me out. Soon we were all separated as we were placed in a huge, social services building. It was a juvenile hall where delinquent children were normally placed. I was hastily put in a dormitory with other children and told to go to sleep.

I hadn't stopped crying since the officer pulled me from under the sofa. It would spawn a fear that would never leave me. A woman who worked there came to my bed and harshly told me to stop crying. I couldn't. Exasperated, the woman jerked me out of the bed by my arm and dragged me into a small room with no furniture and made me stand under a single light fixture in the middle of the room. She told me I would stay there until I stopped crying. It would be more than an hour before she would allow me to return to the bed. To this day, I can't stand to be in a room with a singular overhead light fixture on.

I vaguely remember my mother coming to the Juvenile Hall to see us a few days later. She was not allowed to go beyond the main entrance area and we gathered on a couch as she spoke to us with a supervisor present. I just stared at her, not saying anything; she was a stranger and anything but a mother to us. Yet, I wanted to run into her arms. Now we were here with no idea of what was going to happen to us.

The next few months became a blur of uncaring and cruel treatment from the women in the first foster home where I was placed. It was in the same apartment complex where we had lived. Lola was just a few apartments away with a nice family that took good care of her. We were able to see each other almost daily.

Jackie remained in a confusing situation where he would spend one week in one foster home and then the next week in another foster home. One family was kind and one was not. It would affect him for the rest of his life.

Jimmy also suffered greatly under foster care. He was placed in a separate home away from us. I would learn years later that he was sent to live with a male relative of my mother and was severely sexually abused.

After our being together in the Juvenile Hall, I never saw Jimmy again or knew in detail what transpired in his life until years later. He called me once while I was attending college. It was a strange call as he rambled on for a long time. I thought he was drunk and wondered how he had obtained my telephone number. I learned he had kept the last name of Weible. But then he began to denounce my father for not rescuing us from the terrible mess we were in. The conversation became a long, one-sided and nasty attack on my father. I cut the call off and told him it might be better if we did not talk in the future. I was not going to listen to him put my father down. We never spoke or saw each other again.

The woman of the home where I was placed was one of the neighbors who had called the authorities about our lack of care. Ironically, she mistreated me beyond words and would constantly remind me that she had "rescued" me even though I didn't deserve it. (I remember her name and what she looked like to this day.)

I was so frightened by her verbal abuse and threats that I would sometimes wet the bed. Once when it happened, she grabbed me, struck me and then as punishment made me put on a dress. I was then seated in a corner on the floor near the front door and made to stay there as she hosted a party for friends, pointing me out to each person who came in and telling them I had wet the bed. I was so ashamed and broken-hearted. I just wanted to die.

I do not remember this woman ever telling me she loved me. I felt like a dog tied to a stake outside in the yard and fed but otherwise ignored. It did not take long for the authorities to learn that this woman was indeed cruel in her harsh discipline of me, thanks to nearby neighbors.

Once again, we were moved by the authorities to another foster home location, this one in a little town named Sunland, California. I was filled with fear that it would be another place of abuse. The only good thing was Lola would be with me. Jackie remained in the confusing situation.

As the authorities stopped the car in the yard of the new foster home, all I could think of was to run away. The minute the car door opened, I dashed up the side of a small hill next to the house with Lola yelling at me to stop and come down. It would be more than two hours before I would venture down and stand in the yard, not knowing what to expect.

The foster husband of the new house came out and motioned me to come to him. He firmly told me I would be staying there and it was up to me as to how I would be treated. He then turned and went inside, leaving me standing there. Twenty minutes later I gave in and entered the house, just as frightened as I was when we arrived.

Hardly anything was said to me as I sat timidly at a table as the man's wife placed a plate of food before me. A boy about my age came into the room and slid into the empty chair next to me and immediately began talking to me, asking questions and telling me about himself at the same time. After a few hours, I felt somewhat more receptive to the change, knowing anything would be better than the woman from our neighborhood. The son of the family and I hit it off and spent the rest of the evening together. At least there was someone I could talk to and not be afraid.

Robbie (not his real name) and I became inseparable. I found out he could steal little things at the grocery store far better than I could and before long, he taught me all the tricks of stealing. Robbie also taught me how to smoke cigarettes, which spurred our main goal of stealing them. Most of my time at this home was with Robbie. I didn't care about anyone else, except Lola. The people were good to her and were pleased that Robbie and I got along so well. But there were never acts or signs of affection given to us. As in the other homes, we were just commodities.

Everything was going along nicely—except at night when we had to go to bed. Immediately, it would bring out the worst memories of the past experiences with my mother and the woman I was first placed with. I was afraid to go to sleep, thinking that I would wake up and be back with that woman. Yet, inexplicably there was a feeling—a feeling that something or someone was trying to protect me. Of course, I didn't know what or who it was, but felt it was good. The "feeling" of this presence became a near obsessive incentive for holding out hope that one day all would be different.

That *one day* finally arrived.

rescue

My father's brother Fritz and his wife June came to our rescue. When we were still living with our mother, I vaguely remember them temporarily living in California near us for several months, with Fritz even taking a job as a milkman. They quickly recognized the neglect and what was happening to us. After they returned to Nebraska, Aunt June was determined to come and get us after learning the dreadful details of what we had been going through. Most of my father's relatives were against us coming to live with Aunt June and Uncle Fritz. It created a barrage of negative discussions among the family. Many of them warned Aunt June not to "get involved".

My Aunt June didn't hesitate. She and Fritz took a train to Long Beach, arranged for our release to them and took the three of us to their home in the tiny town of Lewellen, Nebraska (Population 533). The plan was that we would live with them and their three children of similar ages until my father returned from the war.

Uncle Fritz really couldn't afford to take us in, but he felt he had no choice. He was filled with evident bitterness toward his siblings and his parents, who wanted nothing to do with us. I had been through enough by that time to recognize rejection; and, with the exception of my father's twin sisters, Rose and Rita, who were the youngest of the family, we were virtually ignored. Rose and Rita were only 17-years-old when

the JOY *of* MEDJUGORJE

we arrived but they immediately made us feel welcome. I am forever grateful to these girls for their sincere acceptance of us.

On order to make ends meet, Uncle Fritz, who delivered propane fuel to the local farmers would also take in harvest workers in the fall. We somehow managed, and the time in Nebraska will always be special to me. For the first time in my life, someone cared about me.

Until our coming to Nebraska, I never knew about birthdays or Christmas—or about God and going to church. I felt like I was in paradise with the move to Lewellen. There was a tremendous amount of love in our new family. It was the best medicine possible to at least cover for the time of horror of my early years in California.

a new direction

A little more than five years later when I was 13 years old, my Dad, who had divorced my mother and remarried, came to Nebraska to get us and take us to live with him and his new wife in Charleston, South Carolina. Dad was now stationed there as commander of a small ship. He had risen from the ranks of an enlisted man to officer status, eventually becoming a commander.

It was difficult and sad to leave Nebraska and the wonderful life with Aunt June and Uncle Fritz and our cousins. Yet, I was excited to begin a new chapter of life—this time with my father and his new wife, Irene.

At the first moment of seeing my Dad and Irene, I ran to *her* and threw my arms around her waist and said, "I love you, Mom!" From that moment, she would be my stand-in mother. She was never a stepmother to me. She did a wonderful job.

Life in Charleston was also blissful. I missed my cousins and Aunt June but now we were with my father, a man I didn't know very well and who spoke very little. Still, he was our father. He was quiet to a fault and kind, but a stranger to his three kids. Dad didn't know how to be a dad as he was absent from home serving in the Pacific for most of the war. I accepted him as he was, and my new mom more than made up for his awkwardness as a father.

The years of living in Charleston were years of happiness. I did all I could to enjoy life to the fullest. Most of my time was spent outside playing games and just being a kid. With friends, we fished, rode our bikes hard and played baseball and football late into the evening. I always had scraped knees from rough play but I absolutely loved my new life.

We lived in Charleston for three-plus years before my father was transferred to Arlington, Virginia for a new and higher assignment. The move was fine with me. All I could think of was that it would be a new adventure in my now normal life.

Everything was going well with one exception: school. I really did not like going to school, especially the new school of Washington and Lee High School in Arlington. Almost immediately I was getting into fights. There was the survival mode rising again. Also, my grades were no better than average and in some areas, below average. I really didn't care. All I wanted to do was to play and make up for the early years of suffering. The attitude of not caring about school and just wanting to enjoy life made the next major move in my life easy to accept.

One evening shortly after my 17th birthday as we were having dinner, the conversation turned to the fact that school would soon be starting again. That brought on the subject of my grades and then a startling pronouncement by my normally silent father. It shocked us all. He suddenly said in his usual quiet way, "I don't know why you want to return to school since your grades are so bad. I think you should join the Navy and make it a career just as I have."

Having finished the tenth grade and now at the age of barely 17, my answer came easy: "Yeah, that would be great!"

All I could think of was no more school. It was soon arranged by my father that he would do the honor of swearing me into the service. The newspapers came and took photographs and a good write up was in the next issue. Dad was very proud and it was something new and exciting for me to be the center of attention.

Everything was set on entering the United States Navy—until arrival at what is called "Boot camp." The minute all of us as new recruits stepped off the bus at the Bainbridge, Maryland Training Camp, we were blasted by the deafening screaming of our new squad leader. In essence, we were told amidst a flood of expletives that we were now reduced to nothing and would be reshaped as Navy men. I felt immediately I had made a mistake by leaving school!

Life in the Navy was an entirely new way to live and I grew up to some extent. I had to in order to survive. It required survival mode again. In the process, I was assigned to the deck crew, which translated to the janitor crew. Again, I was reminded of the mistake I made in quitting school. However, I soon determined that I wanted more than to be a janitor. By some little miracle, I was accepted into the radar men's division and within the next two years I was promoted to Second class Petty Officer. That single accomplishment gave me the first tiny shred of confidence that I could one day be someone in life.

Only after being discharged from duty did I realize that I had earned the right to attend a university tuition-free if I so desired under what was called the GI bill. However, I had no intention in using it, thinking that there was no way I would be accepted since I had quit high school.

I was living with my sister Lola and her husband in Columbia, South Carolina, trying to decide what to do with my life. It was her husband Allen, who was studying to be a pharmacist at the University of South Carolina, who kept trying to convince me to take advantage of the government bill and apply for college. I kept telling him I wasn't interested.

Within the next six months I worked at odd jobs, eventually landing employment as a dancing instructor in training at an Arthur Murray dance studio. The only problem was income was based on commission with a small salary during training. Days were spent learning the different dances while the nights were filled with giving lessons. I barely made enough income to get by. Surprisingly, I was good at teaching dancing and soon became successful enough to at least earn a meager living.

My career as a dancing instructor did not last long. I met a young woman who was one of my students and after several lessons I was convinced I was in love with her. The studio had a policy that teachers could not date dance students. I didn't care and asked her out. We dated secretly for several months and I soon left the dance studio and went to work for a wholesale distributor company. Feeling I now had a decent job, I asked her to marry me. I was so insecure that I thought if she didn't marry me, no woman ever would. After turning me down several times claiming she needed more time, she finally accepted. Soon we settled into married life. A year later we had a baby girl.

My brother-in-law continued to pressure me to apply to the university. How could I go to college having quit high school, I countered? And now I had a family. He persisted, for which today I am eternally grateful. I reluctantly took the entrance exam to the University of South Carolina not expecting to be accepted but hoping it would get him off my case. But I *was* accepted and the thought struck me that I would actually be going to a university with a chance to be a college graduate. It changed everything.

Reality followed the euphoria of possibly being a college student. I wondered how I could go to school and raise a family at the same time. That fear was offset by the fact that I would be the first male member of my family to attend college. The people I worked for were very understanding and gave me part time work to help out. A month later I walked on campus to begin the quest to earn a degree in journalism. For some unknown reason, I had always wanted to be a journalist or a writer. Ironically while in the Navy I had purchased a small typewriter and had learned to type. The dream was to become a sports reporter since I enjoyed sports above all else.

In the last two years of school, I worked forty hours a week as a detective clerk for the municipal police, sold advertising for the university newspaper (which paid enough to make it worth doing) and carried a full load of classes. The bottom line was the realization that I could actually do all of this. It was another huge confidence booster.

Then, out of nowhere and without warning, the past suddenly invaded the present.

Having settled into a good routine of family, work and school, I was startled one day when my sister Lola called and told me that our birth mother was in town and wanted to see us. She asked to stay at Lola's apartment and not knowing what to do when confronted with such a sudden development, she reluctantly agreed. I hurried over to Lola's apartment, getting there just before our birth mother arrived.

For the next two uncomfortable hours, we listened to our mother's explanation of how we ended up in the Juvenile Hall and then under foster care. I sat there, numbed by the painful memories refilling my mind. There was no discussion or explanation or apology for the days she had abandoned us without care. The summation of it all was the lurid details of relationships, failed marriages (she had now been married four times) and weak excuses.

And then came the shocker.

Our mother began to talk about her disappointment when she found out she was pregnant with me. She then casually stated that she had done everything she could to abort me. I wondered if I had actually heard her say that. How could she tell her son that she did everything she could to abort him?

That did it. Lola began crying and screaming at her to get out and to get out now. Our mother tried to explain but that was enough for both of us. I told her she needed to leave immediately. After she had left, Lola and I just sat there in tears.

However, the encounter was not over. Several days after my sister and I thought our birth mother was gone and out of our lives, I received a call from the jailer during my evening shift in the detective's unit. He told me he had a woman in jail who claimed to be my mother and was asking for me.

I immediately went to the jail and was once again face to face with my mother, who had been arrested for drunk and disorderly conduct. The jailer told me he would release her if I desired. I thanked him and then went to my mother in the cell. I was surprised at how calm I was but I knew I had to bring this to an end. I told her I forgave her a long time ago but that she must leave and never come back. After a pause, she agreed. It was the last time I saw her. When Medjugorje came into my life, I desperately tried to find her to no avail. Recently, in 2015, I discovered through a cousin still living in California that my mother had passed away some time ago after living estranged from the family for most of her life.

During my university years, I experienced several defining moments. I was ready to quit school when a second child arrived. I was sure I would have to leave school and find a job to take care of our expanding family. Thanks to a professor in the journalism school, I did not abandon school. He told me with emphasis that if I left school now, I would never return to studies; he'd seen it way too many times—and that I would regret it for the rest of my life. I took his advice and stayed, determined to do what was necessary to stay in school. Four and a half years later, I graduated with a degree in journalism and with an overall B average.

There was one other critical incident that occurred somewhere in my third year of study. We were assigned in my English writing class to read and then write a paper about the story from the classic book titled "Red Badge of Courage" by Steven Crane. I turned my paper in and stayed for a while going over some notes before leaving the building and making my way to my next class. I'd hardly gone a hundred feet when I heard my writing class professor calling my name. When she caught up with me with my paper in her hand, she bluntly asked, "What are you planning to do once you graduate—what are you going to do with your life?"

I looked at her somewhat taken aback. "I'm really not sure but I think I'll try for a job on a newspaper as a sports writer."

"No, no," she said waving the paper at me, "You've got to write seriously; you have a special gift and you really need to write and you can't waste it on sports stories. You need to think of maybe *writing a book some day!"* With that she smiled, adding: "Don't waste your talent on sports." She then made her way back to her classroom.

I stood there for a while, deeply impressed that this professor thought I could actually write a book. Years later, I realized that this little exchange was the seed that led me to *want* to write a book. It was going to be a great novel or major sports story. Never did I imagine it would be a book about religion, especially about the Blessed Virgin Mary whom I had never given more than a passing thought.

the fruits of insecurity

Upon graduation from the university, I went to work for the local newspaper—but not as a sports reporter. They wanted me in management, which would pay far more than a sports reporter. Due to family needs, I accepted management and began training. Still, the words of my English professor about writing a book were firmly lodged in my mind.

Unfortunately, the schedule of work and a myriad of other factors created the start of severe domestic problems, especially when I was asked to take an assignment in Myrtle Beach, where the newspaper company had just purchased a local thrice-weekly newspaper. I was to convert it into a daily and eventually become the publisher.

Most of my time in the next year was spent away from home. Our marriage continued to suffer, helped along by my resurfaced survival mode. How could this happen? Hadn't I gone through enough? It also created problems with my work. I was so desperate I even pleaded with God not to let our family break up as we now had four children. It was the first time I had ever directly asked Him for something.

But the divorce happened. I was devastated in realizing that I was putting my children through the ordeal of a broken family. On top of it all, I lost my job and was given a month to find work elsewhere.

Life was back to trauma.

My response to it all was bitter anger. Where was this God if He really existed? Hadn't I made the altar call when you go forward in a Baptist church and publically proclaim you accept Jesus as your Lord and Savior? I had even taken on the task of teaching a Sunday school class even though I was totally unqualified. I then made a vow to never set foot in a church again; not even for weddings or funerals or baptisms. I kept that vow for seven long years. As far as I was concerned the people in churches were all hypocrites.

Within a short timeframe, I met and married a woman who felt the same way I did about church. She didn't want children, had been married and divorced and was really not looking to remarry. We lived together for a year and a half before, once again as with my first marriage, I convinced her to marry me. In all honesty, she was not happy with my insistence and agreed with great reluctance. We were married in her mother's home.

Out of the same anger at God, I decided to start my own newspaper. I had found a job selling yellow pages in the mountains of Georgia and ran across a local community tabloid newspaper. *That's what I want to do*, I thought. Having learned as a dance instructor how to convince prospective dance customers to purchase expensive lesson packages, I found that selling was easy to me and I quickly became one of the company's top sales people. The next step was convincing my new wife that I could do it. Why, she asked, would I leave a job when we were doing so well? I persisted and she finally agreed, if somewhat grudgingly.

We worked seven days a week and usually about 15-18 hours a day. In six months, we were established and doing modestly well. Not satisfied and still driven, I started a second newspaper; and then a third and a forth. We then purchased a huge printing press, much to the distress of my wife. How are we going to pay for this she asked? I didn't worry about it. All I knew was that now I felt I could do anything I wanted. I had already been through the worst sufferings and survived; so, what was there to fear? Before long we had a flourishing printing business to go with the papers. An added bonus was competing directly against the daily newspaper owned by my former employer who had fired me.

Six years had now passed since I had made a vow to not go to church. Life took another major turn when my wife told me she thought we should have at least one child. I was surprised and shocked. This woman who had made it clear that she didn't want children was now talking about having a baby? I shrugged and said it was okay with me if that is what she wanted. A year later she gave birth to our son, Kennedy. Two years later, again without warning, she said we should consider having Kennedy baptized. That led to a major argument. I am not going back to a church, I told her. She persisted. A compromise was finally reached when it was agreed that we would go to a church of her choosing for three Sundays, just long enough to have Kennedy baptized. I would then return to my normal life.

We found a Lutheran church just about a mile from our home and because they had a good nursery, my wife insisted this was the one. Ironically, the Lutheran faith was that of my family even though few members regularly attended services. Reluctantly, I found myself back in a church, agitated that I was breaking my vow even if only temporarily. Hardly anyone spoke to me on our first Sunday of attendance, even though I knew many members from business. It was the same the second week of attendance; and then, on the third Sunday, someone came to me and complimented me on a column I had written in our newspapers. I remember thinking: *Well, maybe these people aren't so bad after all.*

Six months passed and amazingly, I was still going to the Lutheran church. By that time, I had been elected to the church council, was teaching a Sunday school class and was president of the Lutheran Men's Club. My feeling was if I was going to go to that church I was going to help run it! I did it all out of business interests—not for reasons of faith.

As the worn out saying goes, God works in mysterious ways. That was surely the case with my return, however reluctantly, to an active role in a church. It was October 1985, that the "reason" for my presence in that church became clear.

The Sunday school class I was teaching became the platform that would change everything. One Sunday morning I announced that for this class we would discuss modern day miracles rather than following the lesson plan. It was a great class and everyone enjoyed it. Near the end, a woman named Becky Ginley raised her hand. "I've got one for you; a Catholic friend of mine recently told me that six Croatian teenagers in a little village in Yugoslavia called *Medugory* – or something like that – were claiming that the Blessed Virgin Mary was appearing to them in daily apparition giving messages from Heaven."

With that, Becky sat down with a facial expression that said *top that one if you can!*

My reaction was immediate: *What utter nonsense! Mary lived, Mary died, so how could she be appearing to these young people?* However, I was immediately thinking such a bizarre claim might make a good column for the upcoming Christmas season.

After the class, I approached Becky and asked her if this person had any kind of written information on this strange event, like a magazine article or newspaper report? I might be interested in doing a story about it to tie in with Christmas. Becky said she has something better than that—she has a video that was made in late 1984 and I could actually watch these kids during an apparition. She was sure she could borrow it for me.

Becky obtained the video for me and several evenings later when there was nothing of interest on the television, I decided to watch the video. *Let me see this great miracle,* I thought as I placed it in the machine. Yet, the moment it began to play something inside of me said: "Pay attention, this is more than just a story for your newspapers!"

Within minutes I was engrossed, shaking my head and thinking: *Why have I never heard of apparitions?* I was mesmerized and when it showed the young visionaries right at the moment of the apparition as they sunk to their knees in synchronization, I thought: *Oh, my God! This is real!* That was quickly followed with: *Oh, my God! If this is real, then . . .you are real!* And then: *Oh, my God! You know everything about me!*

I felt shame and embarrassment. Those feelings were suddenly gone as incredibly, this same Blessed Virgin Mary was speaking directly to me: ***You are my son, and I am asking you to do my Son's will.*** I fell back into my chair thinking, *No, no, you have the wrong person—I'm not Catholic!* She continued: ***I am asking you to write about these events and if you accept, the spreading of my messages will become your life's mission.***

There was no doubt in my mind that all of this was happening. It seemed as if my entire life was flashing through my mind, showing me what would occur if I said yes. I could only answer her by thinking: *How? How can I do this; I don't know you and I don't even know where to begin . . .* and then the hardest part: *I don't even know your Son!*

Deep inside, I knew that my life had just dramatically changed. I didn't know how to further answer. The best I could do was utter a weak "I'll try!"

That tiny little opening was all the Mother of Jesus needed. My mind was filled with rapidly passing scenes of my businesses being gone and my life focused on spreading the messages of the Blessed Virgin Mary at Medjugorje.

By April of 1986 my newspapers were sold and I was free to go to Medjugorje to personally experience it. I arrived on May 1, the beginning of the month of Mary! It was the launching of a mission that has carried me to all corners of the earth to spread the messages of Medjugorje.

The realization came years later that my suffering as a little child was more than recompensed with the discovery of the Blessed Virgin Mary. Her apparitions at Medjugorje have led me to fully experience the pure love of God. She quietly revealed to me that she was the one present with me throughout all of the suffering as a child, waiting for the moment when I would be able to give God my surrender. This indescribably beautiful woman who is the mother of Jesus would become not only my spiritual mother, but also my "Mom."

In summation, the little boy who suffered so much childhood trauma has more than been rewarded.

For I greatly rejoiced when some of the brethren arrived and testified to the truth of your life, as indeed you do follow the truth. No greater joy can I have than this, to hear that my children follow the truth.

—3 John: 3-4.

Dear children! Today I call you to unite with Jesus in prayer. Open your heart to Him and give Him everything that is in it: joys, sorrows and illnesses. May this be a time of grace for you. Pray, little children, and may every moment belong to Jesus. I am with you and I intercede for you. Thank you for having responded to my call.
—Message of March, 25, 2002.

3

words of prophecy

One of the early tours of the mission was on the tiny island nation of Trinidad. It was a hard tour in terms of the number of talks I gave as well as the emotional aspect. But it also yielded a powerful and revealing personal prophecy that would completely define the power and purpose of my mission.

Ronald Grosberg and his family were my hosts and organizers of the tour. He was so filled with the Holy Spirit and excitement of the tour that he had scheduled every possible event he could squeeze into my time there. "Ronald, this poor man is not superman, you know," his wife Charla softly chided him as we went over the schedule shortly after my arrival.

"Oh, he'll survive all right. He's got the Blessed Mother watching after things!" And with a chuckle and a quick pat on my back, Ronald continued his intense briefing of the schedule.

But Charla proved to be right. After a week of nonstop events, I was still filled with spiritual fervor, but the flesh was not as willing as the spirit. I usually managed to squeeze in a morning run during travel but had only been able to do so a couple of times in Trinidad. All I could think of that morning was, *Thank God, it's almost over!*

However, it turned out to be a wonderful morning event at a large school for girls with more than 1,500 students listening intently and later bombarding me with questions.

As we arrived at the site of the second talk of the morning, the Emmanuel Community Center, we were surprised to discover that there would be a Mass before my talk. Even though I was still a Protestant, I loved the Catholic Mass and looked forward to eventually joining the Church.

For the next hour and a half, we shared in a joyful and emotional celebration of love with song and prayer in a packed auditorium. By the time I was to speak, I had long forgotten the weariness of the start of the day.

As I finished speaking, a woman named Violet, who was co-leader of the Emmanuel Community and had served as emcee for the morning's events, took to the stage and began to lead us in song. Suddenly Violet raised her hand and the singing stopped. The auditorium became quiet. In a soft and gentle voice and with eyes closed, she began to speak in prophecy. I sat there, shocked, as I realized it was a message from the Virgin Mary for me! I could hardly breathe as the words poured forth from her, slowly and clearly:

"And you, my little son, whom I have picked up like a little seed, you have been blown by the breath of the Holy Spirit. And I have said to you that I shall speak through you. I now say to you a new anointing is upon your life. The way you have walked, looking back and concerned; now a new way shall be opened for you.

"Your family shall be united with you in the work you are to do. I say to you, my son, you shall go from place to place and as you speak, a new ministry of love shall be poured upon my people through you. It shall be a special and unique gift, one deeper than you have received before.

"I say to you, my son, stand ready, stand ready! For the breath of the Holy Spirit shall blow you into great, great palaces, and into little hovels. I say to you, stand ready, for you are only on the threshold of the work you have offered me. Your little heart, offered to me, I have accepted and placed in my own. I say to you now, as stated in Scripture, behold, greater things than Jesus did, you will do. For behold, today, with the media, with the way the message can be carried, you shall touch millions.

"A new ministry of love, healing love, a renewing love, love that will touch the hardened hearts of sinners and cause them to fall on their knees right then and there. As you go, notice that love shall follow and flow to each human being that you speak to.

"Go now with a new anointing; go now with a new commission, my little seed. For truly, you have been planted. And yet, even though you were like a mustard seed bringing forth a shrub, now I shall make you into an acorn, bringing forth a stately oak.

"Fear not, you are my delight. You are my son!"

As the woman spoke the last words, her voice trailed off. There was what seemed like an eternity of silence; then a few of the people began to quietly sing again the song that had been interrupted a few minutes before. Soon others joined in and the session ended in a spirited rendition that would be hard-matched in Medjugorje itself.

I sat there for a few moments, still stunned, trying to take in all that had happened, trying to remember the words the woman had spoken.

One thing was explicitly clear: the mission had just taken a quantum leap forward.

Suddenly, it occurred to me to get the message and write it down. I looked around, thinking that the woman with the soft voice might already have left. I did not know her name or that she was co-leader of the community. My thoughts were interrupted by Ronald: "Wayne, we must go. They are waiting for us downstairs for lunch."

"But I've got to find that woman. I need to talk to her!"

Ronald gave me a reassuring pat on the shoulder. "Don't worry, that was Violet, and she's downstairs with the others."

I hurried down the stairs with Ronald, relieved to see the woman at a table with other members of the charismatic community. After introductions, I went directly to Violet who had given the prophecy. Dropping to one knee I asked in a low voice, "Look, can you give me that message again, can you write it down for me?"

"Oh, I'm sorry but I can't remember it at all," she answered, shaking her head. "That is the way it is with this gift. The Holy Spirit uses me to say what needs to be said, but I am only a small instrument and I am not always aware of what is being said."

I felt a sinking feeling. "Well, thank you anyway. It was so beautiful!" Resigned that the precious words were lost beyond faint memory, I took my seat at the table.

Listening to the different conversations, I remained distracted by the prophecy. Was this startlingly and mystical personal message given through this woman really authentic? The undeniable fact was, I *did* receive the first message the Blessed Virgin Mary had given me, and part of the proof was the very fact that I was traveling throughout the world and was now here in Trinidad.

It really boiled down to acceptance of a simple but profound scriptural truth found in the words of Jesus in the book of Matthew (18:3):

the JOY *of* MEDJUGORJE

"...Truly, I say you, unless you turn and become like little children, you will never enter the kingdom of heaven."

It certainly took the faith of a little child to accept at face value such direct communications with heaven.

"Excuse me, Mr. Weible." A lady at the next table interrupted my thoughts. "I apologize for eavesdropping but I think I might be of some help. I taped your talk and it includes the prophecy that was given at the end and ..."

"Great!" I interrupted. "Can you play it for me? Can I copy it? Does someone have a paper and pencil?"

"Oh, that won't be necessary," she said. "You can have the tape. My friend also taped it and she will be glad to give me a copy."

"Thank you, thank you, so much!" I happily accepted the tape, feeling interiorly the strong presence of the Blessed Mother. Here was proof of believing with childlike faith; here was also confirming proof of my mission.

It would take a great deal of deep thought and meditation to comprehend the full meaning of the Trinidad message. One fact was sure. All that I would do in the mission in its entirety would be as an instrument of the Holy Spirit. I was nothing special except for this gift given by God.

I quietly vowed to do my best in fulfilling the words of the prophecy.

And he said to them, "Go into all the world and preach the gospel to the whole creation. He who believes and is baptized will be saved; but he who does not believe will be condemned. And these signs will accompany those who believe: in my name they will cast out demons; they will speak in new tongues;"

—Mark 16: 15-17.

I cannot cure. God alone cures. Pray! I will pray with you. Believe firmly. Fast, do penance. I will help you as long as it is in my power to do it. God comes to help everyone. I am not God. I need your sacrifices and your prayers to help me.

—Excerpt from 1983 message.

4

the healing touch of god

We learn over time that God gives us what we need in the way of Holy Spirit gifts to successfully carry out His plans. However, properly discerning the what, when and where of receiving and using the gifts is another thing.

I knew in the early days of this mission that I was given the Holy Spirit gift of healing prayer. The gift calls on us to place our hands on a person and pray for a specific or general healing. There is no way to describe how I knew I had it; it was just there, within me.

I also knew that we are merely instruments of the Holy Spirit. We are given different gifts and serve as the conduit to convey the grace to our brothers and sisters. While most of us can pray over each other in a general sense, the gift of praying for specific healing is a specialized gift of the Holy Spirit.

God always sends confirmations when we are asked to use Holy Spirit gifts. My initial confirmation came during a long, early morning breakfast visit with the incredible Mother Angelica. It was the morning after I had appeared as a guest on her television show on EWTN. The show was called: "Mother Angelica Live" and it included a live audience.

Mother Angelica expressed during the show that she was amazed that the Blessed Virgin had given a Protestant such a mission of spreading God's messages through the apparitions of Medjugorje. She suddenly said, "You know, God can choose any dummy off the street and turn him into a prophet!" the audience broke in spontaneous laughter. "Oh, I didn't mean you," she quickly added.

"It's too late, Mother, you've already said it!" I responded, joining in the laughter.

The following morning, we talked for more than two hours. Within minutes of our meeting the charismatic founder of the highly successful international Catholic television station bluntly told me I had the gift of healing prayer and should use it when called for.

How this charismatic nun knew this, I don't know—and she didn't bother to tell me. "That doesn't mean you hang a sign on the front of your office saying, 'Healing done here!'" she added with a hearty laugh. "You just keep praying and doing what God is asking of you and you will know when to use it!"

Even with such a confirmation, it would take time before I would develop the confidence to actually use the grace of healing prayer. I truly felt I was not worthy to have such a gift—not to mention the enormous responsibility it entailed. I avoided all opportunities to use it on serious conditions and illnesses. Just let me stick with little things, I rationalized.

Several years later, a second confirmation was given to me while I was in Caracas, Venezuela for a series of talks. On the first evening, just before my presentation, a priest approached me as I waited with my translator. He appeared nervous and somewhat hesitant to speak to us. He only spoke Spanish and earnestly began speaking to the translator. My translator in turn told me what he said, including that he knew nothing about Medjugorje or me.

"This is a very holy priest," my translator began, "I know about him. He says he has to meet with us at some point as he has an important message for you—from Jesus."

"What? A message from Jesus for me?" I was startled while at the same time not really sure it was authentic. My skepticism as a journalist was still in place.

The talk was due to begin in a few minutes, so I told my translator, "Tell him we will meet with him later when there is more time and thank him for telling me this."

As it turned out I was only able to meet with the priest after the last talk of the tour. He had reminded my translator of the need to meet with me several times. Finally, at the end of the evening's activities, we found time.

The priest looked at me in earnest while he spoke to my translator. The translator paused a few moments before telling me in a serious tone what he said. "Father says Jesus wants to know why you have not used the gift of healing prayer that He gave you through the Holy Spirit?"

Shocked that a priest who did not know of Medjugorje—or me—would give such a message was more confirmation than I needed. I was chagrined that I had been so reluctant to use the grace. All I could do was quietly thank the priest and tell him I would try not to hesitate to use it in the future. The admonition registered immediately but was overwhelmed as I was in awe that Jesus had given me a message.

In addition to the powerful confirmations, it took a gentle but firm nudge from the Blessed Virgin Mary for me to fully accept the gift and use it when called on.

I think these incredible stories of healing prayer are arguably the most meaningful experiences of this mission; each story is still deeply personal and emotional. Each is unique in its own right.

It is important to fully grasp the *joy* that comes with healing prayer. For those who are so graced to walk again, to hear again, to feel alive again, there is never-ending joy; however, as you will see in these encounters there is also joy *without* the desired physical healing of a loved one. It requires strong belief in Jesus and the Holy Spirit to accept the truth that there is also pure joy in acceptance of God's will. This in itself is a healing.

Stories of the power of Holy Spirit healing underscore two critical points that involve all such healings. First, the actual physical healing of a person is not always perceived in its full ramification; second, the timeline involved from evident healing to the unexpected return or continuation of the illness or condition—or death, can be anything from a few weeks to months or years.

There is a third point to consider: A healing can occur where the disease, illness or condition still exists but in a less aggressive manner or a dormant stage that allows the affected person near normal living. This point adequately describes the "healing" of two-year-old Mary Margaret Marchetti as we begin this chapter with her story.

mary margaret

Mary Margaret was born with the crippling disease of Cystic Fibrosis. Her parents, Gino and Jeannie, were joined by a group of friends from their hometown of Nashville, Tennessee when they took their daughter to Medjugorje in 1987 with the specific goal of seeking a miraculous healing for her. They hoped they could get Mary Margaret into the apparition room during an apparition, as it might be the best chance for her to be healed of the disease.

While wandering along one of the narrow dirt roads in the village they came upon a well-known Franciscan priest Father Svetozar Kraljevac, who had served as a spiritual director for the Medjugorje visionaries. Seizing the opportunity, Jeannie immediately asked him to pray over Mary Margaret in hopes that she may be healed. Father Svetozar paused, looking at the child for a few moments before saying, "Let us pray not so much for a healing but for the child to be well!"

Jeannie was extremely surprised—and acutely disappointed. Later, in answer to the prayers of the supporting group that had accompanied them to the village, the Marchetti family was given the grace to be in the apparition room with their daughter during a live apparition. Afterwards, Jeannie and Dino felt as if *they* had been given a gift of spiritual healing in that they now had the strength to accept the condition of Mary Margaret. For the remainder of their pilgrimage, they were at peace.

As stated many times during talks, there are no coincidences with God. All things happen according to His plan. Several months later, I met the Marchetti family and was given the opportunity to pray over Mary Margaret. It was the first time of actually being called upon to use the grace on a child with such a devastating disease.

The chance to pray for this little girl came about when I was invited by the Dominican Sisters of Aquinas Junior College in Nashville, Tennessee to speak to the members of their order and also at several public events. The day after arriving I spoke at the college, which was open to the public. I was scheduled to speak again that evening and had planned to retire to my room and get some rest. Those plans were quickly changed. A woman pushed her way through the crowd and grabbed my arm, saying, "You don't know me but I've just returned from Medjugorje with a group of people from here . . ."

"That's wonderful! I'm glad you were able to go."

"Excuse me," she interrupted with a smile and a very determined look on her face. "I'm double-parked and I've been sent by several members of our group to invite you to dinner with us, and we just can't accept a no, from you!"

I shook my head and looked at the sister in charge of the order for help. "Well, it's up to you and you do have the time."

"Great!" The woman exclaimed without waiting for an acceptance, I'll pick you up at five o clock sharp and have you back in plenty of time for tonight's talk!"

True to her word, Mollie Gavigan, as she introduced herself, was there on time. During the drive to her home, she gave me a little background on their recent pilgrimage, telling me about Mary Margaret and the desire of her parents to hope for a healing in Medjugorje.

Having met most of the group, I was able to spend a few minutes with Jeannie, who was holding Mary Margaret in her arms. I noticed she was having a difficult time holding in her emotions. As the tears increased she asked me if we could just talk alone away from the crowded room. Mollie directed us to a back bedroom. I noticed that the child was a stark contrast to her mother; she was smiling, calm and seemingly happy.

Jeannie began: "I know that God gave us the grace of being able to accept Mary Margaret's condition, and I do." Jeannie lowered her eyes to her daughter. "But is it wrong for me to keep asking for her to be healed? Maybe I'm not grateful enough for what God has already given us."

I was unsure at first of how to respond to Jeannie's question. Then it came gushing forth without time to prepare. "Jeannie, it is not wrong for you to continue asking for a healing for your daughter. However, you always need to add God's will be done, and then accept it with a peaceful joy knowing that His plan for her will be fulfilled."

I paused, somewhat taken aback by the words that had come so easily. I was fully aware no one but a mother can understand a mother's love for her child.

There was a strong feeling in my heart that Mary Margaret could be healed. I suddenly said to Jeannie: "Mary Margaret is going to be well!" I was unaware at the time that these were the same words Father Svetozar had said to her. I took my rosary from my coat pocket. "Here Jeannie, I want you to have this rosary—it's my favorite one."

"Oh no, I can't accept it—"

"Yes, you must," I insisted. "Listen, I'm going to pray over Mary Margaret now if it's okay with you." In my mind, I'm thinking, are you crazy? Who do you think you are giving this woman such hope that her child will be healed? This is Cystic Fibrosis, one of those big things! Nevertheless, I placed my hand on Mary Margaret's little head and for the first time prayed for a healing of a major condition or illness.

As we left the room somewhat dazed and happy, there was also inner thoughts of, what if—what if she doesn't get well; what if you gave this poor mother false hope?

Three weeks later Jeannie telephoned me just as I was leaving for the airport and running late. "Wayne, we've just come from the doctors. She's well! Mary Margaret is well!"

My insides were churning with awe, happiness and relief.

Two years later my first book *Medjugorje: The Message* was published and it included the story of Mary Margaret. There were many positive letters sent by people to our office telling how the book had changed their life.

Having heard so many wonderful stories of conversion, I was surprised one morning to open a letter from a woman who claimed she had contacted Jeannie Marchetti about Mary Margaret's medical condition. She stated that Jeannie told her that although Wayne was sincere in his attempt, her daughter was not healed from the Cystic Fibrosis; thus, the woman went on to say in her letter that I was not truthful in writing about the healing of this little girl.

I was crushed to hear that Jeannie did not think her daughter was healed. When she had telephoned me after the appointment with Mary Margaret's doctors and exclaimed with joy that Mary Margaret was well, I had taken that to be a confirmation of the healing.

I wrote to the woman defending what I had written about Mary Margaret, assuring her that Jeannie had made that call to me and stated her daughter was well. Nevertheless, I could not get it out of my thoughts. Should I contact Jeannie? What would I say to her?

After much thought and prayer, I felt it best to just let it go. Remembering the words of Father Svet and the nearly same words from me that Mary Margaret would be "well" was enough to satisfy me for the time being. I continued to pray daily for Mary Margaret by name.

The entire matter of Mary Margaret's healing lingered in my mind. In the fall of 2015, I decided to email Jeannie. I told her about the letter I had received and went on to reinforce that the words used by Father Svet, me and her that her daughter was "well" was proof of a healing even though the symptoms of the condition were still there.

Surprisingly, Jeannie responded quickly. She thanked me for keeping Mary Margaret in my prayers. Her daughter, although still having all of the conditions of Cystic Fibrosis had done well in school, went on to obtain a college degree, procured a good job, and was engaged to be married.

Jeannie then added what I perceived as another strong confirmation of her daughter's healing: My email to her had arrived on Mary Margaret's birthday.

She was now 29 years old and doing "well!"

By the summer of 1990, my mission was well underway and it seemed as if I was scheduled to give talks every week. I was physically and mentally drained from twenty-two individual speaking venues in the first five months of the year.

It was time for a break.

Slowly, I settled into a normal life again. Days were spent attending my son Kennedy's Little League baseball games, and my daughter Rebecca's dance recitals. In between, there was golf, daily runs and long walks on the beach

There was one other small task to which I was assigned: it was to pick up Rebecca and two of her classmates every day after school and take them to dance class. Courtney, one of the little girls, was always the last one to the car. "Courtney!" I would fuss with mock-sternness, "why are you always late?"

Smiling, little Courtney would climb in the front seat, hug me and answer in a sweet, little girl voice, "I don't know, I just am!" Of course, I melted. Courtney soon came to be like one of my own children.

It was with shock when we received the grim news on the first Sunday morning in June: Courtney had collapsed at home and had been rushed to the emergency room of the local hospital. She had attended Rebecca's sixth birthday party just a few days before and was noticeably not her usual spirited self. She was tired and did not want to participate in the array of games that had been scheduled.

Then came the devastating news: Courtney had a tumor at the base of her brain and would immediately be flown by helicopter to Duke University in Durham, North Carolina. I was distraught. Intense prayers for Courtney and her parents began immediately.

Early that afternoon, Courtney's mother, Kathian, telephoned just before departing for Durham. "Please Wayne, pray for Courtney," she pleaded. "We have to drive to Durham and we're leaving in a few minutes."

"I've already started," I reassured her.

We really didn't know Courtney's parents Joe and Kathian very well; only through school functions and the dancing activities in which our daughters were involved. They had only recently moved to Myrtle Beach from California and didn't know many people at this point. Kathian had attended one of my local talks on Medjugorje and had read the collection of articles I had run in our newspapers. We had talked several times since as she showed sincere interest in the apparitions, even though they were not Catholic. After her call I sat in silence. I was praying for little Courtney as though she was my own daughter. I didn't know what else to do.

Suddenly I felt that little interior nudge from the Blessed Virgin: I should to go to Durham and personally pray over Courtney. Suddenly, there was no hesitation or worry about being qualified or unworthy. I had to do it.

Reaching Kathian at the hospital the following morning, I told her what I wanted to do and asked if it was okay for us to come. "Oh, thank you! Of course, it's all right!"

Kathian was extremely grateful—and desperate. Courtney was still in a coma and had not responded to treatment. The tumor was inoperable; two of the top tumor specialists were doing all that was medically possible. "They have told us that there is nothing more they can do," Kathian said tearfully. "We can only hope and pray, so please come!"

During the long, four-hour drive, little was said. I prayed constantly with intensity—but also with some doubt that I would actually be able to do it. It was not doubt in the power of prayer but in the fact that Courtney's illness was a very serious one, a major cross.

Somewhere along the way to Durham, I remembered the words of the priest in Caracas. It brought back the often-asked question: Why me? I wondered if I would ever just accept the fact that God asks and we either respond or we do not.

Despite the doubts and questions, I knew I had to pray over Courtney. She was very precious personally, and somehow this was an important part of the mission. I found myself bargaining with the Blessed Mother to please ask her Son through the power of the Holy Spirit to heal Courtney. I would in turn do my part by actually laying hands on Courtney and praying with confidence.

It was late at night when we arrived and checked into a motel, leaving immediately afterwards for the hospital. The elevator door opened to the children's intensive care unit. There alone in the large waiting area were Courtney's parents. "I can't thank you enough for coming," Kathian said, hugging me. "I've already arranged with the nurses for you to see Courtney, so if you're ready I'll take you to her now."

Kathian quickly ushered me into Courtney's room. My heart leapt as I took in the sight before me. There was my sweet little Courtney, tubes attached seemingly everywhere to her little body, and monitoring machines beeping steady signals of vital signs. She was still in a deep coma.

Trembling, I took a rosary from my pocket that had been blessed during the time of an apparition at Medjugorje. "Kathian, I know you're Protestant, but this rosary came from Medjugorje and…"

"Oh, thank you, thank you!" Kathian said as she took the rosary and wrapped it around Courtney's wrist. "I was raised Catholic and I'm familiar with the rosary."

That surprised me. Part of my hesitation in praying over Courtney, beside my own doubts, was knowing that the family was Protestant. They may not comprehend the importance of Medjugorje's message of prayer and fasting so necessary in cases of healing. I hoped they would understand beyond a desperate reaching for anything that might help their little girl. Joe had only recently begun attending church and I was pleased he had agreed to my coming.

I pressed on. "I also have this holy oil and I'd like to anoint Courtney if it's okay with you."

"Yes, yes, please!" Kathian urged. "Anything you want!"

For the next three hours, I prayed over Courtney. Occasionally her eyes would flicker; but that was the only sign of life. Each time doubt seeped into my thoughts the fervor of prayer increased.

Finally, it was time to leave. Joe had come in to give Kathian a break and was bowed in prayer with me, gently holding his daughter's still hand. But there was one more prayer I wanted to say. Silently, I pleaded to my favorite person in Heaven besides Jesus and Mary: "Saint Therese, Little Flower of Jesus, please, *please,* give a sign of flowers — anything. Just let us know that Courtney is going to pull through this."

As I walked out of the ward with Joe, there in front of us on the glass windows across from the elevator doors, was a huge display of posters with all kinds of flowers drawn in crayon by children! I laughed in relief, wondering why I hadn't seen them when we arrived. I knew it was the answer to my prayer to Saint Therese!

Stopping, I grabbed Joe by the arm. "Joe, she's going to make it through this! I know it!" I told Joe about my prayer to Saint Therese. "You may think this is a little strange, but she never fails me!"

Immediately after telling Joe that Courtney would pull through, doubt crept in again. What if she doesn't recover? What if I raise their hopes and then—? However, both accepted that this sign of flowers was real. They were desperately ready to believe anything I told them.

Joe and I returned to the motel to grab a few hours of sleep. I would be driving home later and Joe hadn't slept since arriving. When we left, Courtney's condition had not changed. My prayers now were for peace and acceptance by Courtney's family of her condition. If she survived the entire ordeal, wonderful; if not, let there be acceptance of God's will.

Throughout the mission I had learned in similar life-threatening or terminal crises to first pray for the grace to accept whatever cross is given as a prerequisite to asking for actual physical healing. That, in essence, is why Our Lady stresses penance so frequently in her messages. It simply means we are to take up our daily crosses without complaining.

That evening, I tried to call Kathian at the hospital to see how Courtney was doing. The line stayed busy for over an hour. Finally, I got through. "She's awake! She's awake!" Kathian was practically screaming. "She awoke and began crying and asking for her daddy!"

I prayed a thank you prayer to the Blessed Virgin – and to Saint Therese for her beautiful sign—and, of course to Jesus, hoping He was pleased that I had finally prayed for healing in a serious case.

But then we received an even more beautiful sign.

Kathian, still in a heightened state, added: "Wayne, I have to tell you what happened just before Courtney came out of the coma—" Kathian paused to control her emotions. "My best friend in California called and told me about a strange dream she had last night. She is a Lutheran and doesn't know anything about Medjugorje or you and what you do. And she doesn't know a whole lot about the Virgin Mary."

Again, Kathian paused a moment, overwhelmed by what she was about to tell me. "She said that in her dream, the Blessed Virgin Mary was holding Courtney in her arms. And there was a man she did not know standing next to the Virgin Mary with his hand on Courtney – praying!"

I sat in numb joy in the quiet of my office, hardly able to respond much less comprehend what had happened. I vowed again never to hesitate to pray over a suffering soul, whether the illness or condition was major or minor.

For the next several months, Courtney struggled with her illness. Finally, and mercifully, she died. I knew that the healing prayer had worked even if only for a short time. In those last months of struggle, her family grew closer to God. Friends and relatives did the same. Lives were changed through the suffering of my little Courtney.

In receiving the news of Courtney's passing, I wept as though this little girl was my own child. They were tears of grief mixed with those of joy. She was now dwelling in the one place where there is peace that passes all understanding.

learning to obey

I was back in Ireland for a second tour in a short time frame, with the added grace of having my family with me. The organizers had planned a nice welcoming party, which we were enjoying very much. Included in the celebration was the birthday of son Kennedy, who turned eight years old on April 7.

The lady of the home where the party was held came to me a short while later and asked, "I wonder if you could do me a great favor?"

"Of course," I replied, "What can I do for you?

"Well, it's not for me but for my neighbor," she said moving a bit closer and lowering her voice. "This woman is suffering from cancer and she's only 32 years old and she has a limited time to live according to her doctors. She knows you are here and she has read your tabloid." My hostess again paused briefly before continuing. "Would you be willing to go to her home and pray over her? She's not afraid of dying but she has five little children and a very loving and caring husband and she is distraught over what is to become of them."

My heart leaped in fear. Cancer? I was being asked to pray over a young mother with terminal cancer and five children. My hostess looked at me expectantly, waiting for my answer. "Well, yes, if you think it might help." My insides were churning. What could I possibly do to help this woman?

We went to the house of the woman and entered the bedroom where the young mother was confined. She looked at me with as much exuberant joy as she could muster. "Oh my, thank you so much for taking the time to visit me!"

I smiled and made my way to a chair that had been placed at the side of the bed where she was lying. "Thank you for allowing me to visit with you," I replied. And within minutes, we were talking like old friends, exchanging stories about our children. After a slight pause, the woman looked at me directly and asked, "Can you pray to Our Lady for my children and husband that they will be taken care of when I am gone?"

I didn't hesitate in my answer. Finally, I was learning to obey. If God was asking me to pray over this woman, how could I say no? I smiled at the woman now filled with confidence. "Yes, of course I will; and I will also pray that you will be at peace."

"Oh, I'm ready personally but you know, *I am a mother!* I love my children and my husband. My concern is what is to happen to them when I am no longer here?"

In that moment, the concern and the look on the woman's face said it all. I fully understood her need to be reassured that her family would be taken care of. I did my best to calm her, using the Blessed Virgin as the example of motherhood, how she had to suffer spiritually as her Son went through the horror of crucifixion and how she was now the spiritual mother for all of us who are children of God.

I was amazed how easy the words came to me as a spoke to this woman. I no longer feared or worried that I was not worthy to bring comfort and to pray over her. We talked for a while longer until my hostess suggested we should go. "Yes, of course; but before we go I am going to pray over you," I said to the woman.

I placed my hands on her and prayed for her family and for her peace. Afterwards the woman took in a deep breath, let it out and said, "I am now filled with peace and I thank you for that."

Several months later the young mother died in peace. The family stepped forward and saw to the needs of the children and gave comfort to the woman's husband. I was thankful for the opportunity to meet this woman and pray over her. Somehow, I knew that little act of praying over her had helped.

I vowed to try harder to obey when God called on me to pray over people—regardless of the seriousness of the condition or disease.

praying over mother angelica

Several years after having been told by Mother Angelica that I had the Holy Spirit grace of healing prayer, I was with her at a Marian conference where we were both invited speakers. The charismatic founder of EWTN was still suffering the effects of a recent severe stroke that had curtailed her activities.

As we waited in a cordoned off area from the main area where the talks were presented, I caught her eye for an instant. A slight smile of recognition creased her face.

I got up from my seat and walked over to her. "Mother, how are you? It's so good to see you again." She nodded in response but said nothing due to her condition, which limited her speech.

I quickly realized she was saving her strength, as she was due to speak next. In a sudden impulsive moment, I said to her, "Mother, may I pray over you?"

The famous nun who had committed her life in service to God beamed radiantly and said in a weak, raspy voice, "Yes, I would be grateful." With that, I then prayed over her.

Imagine the irony of God that I should end up praying for the woman who had first told me I had the gift of healing prayer.

Pope Francis: **"When we are in darkness and difficulty, the smile does not come; but there is hope that teaches us to smile on that path to find God."**

the physician saint

The speaking tour in Alaska had been filled with wonderful experiences, as you will hear more about later in the book. I was more than ready for a few days off and half-wished I hadn't agreed to an impromptu talk at a local hospital in Anchorage. Yet, as always there was an underlying reason not seen by me at the time. Feeling the usual nudge, I had agreed. It was Our Lady's quiet way of letting me know it was important.

The crowd was small but it readily filled the little auditorium of the hospital. One family in particular was pleased that I was there. Sharon McMichael and her two teenage daughters sought me out afterwards to tell me about Doctor Richard McMichael, Sharon's husband and the father of the girls. He was a surgeon at the hospital where he specialized in cancer treatment.

"He really wanted to be here tonight, but he is in surgery right now operating on a patient," she told me in a quiet voice. "All of us, especially my husband, have been strongly affected by the apparitions of the Virgin Mary at Medjugorje. We want to go because Richard is himself seriously ill with cancer, but we're not sure he could physically make the trip."

Marie, one of Sharon's daughters spoke up. "We'd like to ask you to pray for our dad, that we can take him to Medjugorje for a healing."

With that tears flowed from the eyes of all three women. Sharon went on to tell me that her husband, despite his illness, was continuing to treat other cancer patients. "Of course, he knows how sick he is but feels it's important to treat others as long as he is physically able. Thanks to your articles, Medjugorje has given Richard the strength to accept whatever God has in store for him. He is not a bit afraid."

I left the hospital auditorium knowing that meeting the McMichaels was the reason for my acceptance of this last-minute speaking invitation. However, as always there was more to come. It was several months later on a pilgrimage to Medjugorje that the story resumed.

"Wait! Mr. Weible, wait!"

Turning around, there was faint recognition of two girls who were calling my name. "Mr. Weible, I don't know if you remember us—from Anchorage, Alaska?"

"Oh, yes, you're the daughters of Dr. Richard McMichael," I said, recognizing them. "How is your father?"

"That's why we stopped you," the older girl replied. "He's here, and he's very sick. He knows you're here also and our mother sent us to find you to see if you would come and visit him."

All personal concerns disappeared. "Of course; let's go."

"This way, we have a car," she yelled as they hurried toward the road behind the rectory.

Within minutes we were at the house. Entering a darkened room, the doctor was laying on a bed, his wife Sharon, on one side and a priest sitting on the other holding his hand. They were softly praying the rosary. Sharon gave me a quick glance of gratitude and then whispered to her husband, "Richard, Wayne Weible is here. He's come to see you."

Dr. McMichael slowly turned his head toward me, and with a weak smile, continued to mouth the words of the prayers. He was as white as the sheets. On completion of the rosary, the priest motioned me to take his place at the side of the bed. This was the most difficult part of the mission—having to face situations like this. It wasn't false humility; I knew who I was and what my life had been before Medjugorje.

Fighting the reluctance, I began to talk to Dr. McMichael, keeping it light, yet realizing the seriousness of his illness. I was relieved some ten minutes later when the priest quietly suggested to Richard that he better get some rest. As I started to leave, the doctor gripped my hand with surprising momentary strength. "Thank you for coming. You are the reason I've come here; your story. Don't worry about me. I'll make it."

Sharon rode with me on my return to Marija's house where I was staying and as we pulled up to the gate, she asked, "I hope I'm not imposing but could you ask Marija to come and pray over my husband?"

"Sharon, I don't know if she will, but I'll be glad to ask her. And please know that I'm going to pray for him constantly."

As I entered the kitchen, Marija was standing near the sink with hands on hips and a mock frown on her face. "You are late for lunch!"

I hastily explained, telling her about Dr. McMichael, adding that I did not think he would live long enough to leave Medjugorje, and then asked if she would go pray over him. "I will try to go later and tonight at the apparition I will recommend him to Gospa."

I hoped "later" would not be too late, but I was grateful for her acceptance. This was Marija's special gift as a visionary: to pray for the sick and handicapped.

Back in Medjugorje a few months later and once again staying at Marija's home, I suddenly remembered Dr. Richard McMichael and his wife's plea that Marija come and pray over him. "Marija, do you remember that man, the doctor who was dying of cancer? The one I asked you to go see and pray over? Were you able to find him and do you know what happened to him?"

She thought for a moment, then exclaimed with a bright smile, "Oh, yes, Dr. Richard. I go *two* times to see and pray for him. He came to the church for Holy Mass, and then, he and his family left for home in Alaska."

"He went home?"

"Yes, he is able to enjoy Medjugorje for a few days and then go home."

I was stunned. Having seen first-hand how critically ill he was at the time of my visit, I was sure he would never leave Medjugorje alive. His family was convinced of the same. Dr. Richard McMichael's temporary recovery was another of the thousands of miracles involving physical healings and cures of people who had come to Medjugorje on faith.

Most of the incredible events of healing at Medjugorje would never be recorded or known by the public. I would learn later that this courageous doctor, who had treated so many cancer patients while suffering the extremes of the disease himself, would die peacefully and without pain several weeks after his return home to Anchorage.

Commentary – Some may ask how it is that a child or adult, who is prayed over and seems to have been healed, suddenly is struck with the terminal illness or condition again and dies. Some may even question as to whether the person was healed at all. I do not.

Here's a question to ponder: How long did Lazarus live after Jesus resurrected him from the dead? A year? Two years—five years or maybe 10 years? We don't know; but does any believer in God doubt that the miracle occurred?

All of us who believe in God are asked to pray for one another. We extend our hands over the sick and ask God for them to be healed. We ask our family and friends to pray for us when we receive crosses.

In one of the most important messages the Blessed Virgin gave in Medjugorje, she gives us the answer to bringing healing to spiritual sickness as well as physical. All of us who believe can do it. She said: *My children, through prayer and fasting one can stop wars; one can alter the laws of nature . . .*

Can you imagine? Through the use of prayer and fasting together, you can stop wars; she means the wars in our relationships, our struggles against addictions, our family strife and divorce and most importantly, our rejection of the gift of life through the horror of abortion. These and many more are the major wars raging inside of us. The worst, of course, is the war of Satan attempting to take us from the love of God. Now, through this message that comes directly from the throne of God, we have the "weapon" to win these wars.

"You can alter the laws of nature . . ."

In short, you can take the very hands that have offended God so many times and turn them into instruments of healing through the gift of the Holy Spirit. Our Lady is telling all of us about these graces. For some the gift is stronger while for others it is less. God alone decides the size of the gift for each individual.

I will forever be grateful to my Heavenly Father for allowing me to meet and use this grace for all of the people in these stories and for many more.

And he called the twelve together and gave them power and authority over all demons and to cure diseases, and he sent them out to preach the kingdom of God and to heal.

—Luke 9: 1-2.

Dear children! In this time of grace, I call you to take the cross of my beloved Son Jesus in your hands and to meditate on His passion and death. May your suffering be united in His suffering and love will win, because He who is love gave Himself out of love to save each of you. Pray, pray, pray until love and peace begin to reign in your hearts. Thank you for having responded to my call.

—Message of December 25, 2013.

5

carrying his cross

It would take time, experience and hard-earned lessons of the cross for me to learn true discernment of God's plan at Medjugorje; and, to accept the call to be part of it by witness through talks and writings. Along the way, I learned that joy can be found in redemptive suffering. Next came discovery that Jesus speaks to our hearts and gives us personal parables and little lessons of the cross as we grow in faith.

The lessons deepen as the relationship between a child of God and Jesus becomes more intimate and personal. One such example occurred as I prepared to return to the village of Medjugorje after a long absence. It had been a little more than a year since the last trip. The reason I had not returned was the raging civil war (1991-95) that was devastatingly wracking many of the republics of the former Yugoslavia, leaving countless villages and towns in rubble; death was everywhere and the atrocities carried out by both sides were demonic.

There was no desire to go into this cauldron of hate—until a priest friend convinced me otherwise. In hindsight, it was a powerful lesson and I discovered an entirely different Medjugorje.

The war had burdened the people with thousands of individual crosses. More than a hundred thousand people had been killed and thousands more left as refugees. Many former pilgrims to Medjugorje had returned in the midst of the fighting to bring aid to the innocent victims desperate for medical, monetary and food supplies. These brave souls had involuntarily learned the lesson of the cross.

Knowing all of this, how could I not return even in the midst of war? Still, there was a lesson to be learned.

I was happy to be returning to Medjugorje—but at the same time, very tentative. This incredible place of pilgrimage was now a bloody, horrendous war zone that was dangerous for everyone. One would have to be crazy to deliberately go into such danger. It was the reason I had stopped going on pilgrimage to the village and I had no desire to return until the fighting ended.

Yet, in spite of deep reservations, I had promised Father Svet that I would come. Father Svetozar Kraljevac was one of the Franciscan priests stationed in Medjugorje. I had met him on my first pilgrimage to the village. We had become close friends and he served as my informal spiritual advisor. He had also served as such to the visionaries of Medjugorje.

Now, because of the conflict Father Svet was consumed with intense fundraising to provide relief funds for food and medicine, and create awareness of the desperate situation occurring in his native Bosnia-Hercegovina. He had asked me repeatedly to make another trip during the wartime conditions. I saw no reason to take such a risk of life and I told him so.

At an October 1992 Medjugorje conference in Denver, Colorado, where both of us were scheduled speakers, Father Svet took up the offensive again as we shared a few moments together in the speaker's lounge. "But why, Father?" I had answered, "I've been there enough times; I know what's going on with the war. Besides, my traveling schedule is already too full."

Quietly, my priest friend pointed out that I did not know the Medjugorje after the last two years of war; I did not know firsthand the suffering penance of the people. It was true. I hadn't been there since August 1991, just before the war began in earnest.

"Come and see," he said, pausing for emphasis. "Just come and see!"

"Okay, Father," I relented, "I'll pray about it, but the only time I have open is the week after Christmas and that's usually family time.

Father Svet reached over and squeezed my shoulder and said with a little smile, "You pray about it. And then we shall see what happens!"

Not wasting any time, I went straight to a little prayer chapel that had been set up near the speaker's lounge. I prayed a special prayer I had learned to reserve for special matters—and it was not a prayer to the Blessed Mother. Instead, I asked my favorite saint, St. Therese de Lisieux, for a sign and I did so rather bluntly: "My dear St. Therese, please let me receive or see a red rose as a sign that I am to return to Medjugorje at this time." A *real* red rose, I added with emphasis. With that I went back to the lounge.

As I sat in silence enjoying a few moments of peace, I thought about Saint Therese. She was my first saint. Known affectionately by her followers as "The Little Flower," she convinced authorities of the church to allow her to enter the convent in 1888, at the tender age of 15. She simply wanted to live totally dedicated to God. And for nine years she did so in a way that has since touched the lives of millions of people. Death came at the young age of 24, but Therese had accomplished her all-consuming goal: she became a saint.

I was surprised when my beloved saint responded so quickly. In less than an hour, a conference volunteer came into the lounge looking for me. "Here's a little gift for you," she said as she handed me a single, long-stemmed red rose!

"Thank you," I laughed, "I've kind of been expecting this!"

The lady looked at me puzzled. "Well, I was simply asked by one of the conference attendees to give you this and to tell you thank you for all you're doing."

I was now sure I needed to return in spite of the war and its impending danger. How could I speak knowledgeably about the messages of the Queen of Peace without seeing personally how the enemy of God and man was attempting to destroy what had taken so long to establish? I wondered why I hadn't thought of that before.

Seeing Father Svet across the room, I told him what had happened. Laughing and repeating several times "Praise God" he hugged me.

My priest friend would be at our home the following week. I had invited him to come for a few days of rest before the next conference in California, where we were both again scheduled as speakers. It was an invitation intended to give him a break from a demanding schedule.

The day after Fr. Svet arrived at our home, I thanked him for coming. "Oh no," he answered with a slight smile, "There is no need to thank me. But, can you do me a small favor?"

"Of course, Father, anything!"

Father Svet paused and then said, "I have been given many things to take back with me and I do not have the capability to do this as I only have a small travel bag. I was wondering if you would bring something very special and important when you come to Medjugorje?"

"Of course. What do you want me to bring?"

Father Svet started upstairs to his guest room beckoning me to follow. "Come, I must show you." In the corner of the room was a package wrapped in brown, wrinkled paper. He carefully unwrapped it to reveal a large crucifix with the figure of Jesus broken in several places. A hand

and foot were missing. It was at least three feet long. "Do you remember this cross?" he asked, holding it up for my closer inspection.

"Yes, it's the cross you had at the Denver conference."

"That is correct. It is a cross from our church in Mostar where it was damaged during an attack. I have carried it throughout the United States to show the people what has happened to the Church in our country. Like Jesus, it has suffered — it has been crucified."

As always, his words were simple and direct. "I would now ask you if you could bring this cross with you when you return to Medjugorje. I do not have room to take it and the other things.

I hesitated before answering, feeling a little uneasy about having to carry a cross through several airports. I also felt immediate embarrassment by my reluctance. However, there was no way to say no at this point. "Well, uh, yes, I'll bring it for you."

"Are you sure?" Father Svet sensed my hesitation.

"Of course, it's no problem. I'll wrap it in a special padding to protect it."

Later, as I prepared to make the return to Medjugorje, I was still disturbed by my hesitation to bring this cross all the way to the village. It would have to fit safely into the overhead on the plane and in a way where it would not be further damaged. I quickly realized that by wrapping it with padding it would be safe—and, no one would recognize it as a cross.

Lugging two carry-on bags and Father Svet's cross, now covered in heavy brown wrapping, I arrived at our local airport bound for New York's Kennedy Airport. From there, I was scheduled for a Lufthansa flight to Frankfort, and then on to Split, for a two-hour auto ride into Medjugorje. Father Svet would pick me up at the airport and drive us to Medjugorje.

Problems popped up immediately. Sending the cross through the x-ray machine, the attendant looked at me rather strangely. "Is that a cross?" I actually flushed as I admitted yes, it was a cross. "Oh," she added, "Are you a minister?"

"No, no," I answered, "I'm just doing a favor for a friend." So much for being discreet about carrying a cross!

To make matters worse, there were many people in the area and I was getting strange looks. I could also feel the guilt about my reluctance in wanting to carry it in public. Having gone through so many spiritual experiences in the last six years, I was dismayed that I was still so worldly as to be embarrassed by outward signs of spirituality.

Little problems at the local airport turned into larger ones at the first stop in Charlotte, N. C. Because of weather conditions and holiday overbookings, the connection into New York was 45 minutes late. As a result, we landed late in New York and I missed my international flight by twenty minutes.

"Well," I replied in disgust when told by an agent that the flight had just left, "Then book me on the next one out of here; I've got to get to Bosnia-Hercegovina!"

I was not in a good mood, having run through traffic to reach the international terminal. To add injury to insult, I was caught in a heavy rain and now the cross was beginning to poke through the wrapping and padding at the corners. "I'm sorry, sir, but there are no flights until tomorrow, and even then, I can't get you on Croatian Airlines," the agent said, adding, "They're completely booked for the rest of the week due to the holiday crowds."

As the agent was giving me the bad news, he kept staring at the now-tattered package of the cross I was holding. "Is that a cross? Are you a missionary?"

"Yes, it's a cross!" I answered with a forced smile. "And no, I'm not a missionary — I'm a journalist."

Desperate now, I pleaded with the agent to exhaust every possible avenue that might possibly get me into Bosnia-Hercegovina. After a futile ten minutes of computer keyboard queries, he apologized again. "I'm sorry, there's absolutely nothing available." And then pausing, he added with a quizzical smile, "Isn't there a war going on there? Why are you going to such a dangerous place?"

All I could do was smile limply. "I told you, I'm a journalist." There was no way to explain that a saint had given me a sure sign to return to Medjugorje and that I knew I was supposed to be able to get there. Finally accepting that I could not get there *any time* in the next five days, I trudged wearily back through the rain to the terminal from which I had just come. I would have to return home.

By now the cross was noticeably visible through the torn wrapping. I was frustrated. Hadn't I received a sign that I was to make this trip to Medjugorje? How could I have come all the way to New York and was now having to return home with a broken cross?

During the return flight to Charlotte where again due to the holiday crowds I would have to stay overnight before returning to Myrtle Beach, I suddenly "felt" the discernment of the day's events. Yes, I *was* to return to Medjugorje, *but not at this time!*

And then came the lesson as I felt Jesus speaking to my heart: ***How did it feel to carry my cross today?***

The exhaustion and frustration of running through airports and missing connections suddenly vanished. I closed my eyes and whispered, "Oh, Jesus, please forgive me for..."

I couldn't even think of the right words.

*

Commentary: There is a story I occasionally use during talks to emphasize the fact that we all have crosses to carry in life, and the fact that some of us are not happy with the cross or crosses we have been given. The story goes like this:

A man, who we will call Joe for the sake of the story, grew weary of having to carry his cross. It just didn't seem to fit him and he struggled with it. So, one day he called out to Jesus that he needed to talk to Him about his cross.

Jesus immediately answered: "Joe, what can I do for you? You seem unhappy with your cross."

"Yes Lord, I am," Joe answered. It just doesn't seem to fit me. It's not that I don't want to carry a cross, but maybe you have one for me that I am better able to handle."

Jesus smiled. "Come with me Joe."

Jesus led Joe to a huge warehouse filled with crosses of all sizes and shapes. "This is where we keep the crosses. Just throw yours on the pile and see if you can find one that better fits you."

Joe was delighted. "Oh thank you, Jesus, I'm sure I can find one that fits me a little better." And with that, Joe began to rummage through the crosses.

An hour passed and still Joe had not found a cross that suited him. Another hour went by and still no luck. Finally, Joe cried out to Jesus. "Lord, I've found one that fits me perfectly! I'll take this one."

"Good, Jesus replied with a slight smile, "That's the one you came in with!"

I'm sure you get the point of the story. Most of us are never fully adjusted to the crosses we are given in life. Humanity causes us to seek the least painful ones; we fail to accept the reality of the death of Jesus on the cross, because if and when we do, we then are chosen to share in His redemptive suffering. As we grow in faith and commitment, we may be given even more difficult crosses.

The good news is our attitude concerning our crosses can change. It changes as we grow closer to Jesus and learn to accept what He asks of us in life. It changes as we go through the spiritual conversion process and begin to develop an intimate and personal relationship with Him. Once we reach the ultimate height of conversion, that is, to be completely open to all that God asks of us, we are able to carry whatever cross we are given.

And that, in turn, brings us joy!

And he who does not take his cross and follow me is not worthy of me. He who finds his life will lose it, and he who loses his life for my sake will find it.

—Matthew 10: 38-39.

...My children, the Father comes to be known through the cross. Therefore, do not reject the cross. Strive to comprehend and accept it with my help. When you will be able to accept the cross you will also understand the love of the Heavenly Father; you will walk with my Son and with me; you will differ from those who have not come to know the love of the Heavenly Father, those who listen to Him but do not understand Him, those who do not walk with Him - who have not come to know Him...

—Excerpt from message of December 02, 2013.

6

the dark night of the soul

It is difficult through human understanding to determine whether the mysterious, inexplicable condition is from Heaven or hell. On the one hand, the victim soul out of humility accepts the penance and continues on; on the other hand, the soul can be so defeated and ostracized as to be pushed into the extreme of no longer believing in God.

This strange condition is known as *The Dark Night of the Soul,* the title of which comes from a poem written by Saint John of the Cross. It creates a feeling of complete and utter abandonment by God in even the holiest of souls, as well as the ordinary striving to follow the teachings of Jesus.

It is impossible to comprehend acceptance of this cross, given to a chosen soul under the most extreme conditions. Only later does the recipient realize that this agonizing form of "pruning" of the soul is pure grace from the Father. To put it succinctly, those who bear fruit, He prunes to bear more fruit.

Newly canonized Saint Theresa of Calcutta is a prime example in today's modern world of this inexplicable suffering. Arguably, she was seen by a predominant percentage of people as a person of pure, simple and holy joy. Yet, this saint felt empty and alone, totally abandoned by the love of God right up to a short time before her death.

Saint Mother Theresa devoted the latter years of her life to serving the desperately poor and dying in India, striving to give dignity of life to all placed in her pathway. Ten years after her death, a collection of her private letters surfaced, revealing her suffering the dark night of the soul, with deep and lasting feelings of desolation and abandonment by God. "I am told God lives in me," she wrote in 1957, "and yet, the reality of darkness and coldness and emptiness is so great that nothing touches my soul."

There is another popular saint of the late 19th century who also suffered the dark night: Saint Thérèse de Lisieux, better known among followers as "The Little Flower." In the last eighteen months of life, not only did she go through the real agony of tuberculosis, which ultimately led to her death at the young age of 24, Saint Thérèse also suffered the agony of perceived abandonment by God. It lasted to the final moments of her short life.

Just prior to her death, St. Thérèse was quoted as saying, "It is true that at times a very small ray of the sun comes to illumine my darkness, and then the trial ceases for *an instant*, but afterward the memory of this ray, instead of causing me joy, makes my darkness even more dense."

Encountering the dark night of the soul among the most devout of believers is not unusual. In fact, it is almost a surety that it will happen. It may last a short while and end; or, for others it may occur, seemingly stop and then return again sometime later.

I learned about the dark night of the soul the hard way: I experienced it personally. It left me perplexed and very frightened. The darkness began in the mid to late nineties. At first I could not understand how my mission of pure joy and dedication could suddenly turn into such emptiness and sudden doubt. No matter how many times I asked this question of the Lord, I received no answer.

It was only through deep prayer and introspection that I later came to understand that we see only as far as our senses will allow us and we become frustrated with the limitations. Slowly, the revelation comes; it requires obscure faith to see with the eyes of the eternal, to view with the lens of our hearts united to His Sacred Heart.

argentina: i don't want to go

At the height of the dark night of the soul, a letter of invitation came during an already difficult time. I had been home for more than a month, getting a good rest from a series of talks around the country. The problem was, I felt spiritually empty and harbored a sense of failure, as though I hadn't given my all in the presentations over the past few months. I did not understand it nor did I know an exact point of when it began.

Now, even after a period of rest and away from the mission, the feelings persisted, perhaps even grew worse. It felt as though my prayers were bouncing off the ceiling. I kept wondering: *Where are you Jesus? Where are you Mary?*

My beloved Virgin Mary who had brought me into this work seemed distant. Attendance at Holy Mass and receiving Jesus in the Eucharist was still sacred and the center of my spiritual life. It seemed to be the only time of relief. However, upon leaving the church the emptiness returned. Praying the rosary, my favorite prayer, was lacking something and I didn't know what it was.

Adding to my distress, the dark night would seem to slowly erode away and leave me with a feeling of spiritual revival. But it would return, little by little until once more I felt totally abandoned. As it progressed, I was sure it was all my fault due to my human failings.

Maybe, I thought, *my mission is over.*

Then a letter of invitation arrived from a Medjugorje prayer group in Buenos Aires, Argentina. I read it without enthusiasm. Normally I would be jumping up and down with joy at the thought of taking the Medjugorje message to another country. They were asking me to come and spend the better part of September 1996, with a full program of talks; and, an extension into the country of Chile for several days before returning home. I sent a letter of acceptance the following day. Several hours later, I regretted accepting the invitation. The thought persisted—*I really do not want to go!*

Not wanting to go on mission had never occurred before. I actually thought that maybe breaking a leg or an arm would give me reason for cancelling the tour. But it didn't happen. The day of departure arrived and I was headed to Argentina and Chile, despite my feelings of abandonment.

Arriving at the airport in Buenos Aires after the 10-hour flight, I was greeted by a large crowd from the prayer group waving welcome signs and singing with exuberance and evident joy. I smiled in acceptance but cringed on the inside.

We loaded in a car belonging to a woman named Mariana, the head of the prayer group, and started the journey to the hotel where I would be staying. No one seemed to drive within a designated lane and I tensed continually as we made our way into the massive city. Mariana smiled and said, "We have a surprise for you; there is a lady named Sara Najun, who lives here. She has inner locutions of Jesus and Mary, and we are planning a time for you to meet her. She is also anxious to meet you."

I didn't respond immediately and then said, "Listen, that's nice of you but I have met many claimed visionaries and locutionists, and I don't really need to meet another one."

There was a pause in the conversation. I immediately regretted being so blunt and—rude. "I'm sorry, that's rude of me, but I just want to concentrate on the talks," I weakly tried to rationalize my remarks.

I settled into the spacious room in the plush hotel where I would be staying during the majority of the tour and soon I was fast asleep. Waking early, I donned my running clothes and headed out of the door of the hotel after asking a few directions. I ran to the point of exhaustion, as though punishing myself for not wanting to be here.

Mariana had planned a luncheon with the entire prayer group in attendance. "We thought you might like to meet the group who is sponsoring your tour," she said as we took our seats. "You only have this event and then the talk in a very large church tonight."

After lunch, I was grateful for the quiet time during the hours before the evening talk. I prayed a rosary asking for a successful tour and in thanksgiving for the hard work of the prayer group to set it up. Time seemed to fly and before I knew it, it was time to leave for the evening's event.

We arrived at a large church with huge open windows along both sides of the sanctuary. People were everywhere! "Oh, look at this!" Mariana said excitedly, "You are going to have a very large crowd tonight!"

The church was filled to standing room only. I should have been humbled and grateful, but all I could think of was how empty I felt. The schedule was set up with my talk and then after a short break, Holy Mass.

I was introduced and the evening began as I spoke for approximately 45 minutes through a translator. Usually, I would pray to the Holy Spirit to give me the words for the people gathered at each talk. On this night, it seemed as if every word was forced. I returned to my seat to a surprising standing ovation, leaving me wondering if they were simply being polite. The applause continued on as I thought: *dear Mother, that is the worst talk I have ever given—I'm so sorry!*

Suddenly there was a commotion in the front of the massive church. Approximately 30 to 40 people were approaching the altar despite the priest motioning for them to return to their seats. They ignored him and came directly to me. A lady grabbed my hand and placed it on her head. I knew immediately that she was asking me to pray over her. *How was this possible*, I thought, *nothing had been said about me praying over people!*

The first lady was followed by the rest of the wave of people, each one doing the same thing. I responded and prayed over each of them while still thinking there was no Holy Spirit in me; but the Holy Spirit was indicating otherwise!

Bedlam began as waves of the attending crowd continued to come up on the altar wanting me to pray over them. After a while, the priest looked at me, smiled and raised his hands in surrender! It lasted close to an hour before order was restored and the Holy Mass commenced.

Getting through the crowd to make our way to the car took another hour. Mariana and the prayer group were ecstatic. I was dazed and now even more confused. How could the Holy Spirit be so present when I felt nothing?

A routine formed for the remaining days of the tour. Each morning I would run to exhaustion. Each evening, the same thing happened with the crowds coming forward to be prayed over. There were healings taking place and the crowds grew larger with each talk. No one had said anything in advance about my praying over people. It just happened.

On the final day in Argentina, Mariana and the group had planned a full celebration dinner with the entire prayer group plus a few others invited to send me off to Chile early the next morning. As we entered the home where the dinner would occur, Mariana glanced at me with an expression of guilt. "I hope you will not be too upset with me but I invited Sara to come tonight. She really wanted to meet you and said it was important."

I took a deep sigh. It had been a wonderful and well-organized tour thanks to the work of Mariana. Meeting Sara was the least I could do for her. "Yes, of course Mariana, I apologize for my initial rejection and will be glad to meet her now."

Mariana's eyes lit up. "Oh, thank you Wayne, Sara is right over there!" With that, she took my hand and led me to a woman standing by a table filled with food. Sara Najun was small and thin to the point of being frail, but with eyes that immediately grabbed my attention. There was nothing about her outwardly suggesting that she had the charism of hearing Jesus and the Blessed Virgin—except for her eyes that seemed filled with holiness.

We began making small talk. Her English was perfect and I soon discovered that she was a teacher of English at one of the colleges in the city. As we were talking, Sara suddenly stopped and said to me, "Please excuse me but I have to go into another room. Our Lady wishes to give me a message for you and also one for the guests here this evening."

As Sara left to go into a small nearby bedroom, I thought: *Well, of course. She is trying to convince me that she has this gift of locution!*

We were then asked to take our places at the dining table. I took my seat noticing that Sara was assigned to the seat next to mine. Approximately five minutes later, she reappeared and took her seat smiling at me and said, "Our Lady gave me two messages; one for the guests here this evening and the other for you. I've written the one for you."

As Sara read the message for the guests, I opened the small piece of paper on which she had written the message for me. My heart skipped a beat as I read its contents:

Tell my son that I love him and I bear him in my heart. His heart fully belongs to me. He loves his Mother very much. His Mother blesses him and tells him not to be scared, because I am in his heart and I hold his hand. I guide him. His mission is to take me to his brothers and sisters. , , I send him to his brothers and sisters and I tell him not to be afraid. I send him. I love him.

I melted on the spot and my emotions could not be contained.

"Thank you, Sara," I said in a quiet, trembling voice, "there is no doubt in my heart that these words come from the Blessed Virgin." I knew it didn't mean the dark night was over but regardless; my Blessed Virgin was still there, knowing that meant everything to me.

After the dinner, Sara and I went into a private area and spoke for close to an hour. I told her everything about the dark night of the soul that had left me in this perplexing condition. We agreed to stay in touch by email after I left the country. Over the years we met many times as I returned to Argentina for speaking engagements, eventually covering the entire country, in that time Sara received more messages for me from the Blessed Virgin. I found them to be as powerful as the words of Our Lady in Medjugorje.

The three days in Chile were a duplication of the talks in Argentina. However, I now had a greater sense of the full purpose of the mission and vowed to continue on with it, despite the presence of the dark night of the soul.

Visionary Marija: **"To experience the beauty of Our Lady's love, and to know that it is that love which gives itself to you, is the most beautiful thing in life. But, when I try to love others and try to give that love to them, then that is difficult and I often feel shame for my**

insufficiencies to love in the light of Our Lady's all-encompassing motherly love."

father jozo's request

Upon returning home from Argentina, the darkness once again filled me. I was beginning to think it was permanent. Even knowing more about it could not ease the coldness and utter loneliness that seemed to shroud my faith journey.

There were, however, treasured moments of relief. An incident that took place in Siroki Brijeg during one of my tours with a large group of pilgrims turned out to be one of those extremely precious moments.

Father Jozo Zovko was a key part of the apparitions of Medjugorje in the early days, having been posted there as pastor of Saint James Church. When the apparitions first started occurring, he was out of the little hamlet on retreat. Upon returning and discovering what was happening, he immediately began an investigation of the claims of the visionaries. His personal interviews with the six youth were terse and pointed and more like an interrogation, leaving the seers wondering if anyone would believe them.

Within two days, events happened that brought the charismatic Franciscan to the defense of the visionaries and into full belief that the Mother of God was truly appearing to them as they claimed. He actually saw the Virgin in apparition along with the children.

Father Jozo would end up serving 18 months in prison for refusing to deny the apparitions were authentic. By the end of the eighties, he was as famous as the visionaries. It was soon a standard part of every pilgrimage to Medjugorje to also go to the parish where Fr. Jozo was stationed after leaving Medjugorje. His talks could sometimes last for several hours.

I met Father Jozo in early 1988 through the introduction of Father Svetozar. Fr. Jozo looked me when we met as though he knew everything about me. He knew my calling and that the Blessed Virgin had chosen me for this mission. We became close friends. On occasion over the years, he would call me onto the platform when he was speaking and ask me to give my story.

On this particular pilgrimage, the dark night of the soul was still very much active within me. We arrived at Siroki Brejig along with hundreds of other pilgrim groups. I hid in the most distant corner of the church from where Fr. Jozo was counseling the priests who had come with the groups on how to pray over the pilgrims. It was a routine procedure he had used for years.

The pilgrims were instructed to line up around the outer part of the sanctuary where they would wait for a priest to come lay hands on them. I was still keeping out of sight near the back of the church when suddenly I hear my name being called by several of the guides: "Wayne, where are you? Fr. Jozo wants you to come forward!"

I was mortified. To get to where Fr. Jozo was with the other priests, I had to walk across the open space now surrounded by hundreds of pilgrims. As I arrived to where he was, Fr. Jozo smiled that familiar smile as he placed his hands on my shoulders. "Please," he said, "I wish you to pray over me." With that, he bowed his head and folded his hands in prayer.

I knew in my heart immediately why he was asking me to pray over him in front of this massive crowd. He somehow "knew" my condition. I did as he asked and prayed over him, filled with humility.

One very important aspect concerning the gifts of the Holy Spirit came to mind as I returned to the far corner of the church; once given, the gift or gifts given by the Holy Spirit remain with the recipient, no matter the decline or condition of faith. Thus, no matter how long the dark night of the soul would remain within me, I was to continue to use them.

Visionary Mirjana: **"The devil prowls around us and sets traps. He tries to divide and confuse us so that we will detest ourselves and abandon ourselves to him. An invisible war rages all around us, but Our Lady is here to help us win."**

i quit

Struggling mightily over many months with the condition of the dark night of the soul, I came to the realization that it would be better to no longer carry out my mission in spreading the message of Medjugorje. It was time to quit.

My spiritual life was in shambles as was my personal life. As stated earlier, the condition of the dark night would come and go without reason or explanation. This had been occurring for several years. It was painful to listen to introductions before giving a talk. I felt like a hypocrite.

One of the final convincing blows came when I was speaking at a conference, along with visionary Ivan. Ivan would actually have his apparition in front of the conference attendees. As he returned to his seat next to me right after the conclusion of the apparition with the Blessed Virgin, he said to me, "Our Lady looked at you for a long time tonight!"

That did it. I would fulfill my obligation to lead a pilgrimage to Medjugorje in November 2001 and then quietly bow out.

Almost as if on cue, it began to rain a steady but light drizzle, adding to the misery of my disposition as I packed my bags. I was due to leave Medjugorje a day earlier than my pilgrimage and would join good friend Steve Shawl and his small group for the trip to the airport. "Sure, come with us—we only have seven people. Just one thing," Steve added, "we plan to stop in Tihaljina for a short visit to see the statue."

That was fine with me, I told Steve. In fact, it was perfect. The church in Tihaljina was home to a famous statue of the Blessed Virgin Mary and its face had become the symbol of Our Lady of Medjugorje. It was only 25 miles from Medjugorje and on the way to the airport. More importantly, it was "my Mary" and I had spent a lot of time in conversation with her in the past in front of this statue. Never was there a more beautiful face of Mary in my opinion.

We arrived at the church and made our way inside, getting soaked as we did. It didn't matter. I went straight to the statue in the front of the sanctuary and prostrated myself at its base. It was here with her that I would bring the mission to an end. The tears flowed and would not stop as I began my apology in silent thought: *I'm so sorry dear Mother; I don't want to embarrass you and Medjugorje any longer . . .*

As I lay there filled with remorse, I suddenly felt that now-familiar presence. After a pause, the Blessed Virgin softly placed her words in my heart: **You are still my son.**

My thoughts were filled with exactly what the Virgin meant: *Get up and stop feeling sorry for yourself; go home, take some time off and then you will resume your mission.*

I did as I was directed by the Blessed Virgin. Scheduled events were fulfilled but I did not take on more. I prayed and prayed asking for relief from this cursed dark night of the soul.

Months later without seeking it, discernment began to set in. The dark night was not a punishment; it was a severe test of faith, a "Job" experience to be exact (If you don't remember or know the story of Job from the Old Testament, I suggest rereading it).

There is no doubt in my heart that the Blessed Virgin, although silent, was with me throughout the ordeal, and because I did not stop praying or attending Holy Mass or going to confession or stop speaking and writing, I *survived* the dark night of the soul. I did not lose my faith. Somewhere in the throes of continuing on with the mission, the condition stopped. Again, just as when it started, I cannot pinpoint an exact date. It was replaced by a deeper, stronger and more intimate spiritual love for Jesus and my dear Mother Mary.

As with Job, my faith became stronger based on two added critical elements that would guide my mission from that time on: true and sincere humility and absolute obedience. I continue to pray and ask daily for these elements to guide me in everything I do in my life.

Commentary: You may ask why the inclusion of this chapter on the condition of the dark night of the soul since the major theme of the book is the "joy" of Medjugorje? The answer is found in the early comments concerning redemptive suffering. The dark night of the soul really is no different than other examples of our God testing the faith of His creation. That, in essence, is what the dark night of the soul is—a test of faith.

Therefore, we can easily compare the case of God asking Abraham to offer the life of his son Isaac, to this horrible condition. Abraham is ready to comply even though he is filled with grief at the thought of losing his beloved son. He is about to offer his son when an angel of God stops him.

I've already mentioned the story of Job who gives up every possession including family out of love for God. Satan tries to make the case with God that if Job is stripped of all that he has, he will no longer love God above all; yet, Job obeys and the reward is that he is given even more than he had before the great trial.

The joy gleaned from this unusual form of testing is derived from obedience and humility. That is why these two elements will from now on be my standards to stay strong in the faith.

For what we preach is not ourselves, but Jesus Christ as Lord, with ourselves as your servants for Jesus' sake. For it is the God who said, "Let light shine out of darkness," who has shone in our hearts to give the light of the knowledge of the glory of God in the face of Christ.

—2 Corinthians 4:5-6.

PART TWO:

abundance of grace

Dear children! Also today, with joy, I desire to give you my motherly blessing and to call you to prayer. May prayer become a need for you to grow more in holiness every day. Work more on your conversion, because you are far away, little children. Thank you for having responded to my call.

—Message of March 25, 2012.

7

special moments

Beyond and within the many wonderful stories, there are dozens of special moments throughout the years of my mission. They are the moments that have defined the work and given it personality and depth.

Special moments are the little nuggets that elevate one's spiritual journey. They also aid others who read about them and then relate them to their own experiences. Some moments take longer to relate, while others may be just a paragraph or two. Regardless they remain special for me—and I hope for you, as you read them. The stories, memories, anecdotes and quotes are not necessarily in chronological order.

the beautiful nun

One of the most difficult—as well as most blessed—tours of the mission was a tour of the Philippines. It was filled with great graces and would consume an entire month of talks and visits packed with spiritual lessons and experiences that would last a lifetime.

It began with a meaningful as well as hilarious story told to me by the charismatic Cardinal Jaime Sin, who was deeply involved in bringing freedom to the people of the Philippines and deposing the long-time dictator Ferdinand Marcos. Within an hour of landing in Manila, I was sitting with the Cardinal having coffee and listening to the story of how it all came about.

Having been in the air for twenty-plus hours, Lydia and her group's enthusiasm was welcome relief as I arrived in the Philippines for the long tour. With little sleep on the long flight, including a two-hour stopover in Tokyo, all I wanted now was a place to lay horizontal for about eight hours.

Dropping into the seat of the awaiting car I heaved a sigh, stating that I was ready for a good rest. Surely Lydia and the group would understand. However, it was not to be. "Oh, but we have a full agenda for the day," Lydia quickly stated when I mentioned how tired I was from the long journey. "And right now, our Cardinal is waiting to personally welcome you to our country."

What could I do? Rest would have to wait.

Since first reading about the "miracle" of the Philippine revolution, I found it very much related to the events of Medjugorje—even to the point that it occurred on February 25 1986, the anniversary day of the apparitions. An audience with the charismatic Cardinal Jaime Sin was high on my list of desires in coming here. Hopefully, I would learn more about Our Lady's one-time sudden apparition, which took place during the heat of the confrontation between Marcos and the people, a fact he had revealed to a surprised international press conference in New York City shortly after the revolution. Not surprisingly, the story was buried near the bottom of page three or four in most reporting newspapers.

Twenty minutes later, after a tense ride through the jammed, toxic traffic of Manila, we were having coffee with the Philippines' most famous church leader. "Cardinal, I've read a great deal about the revolution and the part you played," I said after we had been talking awhile, "and especially about the appearance of Our Lady. I wondered if you could tell me more about this."

The Cardinal laughed. "So, you have heard about that! I will be happy to tell you about 'People Power,' the power of the masses when moved by the truth of Jesus, and about how the Virgin saved our country. But my role in it is exaggerated!"

I sensed he was happy for an opportunity to tell the story again. Settling into his huge chair, the Cardinal began telling of the events that changed two decades of oppression under dictator Ferdinand Marcos, into the beginning of true freedom for his fellow countrymen.

It began in February 1986, as the virtual twenty-year dictatorship of Ferdinand Marcos came to an abrupt and unexpected end through a series of strange events. Corazon Aquino, the widow and reluctant political replacement of slain opposition leader Ninoy Aquino, had won the presidential election in a stunning upset over Marcos. She was elected by an overwhelming margin in the snap election, called for by dictator himself. The Cardinal pointed out that Marcos had called for elections in order to crush the building opposition. However, through ballot box stuffing and other illegal activities, plus a total control of the media, Marcos, flagrantly had himself declared the winner.

Cory, as she was affectionately called by the people, had gained enormous popularity due in part to the reputation of her late husband who had been gunned down as he descended from an airplane on his return to the island nation. Her husband was returning to run against Marcos and hopefully restore freedom to the people. Taking his place, Cory also represented the first true opportunity for democracy.

The rigged election results were blatant and obvious to neutral observers and also to the people. Within days, millions took to the streets of Makati and Manila, spurred to action when a dissatisfied segment of the military launched an unexpected coup attempt. Unbeknown to its perpetrators, it would be this unrelated coup attempt that would allow Cory Aquino, a simple housewife as she described herself, to assume the presidency she had rightfully won at the ballot box. Marcos responded to the rebellion and coup attempt by sending tanks down the streets of the city. He was determined to maintain his grip on the country, even if it meant massacre of the swelling crowds.

As the two elements came to an impasse at a busy city intersection, a full convoy of tanks and other armament manned by hard-core militant soldiers stood poised for action against millions of civilians, many of whom who were virtually laying down in the streets in front of the tanks. Undaunted by the crowds, Marcos gave the order to fire on the people.

Cardinal Sin leaned forward in his chair, smiling. "What I am telling you now was told to me by many of these same soldiers who were ready to fire on the people." Reclining again, he continued. "The tanks were trying to penetrate the crowd. Nuns were pushing against them. People were waving their rosaries and praying.

Then, according to these hardened soldiers, they suddenly saw up in the clouds the form of the cross. These were the Marines who were riding on top of the tanks, the so-called Loyalists (to Marcos). The many sisters had tried to stop them, but they (the soldiers) told me they had already decided to obey instructions and push through. It was now just a question of ten minutes or so. You push the trigger and there you are – everybody will be dead."

Again, the Cardinal leaned forward, very much enjoying relating the story. "Then, a beautiful lady appeared to them. I don't know if she appeared in the sky or was standing down on the ground. Other witnesses told me later they thought she was a beautiful nun dressed in blue and that she was standing in front of the tanks. So beautiful she was, and her eyes were sparkling! And the beautiful lady spoke to them like this: *'Dear soldiers! Stop! Do not proceed! Do not harm my children! I am the queen of this land.'*

When the soldiers heard this, they put down everything. They came down from the tanks and they joined the people. So, that was the end of the Marcos Loyalists. Shortly after this, Marcos and his wife fled the country."

Cardinal Sin paused, turning his hands upward. "I don't know who these soldiers were. All I know is that they came here crying to me. They did not tell me that it was the Virgin. They told me only that it was a beautiful nun. But you know," he paused, laughing heartily, "I have seen all the sisters in Manila, and there are no beautiful ones. So, it must have been the Virgin!"

What a story—and what a sense of humor! Here was a powerful figure of the Philippine Catholic Church, able to add such a wonderful touch to another stunning supernatural visit by Our Lady. But being a journalist, I had to ask: "Cardinal, do you really believe it was Our Lady that the people and the soldiers saw?"

Cardinal Sin did not hesitate. "Yes. My heart was telling me, this is Mary. And since they obeyed this woman who appeared to them and did not follow orders and fire on the people, then Marcos had nobody any more. So, he had to flee away. That was the end of him."

Thus, from the Cardinal himself the story was confirmed; Our Lady did play a direct role in the freedom of the Philippine people. It really is no wonder. They were so consecrated to the hearts of Jesus and Mary that everywhere one looked, pictures of both were displayed. They were on office desks, on dashes of automobiles, even plastered into the brickwork of walls surrounding homes.

Later in the tour, I was scheduled to speak at a large bank at noon. I was not sure about this stop and questioned Lydia about it. "Oh, you will be well received, I promise."

As we walked through the massive bank it seemed every desk had a picture of the Blessed Virgin and the Sacred Heart of Jesus on it. I entered the huge auditorium filled with a tremendous crowd of nearly 1,500 people and a spontaneous standing ovation. The president of the bank had decided to close the bank for this special time so that all of the employees could attend. It was another outstanding highlight of the tour.

Afterwards, I sheepishly felt Our Lady smiling as if saying: *Oh ye of little faith!*

Several days later, I was privileged to meet President Corazon Aquino. It was a huge event with dozens of media representatives recording the event, taking pictures and asking questions. The entire time I was with Corazon, she held a rosary in her hands. She told me that she prayed it constantly and was convinced it was the power of her being able to continue her presidency. She had already survived seven attempted coups.

Corazon Aquino would survive to serve two four-year terms as president. Like the people of the Philippines, faith was deeply entrenched in her. It was this faith that allowed a simple housewife to reach the highest office of her land.

Visionary Marija: **"Her appearance** (the Virgin Mary) **is also a feeling, one best described by the word** *maternal.* **Her expression conveys the qualities of motherhood—care, compassion, patience, tenderness. Her eyes hold such love that I feel like she embraces me every time she looks at me."**

Adding to the incredibility of the entire story Cardinal Jaime Sin shared with me was one more startling addition. I discovered that he had met with Sister Lucia, the last living visionary of Fatima, in Portugal just before his trip to the United States and the press conference where he first told the story of the Blessed Virgin's appearance.

Cardinal Sin related that although living in a cloistered convent, Sister Lucia knew *everything* about the Philippine revolution. She had no access to newspapers, magazines or television. Yet, she related all of the details to the Cardinal.

Sister Lucia then revealed an astonishing revelation to the Cardinal: Corazon Aquino was a gift from God for the Philippines. If she could maintain peace and democracy for a period of two or more years (that is, serve out her second term as president), the Philippine people would be *influential* in leading Communist China to Christianity.

Now, move forward to the spring of 2011. I am in China on tour to bring Medjugorje to this immense country of predominantly non-believers in God. Soon after arriving, I was surprised to learn that a large number of Philippine people were there serving as domestic help. Learning more, it seemed that the Chinese strongly disliked the Philippine workers, much of it due to their open Christian faith in contrast to government enforced atheistic Communism. The Philippine workers felt the same dislike for their employers.

It was evident that the elements of Sister Lucia's revelation to Cardinal Sin were in place to occur.

Visionary Marija: **"To experience the beauty of Our Lady's love, and to know that it is that love which gives itself to you, is the most** beautiful thing in life. But, when I try to love others and try to give that love to them, then that is difficult and I often feel shame for my insufficiencies to love in the light of Our Lady's all-encompassing motherly love."

mary of grenada

I was warmly greeted in the arrival area at the Grenada airport by a beautiful black woman: "Welcome to our country, Mr. Weible, my name is Margaret and I am happy to greet you in the name of Archbishop Sidney Charles!"

A quick visit to the tiny island nation, which was not too far from Trinidad, had been hastily arranged when the archbishop learned of my tour in Trinidad, He had called me and made it clear that I must stop in Grenada before returning home. How could I say no to an archbishop?

Margaret's quiet charm and warm smile were evident from the outset, and in minutes we felt like we'd known each other a long time. It was a comfortable feeling experienced often in the months of travel as I met those who had been called to help spread the Medjugorje messages.

We wound our way through thick, jungle foliage along a narrow paved road as Margaret gave me a quick background on the short history of the Grenada Center for Peace. She and several others had gone to Medjugorje. Now, they were working fervently to spread the messages. "And now, you're here!" She added, "Everyone's very excited about to-night!"

Driving through an area of hills covered with lush growth and a few small homes scattered throughout the hills, Mary suddenly said, "I wonder if I might ask a special favor of you?

"Yes, of course. What is it?"

"This is really unplanned," she said hesitantly, "but since your flight came in early and we've some spare time, would you be willing to make a very old and disabled woman extremely happy?" Margaret looked at me with pleading eyes and optimistic smile, slowly pulling the car to the side of the road in anticipation of a positive response. It worked.

"I guess so," I answered with a little laugh. "What do you want me to do?"

She pointed to a tiny shack approximately 50 yards from the roadway. "A lady named Mary lives there and she loves the Blessed Mother dearly! After reading your tabloid, she wanted in the worse way to meet you. Unfortunately, she is unable to get around on her own due to failing health and no transportation. I was wondering if you wouldn't mind stopping for a moment or two."

"Yes, let's go, I'd be happy to visit with her!" I said motioning Margaret toward the shack.

We drove off the paved road onto a dirt pathway and into a sparse but clean clearing around the little house. "Hello Mary, it's Margaret and I have a special guest with me," my guide called out as she knocked on a fragile wooden screen door.

Standing behind Margaret on the rickety porch, I peered into the dim interior of the little house in time to see a small, frail woman making her way slowly to the door. She was smiling broadly, giving special radiance to her dark, wrinkled face.

"Come in, you're more than welcome!" she said in a low raspy voice. Mary was so thin it seemed her threadbare dress might fall off her stooped, rounded shoulders at any moment. She was a small woman and her bent posture made her appear even smaller. But she had an inner beauty that could only be described as spiritual beauty, the way Mother Theresa is beautiful.

Giving her a light kiss on the cheek, Margaret said, "I've a surprise for you, Mary! This is Wayne Weible from the United States, here to talk tonight about the apparitions of Our Lady in Medjugorje. You said you wanted to meet him, and he was kind enough to agree to stop for a quick chat with you."

"Oh, yes, I know," she answered softly as her eyes, locked on me, began to moisten. "I've been praying to the Blessed Virgin all morning, asking her if she would send him to me, so I've been expecting you." She clasped her hands together, as though in prayer and continuing to stare at me added, "She is so good to me!"

Margaret and I looked at each other. We knew her suggestion to visit this woman was a spur-of-the moment thing; yet, *we also knew* that indeed, Our Lady had given this little gift to an old and faithful child of God.

Commentary: How often we are asked to do something for someone and we hesitate or say no? The world is full of grave sins fueled by ego, pride, greed, addiction and much more. While these are indeed grave sins, the sin of ignoring or refusing to help others, seems to weigh far more heavily on the soul.

Jesus gave us the two great commandments: love God with all of our heart and soul; and, love your neighbor as you love yourself. The latter is really the "penance" Our Lady asks of us at Medjugorje: Do the penance of love by assisting your neighbors in all ways without hesitation.

How many of us are fortunate enough to meet someone like Mary? She trusted in prayer that her desire might be granted. Of course, it would depend on my saying yes to Margaret's request. I was tired; this trip had been added on to a long and arduous tour in Trinidad where I gave 40 separate talks. However, I knew in my heart that this visit with Mary might be one of those special moments.

It was.

miracle of the sun

That evening the church in the little island of Grenada was literally overflowing with people. "Oh my goodness, this is wonderful!" Margaret, the organizer of the tour, was obviously surprised at the turnout and as if anticipating a question from me concerning their preparation for the event, added with a wide smile, "I felt we would fill the church but this is far beyond our wildest expectations! You should feel very welcome!"

Shaking my head, I answered in a low voice, "I feel totally overwhelmed." It registered in my mind that this was the reason the extended tour of Trinidad overflowed to several days in Grenada.

Taking a seat next to the podium, I looked around the interior of the church as the music began to play. It was a large, beautiful structure with huge, open windows along both walls. Faces were peering in from every window as crowds gathered at each opening, swelling the attendance to more than two thousand.

As if to add a final touch to an already spectacular scene, streams of sunlight filtered over the heads of the people crowded into the window openings on the west side of the church. The warm Caribbean sun was just beginning to set.

I began to speak. The words poured easily as I felt myself immersed in the spiritual enchantment of so many souls gathered to hear about Our Lady's appearances. As I was describing the phenomena of the spinning and dancing sun seen so often by pilgrims at the little village of Medjugorje, I was astonished as the full force of the setting sun's rays suddenly came streaming through one of the windows falling directly on me. It was as if someone had hit a switch and turned on a spotlight.

I tried to continue but my voice trailed off; there, before me occurring at that very moment was the miracle of which I was speaking! The sun began to do its dance, throwing off brilliant streams of colors and pulsating erratically, framed in the large window opening! I stood there in silence and stared until the growing buzz of the crowd caught my attention. They sensed something unusual was happening.

I looked at everyone for a moment and then pointing to the sun said, "The miracle of the sun I've just described to you is happening right now as I stand here. All I can say is thank you to Our Lady for she is truly letting us know that she is here in Grenada, just as she is in Medjugorje!"

Heads turned and dozens rushed to the windows on the west side of the church. There were shouts of excitement as others were able to see the phenomenon; soon the place was bedlam.

It took several minutes to restore order. By then, words were secondary. Many of the people in attendance had actually experienced the miracle of Medjugorje through the phenomena of the sun. Others were deeply affected by what was taking place around them. It was pure high-energy spirituality. Conversion truly occurred in many hearts that evening. Long after the talk, many people were still there, not wanting the magic of the moment to dissipate.

Later, in the wee hours of the morning, I lay in a small bed soaked in perspiration due to the remaining heat from the day. I didn't mind. Nor was there concern that sleep was near impossible. The evening's dramatic conclusion of the tour and the phenomenon of the sun during the talk served as a huge exclamation point at the end of an exciting story.

So many people in these small Caribbean island nations had been reached by the love of God. I did indeed feel like a little child of God.

At the moment, nothing else mattered.

Visionary Ivanka: "**All those who do not feel the Church as their home and God as their father; do not call them 'unbelievers' because even by saying that, you judge them. You should think of them as your brothers and sisters. See Jesus Christ in every person you meet. When you pray for them, you pray for yourselves and for your future.**"

fishers of men—and salmon!

"So you've never been salmon fishing, huh?" Homer asked as the two of us helped Paul launch the boat into the harbor waters. Homer was a tall, lanky man in his middle sixties, whose weathered face seemed always to wear a broad smile. He had been my constant companion in Alaska, beginning with breakfast the morning after my arrival in Juneau. It was while sharing meals and stories at these breakfast get-togethers following early-morning Mass that I learned of his own personal little mission. He was totally dedicated to taking the gospel of Jesus into a large prison located in Juneau. I had promised him I would go with him into the prison on Saturday afternoon to talk about Medjugorje.

But first, we were going to do a little salmon fishing.

Dressed in a yellow slicker and knee-high rubber boots, Homer tossed a similar set and pair of boots at me. "Better put these on; it gets a little cold out on the water." As he hoisted the last of the gear to Paul in the boat, he added as an aside, "Everything's set for our talk at the prison tomorrow afternoon. The guys are excited about you coming. And it's not until after 3 P.M., so if you want, we can fish again in the morning and be back in plenty of time for the talk."

I grinned at him. "I guess that depends on if we catch any today!"

"Oh, don't worry, you'll catch more than your share," Paul yelled above the roar of the boat's engine as we headed for open waters.

Less than an hour later, with our fishing lines trolling at the back of the boat, I suddenly felt a hard tug on my line. "I got one! I got one!" I shouted, as the largest fish I had ever hooked jumped high into the air from the end of my line. I began reeling as fast and hard as I could. About ten minutes later, just as I was ready to bring the fish to where Homer could net it and bring it into the boat, He suddenly grabbed my line as Paul snapped his knife open – and then cut the line! As I stood gasping in disbelief, my huge, beautiful Alaska salmon swam off with a last splash of its tail. "What are you doing?" I screamed, as both men roared with laughter.

"This is what we do to all rookies with their first salmon," Paul explained still convulsed in laughter, as he slipped an arm around my shoulders. "Welcome to Alaska salmon fishing, and don't worry, you'll catch a lot more even bigger than that one!"

I smiled ruefully, feeling every bit the rookie fisherman.

But their little joke backfired. I didn't catch another fish the rest of the day, and they only caught a couple, including a large halibut. Homer felt so guilty; he let me finish hauling it in! Paul and I cooked it at midnight as an end-of-fast meal. It was absolutely delicious and marked a super ending to a great day of fun and relaxation from the grind of the tour.

Visionary Marija: **"Our Lady always asks us to live her messages. She doesn't want us to depend on them, but she calls us to be joyful bearers of her words and to be good Christians."**

the JOY *of* MEDJUGORJE

Saturday afternoon proved to be one of the most dramatic stops of the Alaskan tour. After a morning of fishing, I was scheduled to speak at the large prison in Juneau.

As Homer led me into the prison, I felt uneasy. It was mildly exhilarating to have the opportunity to take the message of Medjugorje to those who possibly most needed it. Still, it was disturbing to hear the clank of large, electronically controlled metal gates, as they slammed shut behind me; and, to see the heavy barbed wire strung along high metal fences.

Prisoners stared as we walked across an exercise yard and into a separate building where church services were normally held. Homer waved and spoke to several of the inmates and invited them to come in for the talk. I could see a beautiful peace and sense of accomplishment on his face as we crossed the yard. This was his mission of caring for the poor of heart.

As we entered the building, I was a little disappointed; there were only about 25 prisoners in attendance. They didn't look too friendly or receptive to the impending talk. One in particular, an extraordinarily large man who was an Alaska native was sitting near the front of the room. He began staring at me from the moment I entered.

Feeling a bit intimidated, I prayed that the right words would come and that my fear would not show. I told them that they in particular were the reason for Our Lady coming in apparition. They had sinned and were now paying the price. She loved them; Jesus loved them, and they had this time to make their lives right. "Amens" were emphatically given throughout the talk. I was surprised and pleased.

As Homer and a prison official passed out my articles after the talk, many of the prisoners came forward and extended the tabloid for autographs and began asking   questions. It was just like any other talk and I was filled with happiness and relief when it was over.

The room began to empty as the inmates left. Homer and the official started carrying out the boxes with the remaining materials. Suddenly, I found myself alone in the room with the Alaska native. He hadn't moved throughout the talk; he didn't ask any questions and never changed the expression on his face. He did however take a copy of the articles but he just kept staring at me.

Slowly, the Alaskan got up and came toward me. My heart jumped and I tried not to let the fear show. He stood there, looking first at me, and then at the copy of the articles he held in his large hands. For the first time, his expression softened and he spoke, "I was going to ask you for your autograph," he began in a deep, slow voice, "But now, I don't think I need to. You have written it across my heart." With that, an ever so slight smile creased his face as he thanked me for coming and then slowly turned and left the room.

Commentary – Have you ever been in prison, locked away in a cell as though you were dangerous to the world?

Well, I have.

It is an experience I will never forget—a desperately helpless feeling that engulfs you as you realize that somehow you are suddenly seen as dangerous to all of society.

My incident occurred as I was driving to the Atlanta airport and passing though the little town of Jasper, Georgia. Everyone in the region knows Jasper is an infamous speed trap and true to form, I was pulled over. Yes, I told the officer, I know I was going a little too fast. There was no sense to argue I thought, just accept it and move on.

The officer took my driver's license and registration back to his vehicle. Close to 25 minutes passed and then another police vehicle arrived; more time and more discussions went on as I began to become uneasy and anxious to get to Atlanta to spend the night for a mid-morning flight the following day.

The two officers approached my car. The one who had pulled me over harshly ordered me to get out of the vehicle. I did so, annoyed and agitated that I had been sitting there for such a long time. "What's going on," I asked, "I already admitted I was speeding..."

"Just shut up and turn around and you better change that attitude or I'll lock you up for a week!" I was then roughly body checked and then swung back around.

Now I'm really scared and nearly collapsed as I weakly muttered, "Officer, just please tell me what is going on?"

"You're driving with a suspended license and we're taking you in. Put your hands straight out." With that, I was handcuffed and shoved into the back seat of the police car.

During the next three and a half hours, I was booked, told to change into prison garb (You know, the orange one-piece suit) and placed in a cell with another person who was shirtless and definitely intoxicated.

The long and the short of it is this: two months before I had been in a small auto accident in Atlanta. I failed to appear in court on the set day as I was traveling and forgot all about it. I returned a week later and cleared things up. Unfortunately, the clerk at the court apparently made an error and incorrectly marked my license was suspended. Thus, I was unknowingly driving with a suspended license.

In the early morning hours of the following day, my wife Judi came to the jail and posted my bond. A week later, we returned to Jasper for the required court appearance and it was soon evident to the court judge that I was wrongly listed as driving with a suspended license. The arresting officer offered a forced apology, as did the district attorney.

While sitting in a locked jail cell for nearly three hours, I thought of the Alaskan man in the prison where I had spoken to the small number of inmates. It was later that I learned he had been placed in jail via accusations from his own family. He, too, was an innocent man. He was a gentle giant who had never been in trouble until he was betrayed by his family, all over inherited money from the death of a family member.

Somewhere while sitting in the cell, I silently asked the Blessed Mother how this could have happened to me? Within the flash of a second, I knew it was another little lesson of the cross, teaching us to not judge, but to pray for those suffering in prisons throughout the world—especially the wrongly accused.

Saint Teresa of Avila: **"Whoever has God needs nothing else. God alone suffices."**

a special sign

The country of Colombia, South America was and still is on a lesser degree, a major source for illegal drugs throughout North and South America. I was aware of that as I traveled to the three major cities of the country: Bogota, Medellin and Cali.

It had not been an easy tour. Scheduled events had been cancelled at the last moment due to hesitation by some bishops and priests to allow talks concerning the messages of a controversial apparition site.

Several days later in Cali, I felt the peace return. I was limited to giving talks in a rather small assembly hall located just off a busy street in the uptown section of the city. It was hot and stuffy because of the crowds, which filled every nook and cranny, cooled only by a large doorway that led to an open-air garden in the center of the building. The talks were being broadcast live over a popular radio show and for that reason I was seated at a table, having to speak into the microphone.

It was not my usual style; I liked a podium and having to sit while speaking was difficult. But on this last day, and the last talk of my Colombian tour, there was a pleasant surprise. The audience included five elderly Franciscan priests, their brown robes a familiar sight. In concluding, I told the listeners I wanted to leave them two gifts: "The first is from Our Lady; it is her special blessing which she gives us at Medjugorje, a blessing that is a grace from Jesus. Now, I give it to you."

With that, I raised my hands and extended them toward the audience. As I turned to my right and toward the Franciscan priests, a small bird suddenly flew through the doorway and perched momentarily on the shoulder of one of the priests before flittering away.

There was a murmur from the crowd, most of whom witnessed the scene. I smiled and added, "That, my friends, is a very special sign of her peace. May it remain with you and with all Colombians who respond to her call!"

time without limits

We had a wonderful Medjugorje prayer group composed of members of our parish, the Immaculate Heart of Mary, in Hayesville, North Carolina. The group would meet each Tuesday evening usually at the home of one of the members and occasionally at the church. Our format was based on the basic standards for a prayer group requested by Our Lady of Medjugorje. We would pray the rosary, offer individual intentions and read Holy Scripture or related material for meditation and discussion.

At least once a month, instead of prayer group, we would meet at the church for an hour of Eucharistic Adoration. As it continued, many members wanted to increase our Eucharistic Adoration to two times a month. We did.

One evening as we neared the end of the Adoration hour, Jesus spoke to my heart: **Could you stay an additional 15 minutes with me tonight?**

I was startled and quickly said to the group, "Jesus wants us to stay an additional 15 minutes tonight—and then I blurted out: "I don't know why!"

Several members looked at me somewhat perplexed. Nonetheless, we stayed the extra fifteen minutes.

At approximately five minutes before the additional time was up, Jesus again spoke to my heart and said with a touch of humor in His voice: **I asked this extra time for you to be with Me as an example. I wanted you to know there is no time limit when I am with you!**

I laughed as I told the group the reason why Jesus wanted the extra 15 minutes. It was another "little lesson" of how personal and intimate our Lord is with each of us who accept Him and His gift of salvation.

Visionary Vicka: **"She [Our Lady] would like us to accept the message with our hearts and to live them. Often, we accept the message, we begin to live it, but then we get tired and we remain the way we were before. And Our Lady would like that every day we live her messages."**

a loving, caring mother

Just the thought of the Blessed Virgin appearing in mystical and wondrous apparition to the visionaries daily is overwhelming. However, she is still a human mother and like any caring mother, she admonishes her children.

One evening in the early days of the apparitions, the Blessed Mother reproached the young visionary Jakov because he had misbehaved toward some of the boys at school. *You must love them all*, she told him. Jakov then responded that he did love them but that they annoyed him and provoked him. The Mother gently replied: *Then accept it as a sacrifice, and offer it.*

Jakov would be blessed to have this gentle and wise Mother of Jesus appear to him daily and guide him from June 1981 through the next 17 years of his life. When it ended in September (12) 1998, the Blessed Virgin left him these last words: *Do not be sad, because as a mother I will always be with you and like every true mother I will never leave you.*

While these words were given to young Jakov, they also apply to all of us who become involved in the apparitions of Medjugorje. When we step out of line, the Blessed Virgin will gently correct, as any good mother would do.

a mother's admonition

You've heard it in earlier stories; but I'll remind you again: Our Lady is a mother, and as such, she is always there to comfort us in times of need. And, as a good mother, she also admonishes us when necessary. It has happened to the visionaries—and it has happened to me.

I have to admit that there have been far too many instances where my Blessed Mother has had to gently scold me or to "correct" me or to teach me to be prepared at all times to properly carry out my mission. Unfortunately learning some of these lessons can be painful. The following story is certainly one of those painful experiences.

During a tour in Arizona one of the sponsors had set up a radio interview on a Christian radio show in Tucson, Arizona. "I thought since it was a Protestant Christian radio talk show, I could explain to the audience how the Blessed Virgin is coming in apparition for all people of all faiths," my sponsor Kathy explained as we arrived at the station. "I'm sure they will be able to accept the apparitions and see how God is at work," she continued as we entered the lobby of the station.

We were warmly greeted by the host of the show I would be on. "It's always nice to learn about other faiths," he said with a broad smile. "But I must tell you, I am not sure about these apparitions of the Blessed Virgin—perhaps you can show me in Scripture where she is given this unusual assignment."

Suddenly I felt uneasy. The feeling became worse when the host informed me that there would be a call-in time allotment following my opening comments, which in essence would be to tell the listeners the basic story of Medjugorje and about my own conversion process.

As the show began and I was telling my story, the host interrupted me to ask how could I be sure it was the Blessed Virgin Mary and not Satan who was reportedly appearing in this apparition. Startled, I paused before trying to give an answer. "Well, you may know that she has appeared this way during the centuries..."

"Yes, but even in those cases how do you know it really is her?"

I again paused, totally not expecting the host to be asking direct questions. He continued on the attack, all the time smiling a syrupy smile, "Can you tell me where in Scripture I can find that the Virgin Mary would come in apparitions?"

The show went on in the same manner and the more the host attacked, the more upset I became. It was even worse as callers jumped into the fray, calling me a false prophet and accusing me of being a puppet of Satan.

After we went off the air, I asked the host why he had kept interrupting me. "How did you expect me to tell my story if you felt it necessary to ask questions?" He just smiled the same smile and thanked me for coming.

"Kathy, they ate me alive with all those hostile call-in questions and accusations," I said slumping into the passenger seat of the car. "I mean like the apparitions were Satan disguised as an angel of light; the apparitions were not in the Bible; and, I shouldn't 'worship' Mary and try to take people away from the truth of the Bible."

"Well, you did your best and I thought it was very good," Kathy said trying to calm me. But I knew better. At the conclusion of the show, I was totally embarrassed and downright angry. I couldn't get out of that radio station fast enough.

"Look Kathy, I need to get to a church—a Catholic Church," I added with a flare of anger. At my request, we went straight to a nearby Catholic Church to pray. As I dropped to my knees, still upset, I asked the Blessed Mother, "Dear Mother, how could you hang me out to dry like that? Where were you when I needed you?'"

Instantly, I received her answer in my heart: *If you would spend more time reading Scripture, and less on television and other distractions, you would have known the answers.*

As if in confirmation, I was filled with discernment: I instantly knew the answers to all of the questions that had so embarrassed me!

I learned from that experience that although I was not a theologian, I should at least be prepared by reading Scripture as often as possible, and learn to apply it in daily living as well as in circumstances like the Protestant radio show.

At that time Jesus declared, "I thank thee, Father, Lord of heaven and earth, that thou hast hidden these things from the wise and understanding and revealed them to babes.

—Matthew 11:25.

Dear children, as a mother I implore you to persevere as my apostles. I am praying to my Son to give you Divine wisdom and strength. I am praying that you may discern everything around you according to God's truth and to strongly resist everything that wants to distance you from my Son...

—Excerpt from message of November 02, 2012.

8

a little humor

What would life be without a little humor?

Even an overwhelming event such as the apparitions of the Blessed Virgin at Medjugorje has had its lighter moments. Our Lady is, after all, a human mother and most definitely has a sense of humor according to the visionaries. The first indication of her sense of humor came when in the beginning days of the apparitions one of the visionaries asked her: "Dear Mother, how long are you going to appear to us?"

Our Lady smiled and responded: ***Am I boring you?*** And then added with radiant joy, ***As long as you wish, my angels!***

As long as you wish?

Was she serious?

I would say that time has proven the Blessed Virgin to be true to her word! As of this writing, she has appeared almost daily an unprecedented 36-plus years. In these years, the Virgin has appeared as joyful, radiant, motherly, happy, somber, sad and even in tears. As a human mother transformed into the Heavenly Mother of Jesus Christ, she has been given the greatest of virtues. However, she has also maintained her human attributes—including humor.

I personally discovered the humor of Medjugorje in a rather strange way, as you will see in this first story.

you're a what?

The joy of being back in Medjugorje in 1987 was tempered in that I could not receive the Holy Eucharist in Saint James Church where I had first received it. I had first done so out of ignorance, not knowing I wasn't supposed to since I was not Catholic. Yet, I immediately fell in love with Jesus in the Holy Eucharist. Because of that love and hunger, it was now the one negative aspect in returning to Medjugorje.

On my initial Medjugorje pilgrimage I had received the Holy Eucharist throughout our six days in the village—even though it was later pointed out to me that I should not be receiving because I was a Protestant. I rationalized that Jesus wanted me to receive His body.

On the last day of our pilgrimage we came out of the church after Holy Mass on the morning before we were to leave. I asked Maureen, a young woman in our group from Philadelphia who had become my "Catholic connection" what were all the people doing as I observed dozens of people sitting in front of priests all around the grounds. "They're going to confession," she told me.

"Oh yes, I've seen that in movies," I said and then added, "Well, can I do that? Can I go to confession?"

Maureen laughed, "I don't really know, so you will have to ask someone else."

She then pointed to a nearby priest hearing a confession who stood out with a long white beard, fierce penetrating eyes and white bushy eyebrows to match. "Whatever you decide," she said, "don't go to that priest! He is tough and that's no place for a Protestant to go for a first confession!"

Maureen related her experience with the priest stating that he was very stern and rigidly traditional in the faith. "He drags everything out of you," she added. "He literally scared the "hell" out of me!

I decided to think about the confession thing and decide later. That evening I went into the church and sat on the right side of the sanctuary on the end seat of the last row of benches, staying for the Mass and the apparition. I had finally decided not to do the confession thing in Medjugorje; I could always just go home and "confess" to my Lutheran pastor.

I was feeling homesick about Medjugorje and returning home. How could I be homesick for a place that I had not even left yet! I decided to leave the church and grab a taxi to the home where we were staying in a little village three miles from Medjugorje. As I stood up to leave, I almost ran into a rotund, Franciscan priest who was standing in front of a small booth I recognized as a place where confessions took place. There was a sign on the floor in front of it that read: "Italiano". For some reason, I looked down at the sign and then at the priest who then pointed to me and asked, "Italiano?"

"No, no," I answered, "English." With that, the priest smiled broadly, and literally pushed me into the second little booth and said, "Here—Englaise!"

Suddenly I realized I was about to have a confession even though I had decided not to! With no choice left, I fell to my knees as pain from kneeling so much during the week shot through me. I closed my eyes tightly and then remembered a line in a movie where someone went to confession. I blurted out: "Forgive me, Father, I have sinned—and I'm a Protestant!"

I the priest looked up and said rather loudly, "You're a what?!"

At that I opened my eyes and there I was staring into the fierce eyes of the priest with the long, white beard and hair whom Maureen had pointed out to me. He repeated: "You're a what? A Protestant?" and then added sternly, "Well, I can hear your confession but I can't give you absolution."

"Father, I don't know what that is!" I didn't know what else to say.

After a somewhat awkward pause that seemed to last a long time, the priest said, "Well, go ahead."

Father, I don't know what to do or say—I've never done this."

The priest slowly shook his head. "Of course you haven't, he muttered, probably wondering how he got into this situation. "Okay, then," he finally said, "I'm going to repeat the Ten Commandments one at a time and you answer yes or no to each one!"

I was finally relieved when he got to "Thou shall not kill" and I could say, no!

I left the church in a hurry, grabbed a taxi and once reaching the place where our group was staying, I began walking and thinking about what had just happened. Then I started laughing; that poor priest! However, something wonderful also had just occurred. With or without this thing called "absolution," I felt clean and exhilarated!

Little did I realize that the occurrence of my first Catholic confession, as unplanned as it was, would be the first of many to come in the future.

Several years later, I related the bizarre experience of my first confession at a Marian conference during my talk. The people, more than 3,000 in attendance, roared with laughter. Afterwards, two women approached me and pointing to the large screen behind the speaker's podium that displayed an enlarged image of each speaker, they excitedly told me, "As you were speaking and telling about your first confession, we saw an image of Our Lady on the screen and she was smiling at you!" Yes, my dear Mother Mary does indeed have a sense of humor!

Commentary: A little more than a year after my first confession with the priest with the wild white hair and fierce eyes, I was staying at visionary Marija's home when this very same priest came to visit her. By now I knew a little more about him; he was actually from Ohio and was a hermit priest who literally walked from Marian shrine to Marian shrine hearing confessions. His name was Father Arcadius.

Father Arcadius entered Marija's home and began an earnest conversation with her while I stood aside. When he had finished I said, "Excuse me Father, do you remember me?" The priest that in the beginning was so frightening to me slowly shook his head and said no, he didn't remember me.

"Father, I came to you in confession last year—I was that Protestant who had never been to confession and..."

Suddenly Father Arcadius lit up and excitedly pointed his finger at me and exclaimed, "You're that Lutheran! You're the one who goes around and tells Protestants to pray the rosary!"

I was shocked that he knew this about me. "Yes, Father, that's me and you heard my first confession and told me you couldn't give me absolution."

We talked for a while. The next day I found him on the left side of the church hearing confessions and I got in line. Father Arcadius once again heard the confession of a Protestant.

This time he also gave me absolution.

Visionary Mirjana: "**When everything starts happening, then you will be able to understand why the 18th of March, why every sec-**

ond of the month, why Wednesdays and Fridays are days of fasting; everything will be clear."

an unexpected greeting!

It can get quite hot in Medjugorje in the summertime and in the early years; there was no air conditioning in any home or building in the village. Thus, villagers and pilgrims alike sought ways to stay cool.

One very warm afternoon, visionary Marija and several friends were together in her home having cold drinks and seeking ways to stay cool. Suddenly one of her friends jokingly said she wished someone would just throw cold water on her. Marija, with a mischievous grin slipped quietly into the kitchen, returning with a pitcher of cold water and quickly dumped it on her friend! Within minutes, a full-fledged water fight ensued punctuated with shrieks and screams and laughter as everyone joined in.

In those days, Marija's house was easily identified and the little courtyard in the front was often filled with pilgrims wanting to see and hear from the visionary. As the water fight continued with the contestants hiding around corners and waiting to attack, several Italian nuns came into the courtyard softly calling Marija's name. They were all dressed in white habits. One of the white-clad nuns proceeded up the small set of concrete stairs to the front door of the house calling out: "Marija?"

Suddenly Marija dashed from around the corner and heaved a small bucket of water on the unsuspecting nun, totally drenching her and her impeccably white habit! It was as if it was done in slow motion, Marija would explain later. By the time she realized it was not one of her friends but a nun it was too late to stop the forward motion of the bucket.

For several moments, Marija and the nun looked at each other with shock and surprise. Here was this holy nun who came looking for this humble visionary now standing in front of her soaked through and through! And here is the visionary horrified that she has just drenched a holy nun!

Marija could only apologize over and over as she invited the soaked nun and her companions into her home. She then spent more than an hour visiting with them and making them drinks and coffee.

By the time the Italian nuns left her home, they and Marija were laughing about the incident. It is certain that the nun will never forget her introduction to a Medjugorje visionary!

Visionary Jakov: **"Many people have come here to Medjugorje, they ask themselves, why apparitions are lasting so long? Why Our Lady has been giving us so many messages? Many people say the messages are many times the same. I always say to everybody, instead of why, we should say thank you."**

why this little boy?

From the beginnings of the apparitions at Medjugorje, many wondered why a 10-year-old boy would be included as one of the six visionaries. The Blessed Mother soon put doubts to rest about his being chosen.

Jakov Colo quickly became a "favorite" of the Gospa. Being so young, he was not as in awe as were the older visionaries and thus carried on conversations with the Virgin as he would with anyone. He remained a typical little boy with interest in sports and generally just having fun. However, during the apparition time he was serious and attentive. His witness to the authorities concerning what he saw and felt during the time of the apparition was in line with the others. It was even more convincing considering his youth. How could a small child make up such a story?

Vicka was with Jakov more than the other visionaries. She believed there was something special about Jakov in his relationship with Our Lady, though it was a mystery even to her. When asked by her confessor why Our Lady chose little Jakov, Vicka said: "I can't say that I know that. But none of you really know the little guy! I always remember how the Virgin at the very start said: 'The rest of you go, and let little Jakov remain with me.' That is an unusual boy."

Jakov was not shy in asking questions of the Virgin. Shortly after the apparitions began, he asked Our Lady if she would tell him who would win the upcoming soccer championship. The Virgin just smiled and of course did not give him an answer!

Visionary Jakov: **"I believe that there is nothing more beautiful for a parent but to see his own child pray. When your child comes and asks you to pray together with him. When you see your child going to Holy Mass and coming back from Mass joyful, that is the most beautiful thing."**

"our lady has spoken!"

On the first day of my tour of the Philippines, the organizing group, composed entirely of women, insisted I see the statue of the Blessed Virgin Mary that had been erected at the site where she had mysteriously appeared to protect the people from the murderous wrath of dictator Ferdinand Marcos. Although exhausted from the lengthy flight to Manila, I wearily agreed.

More than a million people had taken to the streets in protest to the rigged election of Marcos to yet another oppressive term as president.

Troops were called to quell the so-called rebellion. Just before the troops were about to fire on the people, Our Lady suddenly appeared above the troops and told them not to fire, as the people were *her* children. Of course, they did not and without support from the military, Marcos had to flee the country.

We reached the shrine just as the stress of Manila traffic was about to overwhelm me. Situated at a busy intersection was a beautiful large chapel, and on top of it was a huge, rather homely statue of the Blessed Virgin Mary constructed out of dark grey metal. Its head was far too big for the rest of the statue. Two arms stretched out seemingly over the entire city with unusually large hands turned upwards. The women were staring at me for a reaction. "What do you think," Lydia, the leader of the group asked, "Isn't she beautiful?"

"Well– "I didn't know what to say. It was one of the ugliest statues of the Blessed Virgin I had ever seen. "It's certainly different . . ."

They all burst out laughing. "We know it is not beautiful, but it is special to us because of what happened shortly after it was completed," Lydia explained. "You see, after the revolution, the people wanted a large statue of Our Lady to permanently mark the spot where she appeared and saved us from Marcos' soldiers. But after it was completed, much criticism came to the artist and finally, it was decided to fix the head and the hands, so as to present a more beautiful Mary to the public."

Lydia took my hand, pulling me toward the edge of the street. "Come out here so you can see it better. There, all around it," she said pointing to the statue, "They built scaffolding and everything was in place to make the corrections. All of a sudden, a small tornado came out of nowhere, heading straight toward the statue! All of the workers fled to safety and as the tornado passed over, miraculously no one was harmed and no damage was done to the shrine or any other building. Only the scaffolding around the statue was knocked down! Our Lady had spoken! The statue would remain as it is."

I looked at Lydia. "Is this true? It just doesn't sound…" Lydia cut me off, "Oh, but it's very true," she said. "I know people who witnessed it themselves. And, so that you can see it was Our Lady behind this, you must know we do not have tornados in the Philippines!"

Once again, the Blessed Virgin had shown her sense of humor!

confession incognito

I'm certain many of you reading this little incident can associate with it. When many of us go to confession we want to go to a priest who does not know us.

This was especially true for me after having been involved in spreading the Medjugorje messages for several years because of the high profile it created. When I was in Medjugorje I always wanted to find a priest, who did not know me. How could I possibly go to a priest who knew me and confess things that would make him think less of me as a messenger of Medjugorje? That, of course, was pure ego.

To assure that I would find one who fit the need, I would walk along the front perimeter of the rows of booths looking inside the confessionals as people were leaving in order to locate an English-speaking priest possibly from another country. On this one occasion, I discovered a Filipino priest and quickly got in line. When my time came, I entered and gave my confession. He in turn gave me absolution. Just before leaving the booth I said to him, "Father, I will pray for you as I do for all priests who hear my confession."

The priest then reached over and hugged me and said, "God bless you Wayne, keep up the good work!"

Pope John Paul II: **"Pray for me in Medjugorje!"**

are you . . ?

When the outside altar located behind Saint James Church in Medjugorje was first constructed, it immediately became a special place for me to give talks to different English-speaking pilgrim groups. Non-English speaking pilgrims occasionally joined the talks, with one member doing a quiet translation. Thus, I was not surprised one afternoon when a small group of Italian women stood by and listened.

After the talk, I moved to the side of the church and began inter-reacting with the people. Soon a line formed for me to answer questions and sign autographs. I immediately noticed the group of Italians getting in line with the others. When it was the turn of the first of the Italia lady, she handed me a small scrap of paper indicting for me to sign it; so, I did. The second woman did the same. However, when the third one came to me and handed me the little slip of paper, she suddenly pointed at me and asked as I was signing the paper, "You Ivan or Jakov?"

"Oh no," I responded, "I am an American—Americano!"

With that the woman snatched the paper from me, gave me the look and quickly walked away with the others, all of them excitedly chatting and looking back at me with disgust.

I laughed so hard I had tears in my eyes! It was another hilarious incident that was so common with the Italians. They fill Medjugorje and without their strong support in the number of pilgrims coming to Medjugorje, the site would probably not be the success it is.

The Italian daily morning Mass follows the English Mass and it is frustratingly common for the pews near the front of the church to be filled with the Italians, mostly women, in anticipation of *their* Mass, which follows the English Mass. Almost always, they come into the church just before the Holy Eucharist. Upon receiving, many an American has returned to where they were sitting only to find an Italian in their seat! They simply smile and utter "scuami!"

One day when I was staying at visionary Marija's home, there were several young Italian men and women who had come to visit her. As always, Marija would accept them and spend time with them. One of the young men began proudly bragging there were more saints from Italy than any other country. I couldn't resist as I answered him: "Yes, and you need every one of them!"

setting new zealand on fire!

It had been a good tour. We covered the rim of cities on the exterior of the outback in Australia and now we were beginning a final three-day tour in New Zealand before heading home. I was filled with a fiery zeal and wanted to share it with the rugged, independent-minded New Zealanders.

As it turned out, I shared it in a very different way.

The first two days of the tour went well, topped off by large crowds eager to hear the messages of the Blessed Virgin coming from this little hamlet of Medjugorje. As I prepared for the third and final day, I discovered that I had run out of clean socks and undershirts. I was desperate—how could I wash them by hand and get them dry enough before the talk? There was little time to spare before I was to be picked up.

As I glanced around the room it suddenly struck me that I could dry the wet garments quickly by placing them over the neon bulbs in the lamps by the bedside. So, I did.

In the process of preparing for the night's event and also attempting to begin packing for my departure the next morning, I forgot about the drying clothes—until suddenly I heard a loud ringing noise outside. At the same time, I smelled something burning and of course it was my clothing hung over the lamps!

It didn't take long to realize that my burning clothes had set off the alarm. Within minutes there were two fire engine trucks in the parking area, which was now filled with the other guests of the motel. The firemen were making the rounds of each room to determine the source of the fire. I opened my door as a fireman was about to knock. "I'm afraid I am the guilty party," I said sheepishly, pointing to the charred clothing now in the bathroom sink where I had doused the flames.

"Don't worry about it Mr. Weible, there's no harm done." I was shocked the fireman knew me. He continued: "I'm looking forward to your talk tonight and just wanted to say thank you for coming to our country with this wonderful message."

I did my best that night to match the "fiery" event of almost burning down a motel in New Zealand!

holy protection

As I returned home from a speaking tour and emptied my brief case, there were scattered papers and prayer cards that people had given me during the various presentations. My 10-year-old son Kennedy began rummaging through the pile. He picked up one card, read it and then turned to me and asked, "Dad, is this true? It says on this prayer card that if I pray one Our Father, Hail Mary and Glory be daily for three years, I will never drown."

I took the card, looked at it and replied to my son, "Well, that's what it says, so, why do you ask?"

Kennedy's eyes lit up. "Dad, if I do this, you won't have to worry about me drowning when I'm surfing. I'm going to do it!"

Living in Myrtle Beach, South Carolina was a surfing paradise for the kids. Of course, there was always concern from the parents for their safety. However, I was pleased that Kennedy would take on the task daily for three years and I encouraged him to do it.

Time passed and finally the last day of the three years arrived. Kennedy came into the kitchen that morning fully excited. "I did it, Dad, I really did it! Now you won't have to worry about me drowning when I'm surfing!"

As proud as I was of my son for completion of three years of daily prayers, I couldn't resist the temptation. "That's great Kennedy, but what about sharks?"

Kennedy was crestfallen. After a few minutes, he asked, "Is there a prayer for protection against sharks?"

Go, therefore and make disciples of all nations, baptizing them in the name of the Father and of the Son and of the Holy Spirit, teaching them to observe all that I have commanded you; and lo, I am with you always, to the close of the age.

—Matthew 28: 19-20.

...I desire to be a mother to you, a teacher of the truth—so that in the simplicity of an open heart, you may become cognizant of the immeasurable purity and of the light which comes from it and shatters darkness, the light which brings hope...

—Excerpt from message of May 02, 2014.

9

more special moments

Just writing about the extraordinary special moments brings back priceless memories and a sense of awe. Of course, all special moments are precious gems. However, those contained in this chapter rise above just meaningful. I'll let you, the readers judge for yourselves!

sister trinity

I spoke twice at two different locations in Anchorage, Alaska and managed to work in a special visit at the hospital to a 92-year-old Episcopalian nun named, Sister Trinity. Cathy, a member of the group that brought me to Alaska had met her while doing voluntary work at the hospital. She was ecstatic that I was taking time to visit with this elderly nun, of the Episcopalian faith. Admittedly, I was also curious that the Episcopal church had nuns.

Although frail and weakened by her present condition, Sister Trinity greeted me with enthusiasm. Her small room was filled with flowers from well-wishers. I knew in my heart that her time on this earth was fast running out, as the pain and intensity of her illness was clear on her thin, angular face. But as with so many others of great faith facing the inevitable, there was peace and full acceptance in her eyes.

"It's wonderful that you, a Lutheran, would be chosen to spread these messages," she said weakly as I took her hand. And of course, she fully believed that Our Lady was appearing in Medjugorje. "She loves us all, no matter what faith we claim," she added when I mentioned my surprise that first of all the Episcopalian Church had nuns; and secondly, that she believed in apparitions so readily.

"Oh, yes," Sister Trinity answered when I questioned her about the order; "we have a great devotion to the Blessed Mother." This ethereal woman, who was so near death now, had served God in her Protestant order for more than fifty years. I quickly recognized her as another "Mary," like my Mary of Grenada.

I was happy to respond when she asked me if I would pray over her. I prayed for a peaceful death. Later, after returning home from the tour, I would learn from a member of the group that had sponsored my trip that Sister Trinity died on August 15, the Feast of the Assumption of Our Lady. I knew her departure for heaven on this particular day was no coincidence.

Visionary Mirjana: *"I cannot divulge much about the secrets but I can say this…*Our Lady is planning on changing the world. *She did not come to announce our destruction; she came to save us and with her Son she will triumph over evil. If Our Mother has promised to defeat evil, then what do we have to fear?"*

It was one of those rare moments with visionary Marija when there were no crowds waiting in the small front yard. We had just enjoyed a nice meal and were now relaxing, discussing the possibility of the fast expanding Yugoslavia civil war encroaching into Bosnia-Hercegovina. We wondered how the horror of war could come to the country that was home to Medjugorje, where the Blessed Mother was appearing as the Queen of Peace?

A mutual friend Margaret, who was from Scotland, was with us along with a fellow pilgrim, Terry from the states. We settled into a small room to watch an old black and white television that had been given to Marija. She loved old movies and had significantly increased her use of English from viewing them. We talked and watched simultaneously, munching on popcorn and generally enjoying a quiet evening despite the growing threat of war.

Suddenly, the quiet was broken by a disturbance on the street in front of Marija's home. Shouts could be heard followed by the sounds of scuffling. Peering out the window, Marija turned and quickly headed for the door. "It is Croatians and Serbians fighting," she said over her shoulder as she quickly bounced down the stairs and into the small courtyard of her home.

We watched from the window of the room as she walked directly into the middle of the men and talked calmly yet firmly with them. Even in the dimness of the evening it was clear they were young and had been drinking heavily. Ten Croatians had one Serbian surrounded and were pushing and shoving him around because he had been shouting Serbian nationalistic slogans.

Within minutes they began to disperse and Marija returned to the room. Her cheeks flushed and eyes dancing, she shook her head slowly.

"They drink and then the fighting begins. One day soon it will turn into real war. That is why Gospa asks us so many times to pray for peace."

Unfortunately, Marija was right.

On the tenth anniversary of the apparitions, June 25, 1991, the war came to Bosnia-Hercegovina. The men of the village of Medjugorje joyously joined with the vast majority of the male population of the country "celebrating" their entry into the conflict. The dark stain of nationalism soon overshadowed the incredible grace of the apparitions.

Forgotten in the heat of the moment was the second encounter for Marija with the Blessed Virgin on that first day of the apparitions in June 1981. After Our Lady's first session with the six visionaries that day, Marija had become separated from the others due to the excited crowd of villagers who had followed the young seers up the hill. She was on her way down the hill when suddenly Our Lady appeared in an open space to the left of the pathway—this time not smiling and happy. She was somber and serious as she said to Marija: *Peace, Peace, Peace! Be reconciled! Only Peace! Make your peace with God and among yourselves. For that, it is necessary to believe, to pray, to fast, and to go to confession.*

It was an impassioned warning that would be repeated over and over again by the Virgin in the succeeding days, months, and years. This second message, on that first day of intimate conversation with the Mother of God, was a pointed warning not only to the three ethnic groups that formed the population of Yugoslavia, but most emphatically, to the entire world.

Three and a half years later, nearly a million people had been killed in the civil struggle. More than 100,000 were now homeless refugees. Yet, the Blessed Virgin continued to appear in apparition in Medjugorje.

The Queen of Peace was doing all that she could to be the peacemaker for the world.

Archbishop Fulten J. Sheen: "**Joy is not the same as pleasure or happiness. A wicked and evil man may have pleasure, while any ordinary mortal is capable of being happy.** Pleasure generally comes from things, and always through the senses; happiness comes from humans through fellowship. Joy comes from loving God and neighbor."

loretta

During an early tour in Los Angeles, California I was invited to the home of Loretta Young, one of Hollywood's legendary movie and television stars whose durable career had delighted milllions of fans for years. She was in her time arguably the biggest star of television.

Loretta had journeyed to Medjugorje with her son and had been spiritually renewed by the pilgrimage even though severely spraining her ankle on the pathway up Podbdo on the first day. Despite this annoyance, she had become an advocate of Medjugorje, and hearing of my coming to Los Angeles, she wanted to meet me.

As we drove into the heart of Beverly Hills, I could hardly believe this woman whom I had admired for so long had read my articles and was open to meeting me to discuss Medjugorje. My admiration stemmed not only because of her acting ability, but the fact that she always ended her popular weekly television show with a moral message based on Scripture.

At a church near Loretta's home, we met two other people who would join us that afternoon. Karen Kopins was a rising young starlet who had also been to Medjugorje, creating a change of perspective in her budding television and movie career. With her was a priest, Father Susa, who worked in Calcutta, India with Mother Theresa. He had known Loretta for years and had a deep interest in finding out more about Medjugorje.

We quickly got to know each other and I hastily arranged with my escorts to meet them at the church in a couple of hours.

At the door of a spacious but modest home by Hollywood standards, we were greeted by Loretta herself. The conversation immediately turned to Medjugorje; stories flowed as we sipped hot tea. It was apparent that Loretta was indeed what she appeared to be on stage and screen. Here was a woman whose life as well as career revolved around her faith. Just as any other pilgrim to the little village, she told of its effects not only on her but also on her son.

I was mesmerized as this famous movie and television star related the story of going to Lourdes at a critical point in her career to do a show about the shrine. "Things were not going well at all at that time," she told us, "But I wanted to do something special for my faith and the Lourdes show was it."

Loretta had just received cancellation from her long-time sponsor who had requested repeatedly that she stop doing her trademark moral and scriptural references at the end of each show. "There was no way I was going to do that," she added with emphasis, "So they cancelled me."

Things became worse once they arrived on location at Lourdes. Heavy rains caused long overruns and extended expenses, which she was forced to assume personally when her insurance company balked at paying for the extra time.

"But it wasn't all bad," Loretta continued. "One of the executives with the production company was an alcoholic and with nothing to do and nowhere to find a drink, he went out one evening walking up the hill where the Stations of the Cross were located. Suddenly, there is this deluge of rain with fierce thunder and lightning. As he struggled up the pathway in the dark, a bolt of lightning struck, lighting everything in brilliance and he found himself staring directly up at the huge cross at the top of the hill – and there was Jesus, staring down at him!"

Loretta laughed at the memory. "Needless to say, he was converted – and cured of alcoholism. On the flight home, I'm happy for him but I'm thinking, that was a mighty expensive conversion!"

"That's quite a story," I said.

Loretta held up her hand. "Wait a minute, that's not all. We arrive home and my agent is waiting for me at the airport with a big smile on his face. He informs me that we already have a new sponsor for the show. And, the insurance company has decided to cover all costs of the production overrun! All this and a conversion too!"

I returned to Loretta's home the following day at her invitation to watch the now-famous show that was filmed on location at Lourdes. It was another opportunity to spend time with her and to further admire a star of such magnitude who lived her faith and had the tenacity to defend it.

Another grace also came from this incredible meeting with Loretta. Karen Kopins made the decision to leave the Hollywood scene and to marry and raise a family. Hollywood's loss was Heaven's gain.

a special grace

You know, Mary Virgin makes me feel as though every message given at Medjugorje is just for me. All of us should feel that way. It is the basis of developing an incomprehensible intimacy with her. Even greater, she brings us to the reality of her Son Jesus in the Holy Eucharist. I remember visionary Marija saying once, "If I had to choose between receiving Jesus in the Eucharist or having Gospa appear to me in apparition, I would choose receiving Jesus."

Developing an intimate relationship with the Virgin Mary is no different than developing one with Jesus in the Holy Eucharist—and as always, Mary is intrinsically involved. And why wouldn't she be involved?

She is the daughter of the Eternal Father, spouse of the Holy Spirit and mother of the only begotten Son of God.

The Blessed Virgin Mary is given two major roles in the plan of salvation. She is chosen to be the Mother of God and she is given the role as spiritual mother to the children of God. Holy Scripture tells us the story: Mary Virgin was there with her Son in many of His travels during the three years of mission. She was with her Son and His disciples in the Upper Room for the Last Supper where the Holy Eucharist originated. She was there at the foot of the cross to see her Son die for the salvation of the world. She was with the disciples and followers of Jesus when the Holy Spirit came down upon them.

Mary is given the title: "Mother of the Eucharist." She is the first tabernacle; she is the first Christian and, she is the messenger and teacher to all who will listen to her words that come straight from the throne of God. She is …Our Mary!

All of the above concerning the Blessed Virgin Mary is why I share this next story with you. It is, without doubt, the greatest compliment I have ever received. I know you will comprehend why I share it even though it could easily be construed as self-promotion.

When I returned home from my first pilgrimage to Medjugorje in May 1986, I immediately started attending daily Mass at the local Catholic Church. Before long I had become a familiar face there and was known as "that Lutheran Protestant" to whom the Blessed Virgin had spoken, and given a special mission to spread her Medjugorje messages. I paid little attention to such accolades far too engrossed in fulfilling as best as I could what she was asking of me.

One day as I entered the narthex of the church and stopped in front of a Sacred Heart statue of Jesus to say a few words of prayer, one of the three elderly nuns stationed at the parish came up behind me and tapped me on the shoulder. I turned around to see Sister Anne (not her real name). She was the oldest of the three and wore large coke-bottle thick glasses. "Pardon me Wayne, could I ask a special favor of you?" she said, her frail face dominated by the thick glasses hovering inches from mine. I could immediately tell that she was stressed about something.

"Of course, Sister Anne, what can I do for you?" Sister Anne looked around to make sure no one else was near enough to hear her and said, "Well, they want me to retire and return to the main convent in Baltimore, but I don't want to retire and I don't want to leave here. She paused for a few seconds, reached over and grabbed my hand and then added, "Could you please ask Our Lady not to let them retire me and to let me stay here?"

I was deeply touched at the request of this beautiful little nun standing before me in full habit—and also taken aback momentarily. "Sister," I finally responded, "I'll be glad to ask Our Lady to help you; but Sister, you're a *sister*! You've given your life to serving as a nun in the convent. I'm sure you could ask for yourself as well."

The little nun moved even closer to me and said with great seriousness, "Yes, that's true, but you're Mary's boy!"

To say that I was stunned and deeply touched would be an understatement. It is the greatest compliment I have ever received. Yet, as "Mary's boy" I knew that all who held her in veneration and saw her as a personal intercessor, were all "Mary's boys and girls!"

Visionary Ivanka: **"Our Lady is here with us today, now and we have to make the decision whether we want to let Her in and to open our hearts and accept Her messages. That is why, carry peace in your hearts, and carry peace to your families, to your countries, to your churches."**

The second greatest compliment I received during the mission came from a resident of the village of Medjugorje---a very special resident. It was given by the mother of locutionist Jelena, one of the two young girls who at the age of 10 began receiving inner messages from the Blessed Virgin.

Jelena and her cousin Marijana were given many powerful messages concerning the Church. They would see the Virgin interiorly in their minds as she would come to them without warning. The Virgin even dressed differently then when she was appearing to the six visionaries. Jelena was by far the recipient of the more powerful messages and the dominant one, as Marijana was very shy.

Sadly, the two locutionists of Medjugorje are all but forgotten today, with the majority of the public interest on the three remaining active visionaries. It has been my thinking that the messages given to them will become dominant at the end of the daily apparitions.

I was blessed to be able to stay at the home of Jelena's family on a number of occasions in the early years of pilgrimage to the village. On a summer visit; I had met a lady at the top of Cross Mountain early one morning. We struck up a conversation. I told her that I didn't have a place to stay beyond that night as the village was packed with pilgrims. "Oh I'm staying at the home of one of the locutionists," she told me. "They do not take in many pilgrims but I know they have an open room at this time. I will be glad to take you there."

Incredibly, I was welcomed with open arms. Jelena's father Grgch was very devout and humbled that his daughter was receiving locutions. He had actually built a special prayer room and the entire family gathered there every morning for prayers. Jelena was 13 years old at the time. She spoke no English but somehow, we developed a bond despite the language barrier. Additionally, I was accepted by the entire family and developed a friendship that lasts to this day.

Over the next two years I watched Jelena grow into a young woman. She had learned to speak English so well that it was difficult to detect an accent. I went to the house one day to see her and the family and found her speaking to pilgrims from the steps of her home. Of course, she had a translator and was speaking in Croatian. However, when she had finished and the pilgrims were gone she greeted me with: "Hello Wayne, how are you?"

"Oh wow, listen to you," I answered, "It seems you have learned a little English!" Jelena gave me a look of pride as she said, "I have not just learned a little English—I know it all!" "Well then, I said, speaking rapidly, tell me what I am saying right now!" She then translated all that I had just spoken. "I believe you and I'm very proud of you for learning it so fast."

Jelena would continue her education in the United States, attending Steubenville University in Ohio. I was blessed to spend time with her while I was there speaking on Medjugorje. We shared a few stories gleaned from her role as a locutionist.

The little girl from Medjugorje had grown into a strikingly beautiful young lady, graced with the looks of her mother as well as having extraordinary intelligence. Jelena married an Italian man and moved to Rome. She would eventually earn a Doctorate degree in theology. While undertaking such demanding studies, she also became a mother of three children.

It was during another summer when Jelena and her family were back in the village for a visit that we met at her family home, catching up with each other. Later in our conversation, Jelena looked at me and smiled. "You know," she began, "My mother has only read two books in her life—the Bible and your book, The Message."

I was totally surprised. As Jelena translated to her mother what she had told me, her mother looked at me and nodded with a smile as if to confirm.

These little graces are not only sources of personal happiness but strong confirmations that the Holy Spirit guides the mission—and also anointed my first book!

Visionary Vicka: **"Many times we see Lent as a time when we make sacrifices and practice self-denial by giving up coffee, alcohol, chocolate, cigarettes, TV, or whatever we are overly attached to. But we must renounce those things out of love for Jesus and Mary, and be careful not to do it for our own glory."**

the penance of love

After writing about an important charity I was working with known as *Rebuild For Bosnia,* we began to accumulate funds to begin building homes for refugees in the area surrounding Medjugorje. As the chosen patron for the charity I decided to take it a step further.

I was leading a pilgrimage to Medjugorje in November 2000 and had sent a letter to each pilgrim asking for donations of essential toiletries and clothing. The group brought large suitcases full of these items and we distributed them to the waiting families who were still living in squalid conditions. More importantly, the pilgrims generously donated toward the building of a house. That was my goal: to collect enough funds from this group of pilgrims to build at least one home as a permanent legacy for this particular pilgrimage.

After speaking about the charity in my opening talk, I was approached by a couple from the group the following day. "We'd like to donate a house," the husband told me, "but we ask that you keep our names confidential."

I was not sure if I had heard him right. "You mean you want to make a contribution?" I asked.

"No," he said, "We want to donate an entire house!"

I was nearly speechless – and immediately filled with emotion. I couldn't thank them enough and later in the evening talks, I told the others in our group about the extraordinary offer without identifying where it had come from. Soon two more people came forward and pledged to work toward obtaining funds so that they, too, could donate a full house.

Several days later, the first couple who had promised to donate a house approached me again and said they would *match* each house pledged by the rest of the group! The result was that this pilgrimage left a legacy of at least four homes, with a strong possibility of two more from donations that continued to come in from members of the pilgrimage.

I returned home spiritually refreshed and filled with renewed fervor to live the messages of Our Lady. A beautiful bonus was the development of a friendship with the couple who donated a complete house and spurred others in the group to do likewise, which continues to this day.

God is good.

a special visit

As stated in a previous story, Our Lady took Vicka and Jakov with Her to visit Heaven, Purgatory and hell. It was an incredible time of great discovery, Vicka would later say. However, the visionary was most deeply moved to great compassion for the souls in Purgatory.

Vicka asked Our Lady if there was something she could do to help these poor souls, if she could offer herself for their expiation. Our Lady accepted her offer when she was certain Vicka understood the seriousness of what she was asking. Shortly afterwards, a mysterious illness afflicted Vicka, causing her to suffer from extremely painful headaches and high fevers that were so severe, she would fall into comas. Often during these episodes, she was semi-conscious and obviously suffering, though she always would awaken a few minutes before Our Lady's apparition each evening and would approach the moment of the vision smiling and happy.

At one point, Vicka's mother begged her to ask Our Lady to cure her, but Vicka responded that if her mother knew how much expiation her suffering was doing for the poor souls, she would not ask this of her.

In January 1988, Our Lady told Vicka her suffering would soon come to an end. She gave her the exact date her illness would disappear, though Vicka was to tell the date to no one with the exception of her confessor. The bishop's commission which was investigating the apparitions was given the date in a sealed envelope.

On September 25, 1988, the headaches and symptoms disappeared, never to return. Members of the commission, upon opening the envelope, discovered the same date therein.

Through these years of carrying this cross, Our Lady brought Vicka through the school of suffering, an education that has helped countless individuals learn how to accept suffering with joy. She became a witness not only for all those who carry the cross of physical illnesses or handicaps but for all people who carry a cross, whatever shape or form it may come in. Our Lady has often asked Vicka to offer up other sufferings as well, the most difficult being to give up her daily apparitions for extended periods of time. This has been asked of Vicka on several occasions over the years.

Vicka suffers greatly during these times of not seeing Our Lady for specific intentions that Our Lady has asked of her. They are the most difficult—and also the most extraordinary special moments of sacrifice.

One day in the early months of the ongoing apparitions, visionary Marija was so ill she could not attend Holy Mass. The singular day of missing Holy Mass stretched into several more adding to her misery of being sick and bedridden. She had been ordered to stay in her bed as much as possible, arising only just before the time of the apparition.

Father Slavko Barbaric, who was serving as one of the spiritual directors for the visionaries, was well aware that Marija had not been to Mass for several days. He telephoned her and said, "Marija, please prepare yourself in some of your nicest clothes—I am bringing Jesus to see you!"

Marija was filled with excitement. Jesus was coming to see her! Even though it was not the time of the daily apparition, maybe the Gospa would also come. She quickly dressed in some of her finest clothes and anxiously awaited the arrival of Father Slavko and Jesus. The visionary's heart fluttered in anticipation. After all, hadn't the Mother of Jesus continued to visit her in spite of her sickness?

Father Slavko arrived and knocked on the door of Marija's home. The visionary ran to the door and opened it with great anticipation. There stood the priest cradling a pix in his hands, which he then extended to Marija and said: "Here is Jesus—He has come to make you well!"

Visionary Vicka: **"When you look at Our Lady the beauty of her face is so wonderful that words can't describe it. She herself has said that she is beautiful because she loves. This is the way we must be beautiful – above all, beautiful inside – so that our faces can radiate this beauty too... Unfortunately, we hide our faces behind many types of masks; we hide everything inside. We have to begin to love to be beautiful."**

Here is another story when visionary Marija was too sick to go to the usual place of the apparitions. As it turned out, she would have the apparition with the Blessed Virgin at her home; and, for the first time, her mother and father would witness their daughter during an apparition.

It was a very special occasion for Marija's parents. Also, present would be her sister Rusica, her future husband Paulo Lunetti—and me!

But there were more people present. Three of Marija's nephews and nieces, all of them aged three years or younger, were also present. As we settled in for the time of the apparition, the small living area was filled with screeches and laughter as the children ran around in total abandonment.

The noise continued and I wondered how Marija could possibly have her apparition in such a setting. However, as she knelt in front of a cross on the wall, she motioned to the three children to come and kneel next to her. Suddenly they were all silent and still. The Blessed Virgin came and the apparition lasted for a little more than four minutes.

Marija beamed with joy when the post apparition prayers were completed. She then told us what had occurred during the apparition. "Our Lady came with three little cherub angels and she then looked at the three children and said 'You also have three little angles with you!'"

I could only shake my head as I discerned that this stupendous experience was another lesson straight from the Mother of God!

"The Holy Eucharist is the dominant expression of God's unconditional love."

How many times have you heard that question from believers and unbelievers alike? Most people who have dogs, cats, horses and a variety of other animals truly believe that animals that are close to them go to Heaven.

After my own personal experience, I am now one of them.

Many animals seem to have surprising intelligence: not just apes or dolphins, but also birds like the African grey parrot. They can put together meaningful phrases and even sentences. African greys are said to have an intelligence comparable to a three or four-year-old human.

Recently, there was a story carried in many major news outlets about a man who while watching football ventured just outside of his back door to fetch additional wood for his blazing fireplace. Dressed only in pajamas, a robe and thin slippers, he slipped on a small patch of ice severely hurting his neck. He couldn't move and within minutes his dog rushed to his side and began barking constantly. Meanwhile the man kept shouting as well, hoping a neighbor might here and come to his rescue.

No one came to the man's rescue. Yet, the dog kept barking and as the chilling air caused the man to shake with cold, his dog jumped on top of him to keep him warm. Early in the morning, with the dog still barking and intermittently howling, a neighbor finally heard and came to investigate. The dog stopped barking but would not leave his owner's side until he was taken by ambulance to the hospital.

Even with familiarity of several stories like the one above, I did not believe that animals went to Heaven. I recall an encounter with a woman in Virginia Beach, Virginia who picked me up at the airport as part of the group sponsoring my talk there. She had a beautiful poodle with her and hardly paused talking about her dog. Somewhere in the conversation she said, "I just can't wait to go to Heaven with my dog!"

That did it for me. I said as gently as possible: "That's a nice thought, but I don't think your dog is going to Heaven."

Suddenly the woman sharply pulled the car to the side of the road and stopped, turning to me and very pointedly said, "If my dog can't go to Heaven, then I don't want to go either!"

I was stunned. Surely this woman must realize how foolish this statement was. No one with real faith would believe such a thing.

It would be nearly 10 years later that I would change my mind about animals going to Heaven, due to a personal experience that involved my own dog. Brandi was a beautiful little sheltie and was extremely shy. Only on a few rare occasions did I see any temper from Brandi and that was when a male dog was nearby. She exuded femininity and her coat was like silk. I bonded with Brandi like with no previous dog I had owned.

Brandi was 10 years old and supposedly in excellent health. The day before a pilgrimage to Medjugorje, I played with Brandi for an extended period of time tossing a Frisbee toy, which she would expertly catch in the air and return it to me. It was her favorite thing to do. In fact, the shy little dog would noticeably change from shyness to full happy participation in this game.

Therefore, it was a complete shock to receive a call the evening of my arrival in Medjugorje from my wife Judith that Brandi had taken ill and had to be rushed to a veterinarian for treatment. She added that the vet had stated that Brandi was extremely ill and may not survive. At six o clock the following morning Judith sadly informed me that my Brandi had died. I was devastated.

As members of the pilgrimage group came into the breakfast, they immediately noticed that I did not look well. I shared with them through my tears about Brandi's death. Soon most of the group was also in tears. To make matters worse, I had to speak to a group early that morning and was thankful it was a Korean pilgrimage and not English. I don't think I would have made it through a talk to Americans with such feelings of sadness.

Our group met at a small chapel for a private Mass just outside of Medjugorje, where I joined them following my talk to the Koreans. Still filled with emotion, I turned my thoughts to the Mass saying several prayers in preparation and momentarily forgetting about Brandi's death. I noticed that on the wall between two tall windows behind the altar there was a display of three ceramic oval plaques hanging vertically. Each plaque had a picture on it; the top displayed a fish, the middle one a lamb and the bottom one a dove.

As I was looking at the plaques, suddenly they were overshadowed in a brilliant burst of light. In the middle of the light was my Brandi, barking with great joy, her breast as white as snow. I sat there stunned. There was no doubt of what I was seeing and I knew in my heart that it was a special gift of the Holy Spirit.

I also knew without doubt that animals did indeed go to Heaven! Brandi was letting me know that and also that everything was going to be all right.

Therefore do not pronounce judgment before the time, before the Lord comes, who will bring to light the things now hidden in darkness and will disclose the purposes of the heart. Then every man will receive his commendation from God.

—1 Corinthians 4:5.

"Dear children! Today I desire to share Heavenly joy with you. You, little children, open the door of your heart so that hope, peace and love, which only God gives, may grow in your heart. Little children, you are too bound to the earth and earthly things, that is why, Satan is rolling you like the wind rolls the waves of the sea. Therefore, may the chain of your life be prayer with the heart and Adoration of my Son Jesus. Give over your future to Him so that, in Him, you may be joy and an example with your life to others. Thank you for having responded to my call."

—Message of August 25, 2016.

10

even more special moments

common sense faith

There are occasions when good old common sense prevails at unexpected times. Such was the case one warm afternoon in Medjugorje when a small group of us were making our way to my favorite restaurant in Medjugorje, Columbo.

There was a silence among us, one of those odd moments when no one had anything to say. Suddenly, Father Moyna, a priest from New York with a strong accent and a penchant for coming out with what may be considered somewhat eccentric statements, suddenly said in a rather loud voice: "If you don't want to go to hell, then you won't!"

We all stopped and turned to Father Moyna, as if expecting him to explain the strange statement. But he said nothing.

Almost in unison, all of us came up with the same explanation as we looked at each other with a look of realization: If you do not want to go to hell, then you will work hard not to—you will do everything you can to prevent it.

It was only good common sense!

Visionary Mirjana: **"Our Lady asks us to pray for those who do not believe—those who have not yet come to know the love of God."**

in defense of faith

With the publishing of my first book, *Medjugorje: The Message* came a new obligation: autograph sessions. They would take place mostly in bookstores. But there were exceptions, some of which led to confrontations with people of other Christian faiths—that is, Protestants.

In many of the autograph sessions, someone would inevitably bring up the question: How could I as a Protestant write about something so Catholic? The question was first asked by my Lutheran pastor, who was incredulous that I was involved in what he said "was pure Catholic error." He had actually taken a red marker and highlighted the so-called errors of Catholicism in my first article on Medjugorje published in our newspapers. There was no way to explain that the Blessed Virgin Mary, the mother of Jesus, had spoken to my heart in asking me to spread the messages she was giving in Medjugorje. That would only have made things worse. Besides, I was not about to tell anyone at that time that the Virgin had actually spoken to me. That would certainly threaten my journalistic reputation.

One such autographing stop was inside a massive mall in front of a Catholic bookstore. However, the table filled with my books was placed away from the store and near a busy post in order to reach more people. Most of those who came to the signing were polite and asked reasonable and interesting questions. It was a good session and many books were sold.

At one point, the foot traffic slowed down noticeably. It was a welcomed break. I leaned back, grateful for the opportunity to relax for a few minutes.

Earlier, I had noticed a man standing close by observing what was occurring. He had been there for a while but had not come near the table. As I was straightening the stack of books left, the man approached the table obviously waiting for a time when no one else would be there. As I glanced up, he said with a strong southern accent, "Can I ask you a question?"

I smiled and answered, "Of course, what would you like to ask?"

The man stared hard at me. "Are you the anti-Christ?"

My heart jumped a bit as I smiled and responded, "Excuse me?"

The man leaned down toward me now, glaring in judgment. "I asked you, *are you the anti-Christ?*"

I could feel the heat rising in me as I searched for a civil answer to his startling question, which I took as more of an accusation than a question. "Sir, first of all, no, I am not the anti-Christ. I am a Christian." Now I was the one staring hard at him. "Why would you ask such a question of me?"

The man straightened up and crossed his arms. "Well, obviously, you worship the Virgin Mary and other so-called saints and not Jesus. Mary was just another sinner who had other children. Unless you accept Jesus as your Lord and Savior, you cannot go to Heaven!" he paused a moment and then continued: "Scripture says that Jesus is the only way to salvation, and that you shouldn't have other gods before you!"

I relaxed somewhat and smiled again, hoping to calm the situation. "Sir, I can assure you that Jesus is my Lord and Savior. The Blessed Virgin Mary is His mother and she comes to this village of Medjugorje in apparition to six young visionaries with the express purpose to lead us to Him."

The man quickly cut in: "But you Catholics pray to Mary. The Bible says we should only pray to God the Father in the name of Jesus."

I countered quickly: "Look, when you have a problem or a crisis, don't you ask other people to pray for you? That's what we do with Mary; we ask her to intercede for us."

That seemed to slow the man down a little but then he responded, "Well, can I ask you another question?"

"Of course."

Finally, the man smiled slightly. "How do you know this apparition thing is the Virgin Mary and not Satan?"

I was ready for this question. It had been asked of me several times at different venues. I moved a bit closer to him and lowered my voice, looking directly in his eyes. "Well, if this is Satan, it's the greatest mistake he has ever made because millions of people are converting and accepting Jesus as their Lord and Savior!"

The man slowly shook his head, smiled in acceptance and began walking away. He paused a moment, turned around and said, "Can't argue with you on that one!"

Commentary: How often are Catholics confronted by non-Catholics about their faith and intimidated when the confronter begins quoting Scripture? The Blessed Virgin has asked through her messages at Medjugorje that we read a little Scripture daily, meditate on it and then try and put it into everyday life. If we do this, we will grow in comfort with the Bible, enhance our faith and have the answers to defend our spiritual beliefs. Most importantly, we will find emulsion into holiness at the intimate level that will bring deeper discernment of the words of God.

There is nothing new in the messages given to us at Medjugorje. They all can be identified in Holy Scripture. Apparitions of the Blessed Virgin come in times of crisis. Sometimes it is for a community, a prayer group, a region, a country—or for the entire world. I don't think there is any argument that the world is deep into crisis where faith is being overshadowed by the darkness of evil. Most importantly, she does not come just for Catholics but for all of the children of God.

Thus, the mission for those of us who know the spiritual role of Mary as a "first responder" in times of crisis is to live the messages she has given to the world for the past 36 years and let others see it. Secondly, we should arm ourselves with familiarity of Scripture in order to reasonably defend Mary's role as messenger in times of spiritual crisis.

a cool evening

As we arrived at the church in Moscow, Russia, the visible breaths of the masses of people waiting to enter the sanctuary underlined the extreme cold of the evening. Even though dressed in a suit with a thick topcoat, warm gloves and a typical Russian fur hat, I was freezing!

We had to make our way through crusted snow to the rear entrance of the massive old church, thus exposing us to the cold even longer. As we entered the building, expecting relief in a warm environment, I was shocked to find that there was no heat inside the ancient church.

Welcome to Russia! I thought.

Despite the cold, I was filled with joy just to be able to speak to the Russian people about Medjugorje. It had been a long and hard tour up to this point. Earlier in the day, we were not sure we could even get to Moscow due to fuel shortages that grounded many flights. But somehow here we were making it all worthwhile.

Once the crowds had entered the church, it was standing room only, a rather odd looking crowd with everyone wearing heavy coats.

Soon the cold surroundings were forgotten as the evening began with Holy Mass.

When it came time for the talk, I did something that shocked the people; I walked to the podium, stopped and removed my topcoat and gloves, which created a loud and startling united gasp from the assembled crowd. One man quickly rushed to me indicating I should not remove my topcoat. My translator explained in hesitant English, "He is saying you will freeze!"

I simply shrugged and explained to him that I could not talk with the heavy coat in that it would be a distraction. With the translator relaying my explanation, he nodded in resignation and returned to his seat.

Amazingly, I did not feel the cold once I began the talk, which lasted a little more than an hour and ended in a rousing standing ovation. In fact, I was warm as I could be. As I put my topcoat and gloves back on, the cheers became louder—and, I instantly felt the chilling cold again!

After another hour of greeting the people and by now thoroughly frozen from head to toe, I silently thanked the Blessed Mother for the little miracle of keeping me warm during the talk. Just another instant of letting me know she was there.

Saint Louis de Montfort: **"Blessed is the Rosary, which gives us the knowledge of Our Blessed Lord by meditating on His life, death, passion and glory."**

the medals

There is no memory of when I began passing out medals to people attending my talks. It's just something that started. Usually in preparation for each talk, I would place five Medjugorje medals of Our Lady in my coat pocket. Following the talk, I would hand out the medals as

I felt directed. It became a standard part of each talk. There were times when no medals were given out; or, only a couple. I soon realized that this little gift was very special and that Mary would make it known to me to give a medal to someone—usually at the last second. That served as confirmation for me. On rare occasions, the medals were rejected for a variety of reasons. Over time great stories immersed about the effects the medals had on the recipients. There have been enough that they could fill an entire book! The following episode concerning the medals is one of my personal favorites:

After a talk in Sacramento, California, there was a reception for meeting the people and signing books, a time I eagerly looked forward to as it gave me opportunity to share with those in need of prayer or special support. It was during these times that I most often gave medals to individuals. A man and his wife next in line approached me with the man smiling somewhat sheepishly. "You probably don't remember me . . ." He then turned and added, "Or my wife."

Of course, I didn't, but smiling I said, "Well, you look familiar."

The man's expression changed to seriousness. "You gave me a medal a year ago in Baton Rouge, Louisiana. We've been transferred here now, but a lot has happened to us since then."

Surprisingly, I then did remember them, especially him. A year earlier at one of my talks, as they had come through the line with my book for an autograph, she was thrilled and he was impatient and obviously not happy to be there. "Yes, I gave you the medal and you insisted it wasn't for you and you told me to give it to your wife. If I remember correctly, you told me you didn't want to be there."

The man answered somewhat embarrassed, "That's right. I only came to the talk that night at my wife's insistence. In fact, I didn't even like the Catholic Church or anything associated with it. I only attended for her sake because she is Catholic. I couldn't believe it when you said the medal was from the Blessed Virgin Mary and she wanted *me* to have it."

"And now, my husband's taking instruction to join the Church," his wife added quietly. "We wanted to let you know what that medal did for our family."

Quietly thanking them, I knew I would never again hesitate to call all Christians to their historical church beginnings, the Holy Catholic and Apostolic Church of Jesus Christ.

the proposition

"I don't know why I am here or even how I got here," she began through tears and genuine sadness. I shook my head. How many times had I heard this statement in bringing pilgrims to Medjugorje? I asked her to continue.

Susan (not her real name) told me her life had been "a real mess" just a year ago. She had become addicted to drugs and had turned to prostitution to support her habit. Then something happened that frightened her into taking a long, hard look at her life.

"Almost exactly a year ago, I was picked up by a man one evening, a huge man, who went wild after sniffing too much cocaine. He became enraged and began taking it out on me. We were in his car when he just flipped out and started shouting and cursing at me. Suddenly, he pulled out a gun, and shoving me to the floorboard of the car, he put the gun to my head and said he was going to kill me."

Susan spoke in a low monotone. I wondered how she could have possibly reached such a point in her life. She was in her middle thirties, slender, attractive – and intelligent. The look in her eyes was the only indication of what she had gone through. They were large, hauntingly sad brown eyes, now filled with pain and embarrassment as she related her story.

"I stayed on the floorboard of that car for six hours," she continued, "And he kept on cursing me and telling me he was going to kill me. It was as if I saw my whole life in that horrible time. And then I reached a point where I didn't care anymore. I pushed the gun away, got out of the car and began walking away, telling him if he was going to kill me he better do it now. I was shaking, knowing I could die at any second. But instead, he just closed the car door and drove away. I don't know how long I stood there, but something deep inside of me told me to go and see a priest."

In the following months, Susan learned about Medjugorje and as she put it, "I felt I had to go, somehow. I was raised Catholic and knew of the Virgin Mary, but it all got lost in my teenage years. I learned of this trip through a friend, and felt I had to come. Now, here I am, wondering how I deserve to be here after all I had done."

Jan, a fellow pilgrim who had befriended Susan and had arranged for her to speak to me was right; she had told me I needed to hear Susan's story. It was one of the most incredible experiences I had heard since becoming involved with Medjugorje. And I knew Jan was there to assist her in understanding why she was in Medjugorje. The three of us talked a long time. Then Susan related an incident that had occurred the past evening after the Croatian Mass, adding, "It let me know the struggle wasn't over."

Standing on the front steps of Saint James Church after Mass waiting for Jan, two Croatian men had approached her and very directly asked her to sleep with them saying, "We have never had an American woman."

Susan gave a little laugh. "I couldn't believe this was happening here in this place. I guess that told me Satan wasn't going to let me go without a fight. Anyway, I calmly asked them if they realized where they were standing while making such a proposal. They just smiled and then left."

Susan paused a moment and then began to cry. "How did they know?" she asked. "How did they know I had been a prostitute?"

We talked long into the evening as I tried to assure her that Satan doesn't give up easily. "You just keep on praying and know you are now a child of God. He can't hurt you," I added, "But he makes you think he can!"

Two days later our pilgrimage journeyed to Siroki Brijeg to listen to Father Jozo.

After his talk, he went through the crowd praying over people. When he came to us, Susan immediately went down completely and deeply "slain in the Spirit" as it was called. Several minutes later, as Jan helped her to her feet, she was overcome and ran out of the church in hysterical tears. I quickly followed after her. Seeing me, Susan's tears increased. "It's all wonderful, but it's just too much—it's just too much all at one time. I need to go home and sort things out . . ."

I put my arms around Susan as she shook with sobs. Holding her for a few moments, I told her, "Susan, you *are* home. You belong to Jesus now!"

I later learned that Susan became involved in raising funds and goods for the people of Bosnia-Hercegovina who suffered as refugees from the horrible civil war.

The Blessed Virgin Mary at Medjugorje: *I wish to keep on giving you messages, as it has never been in history since the beginning of the world!* —an early message (date unknown) from the Blessed Virgin to the visionaries.

the multiplication of food

The story goes that a villager named Josip had become modestly successful through the business of housing pilgrims during the early days of the apparitions. He had been one of the first to open his home to visiting pilgrims with no expectation of material gain. However, he was soon blessed with earnings far in excess of what he had earned by his own labors in the past.

Yet, Josip and his family continued living as they always had. His family was in attendance at the church each evening for the apparition, the Mass and all of the prayers. He had been struck by the Blessed Virgin's message and was determined to live it to the best of his ability. Josip knew and acknowledged where his personal success had come from and he remained a man of prayer and fasting.

Success had allowed Josip to expand his home to take in even more pilgrims, and to purchase material goods beyond his wildest expectations. Among his possessions was a large freezer that, during pre-war days, was always well stocked with freshly butchered meat. With the influx of refugee relatives during the devastating civil war, Josip's meat supply was fast dwindling, forcing him to butcher one of his cows.

He carefully wrapped the meat and placed it in the freezer, with the intention of rationing it sparingly. Soon, however, his neighbors had as great an overrun of refugee guests as he did. And they had no meat. So, Josip generously shared the meat with all in need, attempting to live the messages as he had since the Blessed Virgin had first appeared in the village.

Each day, Josip would take meat from the freezer for his family and his neighbors in need. The meat lasted far beyond the time when it should have run out. Yet, Josip was able to disperse the meat daily. Finally, a neighbor asked, "Josip, did you have to butcher your other cow?"

"No," Josip answered with a quiet smile, "it just keeps coming! Every time I open my freezer, there is the same amount of meat as the day I first butchered my cow."

Months later, Josip was *still* taking meat from his freezer. His explanation was simple and straightforward: "Gospa said we could stop wars with prayer and fasting, and that we could *alter the laws of nature* . . ."

a golden moment

Kevin was a New York City police officer, divorced and as ordered by the court forced to share limited visitation time with his 13-year-old daughter Katie. He had discovered the grace of the apparitions of Medjugorje and it had changed his life. The burley police officer signed on for my youth festival pilgrimage in August with his daughter who had become unruly, disrespectful, rude and often sullenly silent as she entered her teen years. He hoped for a miracle that would change his daughter into a happy and well-adjusted person.

For Kevin, the miracle of helping his daughter began when his former wife agreed to allow Katie to come to Medjugorje with him. Both parents were worried by Katie's attitude. Out of desperation, Kevin's wife had agreed to the trip.

I did my best to talk to Katie when presented a chance. I tried to keep it light. I pointed out to her how many young people were there for the youth festival. Little in her demeanor changed. Kevin also noticed and was discouraged. "Don't worry, Kevin, something will happen to touch her. Our Lady didn't bring her all the way here without purpose. You just have to maintain hope and keep praying!"

Several evenings later as we sat outside on the left side of the church during the praying of the rosary, that little "something" happened. Katie was seated next to her father but refused to say the words of the prayer.

As Kevin prayed, each bead of his rosary instantly turned a golden color. Kevin was lost in the prayer and did not notice what was occurring; nor did Katie who gazed in the distance, lost in her own thoughts.

I smiled and gave Kevin a light nudge. "Kevin, look at your rosary beads."

Kevin looked at the beads, frowned and said, "What?'

"Look at them, Kevin!" I said with a little more force.

Again, Kevin looked at them and then at me. *"Look at them Kevin!"*

Suddenly Kevin's eyes became big. "Oh my God, yes, I see it; they're gold!"

With that, Katie turned to her father asking what was happening. Now it was Kevin's turn to nudge his daughter. "Katie, look at the beads—they are turning gold as I pray each one of them!"

From that point on, the sullen, unhappy Katie changed. She began praying the rosary as she watched for herself the beads change to a golden color. And, for the remainder of the pilgrimage, Katie slowly began to enjoy her time with her father.

Kevin's prayer was fully answered!

Visionary Ivanka: **"Our Lady invites us all to renew the family prayer, so that the Word of God and the Holy Bible is in the center of our lives. Every day I pray for the families in the world, but at the same time I'm kindly asking all of you to pray for our families."**

a special table

Touring in Krakow, Poland was special. This was the city where Saint Pope John Paul The Great had served prior to becoming pope.

The ancient church that was the site of the evening's talk was beyond crowded. People were in the streets surrounding the church. "It is because of your book," Zofia related. "It is very popular!"

There was a near riot afterwards, as people literally stormed the sacristy, wanting books signed, or to grab my hand. The priests pleaded with the crowd, reminding them that Mass would begin shortly. Thirty minutes later, order was restored when the priest announced that I would remain as long as necessary to sign books and speak to the people.

After Mass, we were escorted to an area in the front of the church. The priests placed a large, oval-shaped table into the doorway, and people lined up outside in extreme cold and misting rain, singing and praying the rosary as they waited in penance to have a book signed or to simply say thank you for coming to Krakow. I felt as if I was on the edge of heaven as the singing grew in volume.

Zofia, standing nearby began to laugh. "What is it?" I asked, taking a brief respite from signing.

Zofia pointed to the table. "The priest just told me that this table on which you are signing the books, was often used by Pope John Paul II, as a ping-pong table when he was assigned to this church for several years!"

All I could do was join her in laughing, imagining Our Lady smiling at this little gift of grace, and sure that she had arranged it!

I have yet many things to say to you, but you cannot bear them now. When the Spirit of truth comes, he will guide you into all the truth; for he will not speak on his own authority, but whatever he hears he will speak, and he will declare to you the things that are to come.

—John 16:12-13.

the JOY *of* MEDJUGORJE

Dear children, with joy, persistently work on your conversion. Offer all your joys and sorrows to my Immaculate Heart that I may lead you all to my most beloved Son, so that you may find joy in His Heart. I am with you to instruct you and to lead you towards eternity. Thank you for having responded to my call.

—Message of September 25, 2009

11

amazing grace

There are many amazing moments of grace in our lives even though at the time of receiving them we may not recognize it as so. They are the personal events that cause immediate, momentous spiritual changes in our lives. They are the moments that make us say with awe, "I really believe in God!"

The most plenteous grace I received was the evening the Blessed Mother of Jesus spoke to my heart, asking me to change my life and help spread her messages given at Medjugorje. Reflecting back, I shudder at what my life would be like today if she hadn't come that evening and called me her son. Would I still be alive? Would I have found faith on my own? The answers are really of no consequence now because I did respond, even though it was a weak, hesitant "I'll try."

I have preached in the many years of this mission that all the Virgin Mary needs is that one little opening of our souls, that will allow her access. Once we let her in, she begins the preparation for those amazing moments of grace that bring us to the desire to become children of God.

As Mary instructs us as she has through the message at the beginning of this chapter, we must with joy persistently work on our conversion. She will assist whenever and wherever she can as long as our hearts remain open to her. But what if we know little or nothing about this Mother from Heaven, or about her Son? How do we begin the process of conversion? In that case, it can only come directly from God. The first occurrence of grace in this chapter illuminates how such a God-moment can come to us even though we know little about God.

the call

Having just received my discharge from the Navy, the local YMCA in Columbia, South Carolina was my new home. Rent was only five dollars a week, which fit my very limited budget at the time.

One morning around three o clock I was awakened and knew immediately it was God who woke me. There is no way to explain how I knew, but in response, I slowly got out of bed and went directly to my knees. It was unusual in that I had never thought of God or about faith in general.

I did not hear a voice, just a powerful feeling that God was asking me to pursue a life of ministry. Of what kind, there was no mention. I knew virtually nothing about organized religion. However, I had been going to a Baptist church with my fiancé. I even made what Baptists tab as the altar call, that is, to come forward publicly and accept Jesus as your Lord and Savior.

In response to this call from God and almost without hesitation, as though there was a choice, I quietly said out loud, "Oh no, I'm going to get married." And with that the "presence" was gone. I slowly got up and returned to my bed and was soon fast asleep again.

That strange but special moment has never been forgotten and of course when I became involved with Medjugorje, it immediately resurfaced in my memory. I realized that I was now in a mission and that it was a special ministry in answer to God's call, even though it came from the Blessed Virgin.

Looking back, I wonder what would have happened if I had said yes to God in that early morning call. Would I have married even though far too immature and unprepared? Would it have ended in divorce? God only knows.

It took nearly 30 years to finally answer God's call—and to learn that He never gives

up on us. He just waits for the right time.

the anointing

What I am about to describe is a vivid and very real early morning dream or spiritual vision, which I experienced in the early days of my mission. It remains even today far beyond my understanding.

In retrospect, I somehow comprehended the intent and meaning of the vision but not the fact that it was happening to me. Who was I to receive an "anointing" from what I could only perceive in my heart as God the Father? That was the immediate thought.

No matter how we progress in our spiritual journey, God is always mysterious and secretive and hidden. Who can understand the Trinity? How do we rectify the Old Testament God with the New Testament God? For most of us, we leave these matters to the theologians and do the best we can to live the message of Jesus given in the New Testament. We receive without warning or understanding special spiritual graces of varying degrees and wonder, why me?

This amazing vision was in lucid detail with the most indescribably, beautiful musical singing in unrecognizable tongues. It was angelic and mesmerizing. As it filled my presence in a way known only to my soul, I felt myself being slowly elevated in a horizontal position with my hands crossed on my chest. As I was gracefully moving upward, the singing and music increased in volume—until I gently came to a stop.

The mesmerizing singing lowered to almost a murmur. After a noticeable pause, a brilliant white light surrounded me and as it opened just above me, a huge eye encased in a triangle emerged and looked directly at me for what seemed to be an eternity.

Just as in that early morning call when I was living in the YMCA, I perceived this again as the presence of God. There was no doubt in my heart that He had just anointed me and my mission.

Slowly, I began to be lowered, still in the horizontal position as the brilliance of light closed and the eye was no longer visible. The singing in tongues continued until suddenly I was awake, the reality of what had just occurred in the dream/vision dominating my whole being. I lay there replaying it over and over, not realizing at first that tears were flooding from my eyes as I wanted the singing in tongues to go on forever.

I shared this special grace with my wife and no one else—until now.

The Blessed Virgin Mary's words to Juan Diego: *"Listen and let it penetrate your heart . . . do not be troubled or weighed down with grief. Do not fear any illness or vexation, anxiety or pain.*

Am I not your Mother? Are you not under my shadow and protection? Am I not your fountain of life? Are you not in the fold of my mantle? In the crossing of my arms? Is there anything else you need?"

our lady's hug

The majority of the early talks I gave on the apparitions at Medjugorje were predominantly in Protestant churches. That was understandable since Protestants made up 97% of the population in the state of South Carolina.

Most of the speaking venues took place in our home town of Myrtle Beach and the surrounding area. That was due mainly to the fact that there was only one Catholic church in our town—and I had already received an unexpected reprimand from its diminutive, Irish pastor, whom I had known from local civic clubs for at least ten years.

Having been invited to come to the church one Saturday evening to receive a gift for writing about the apparitions, the gift turned out to be a rosary, which I thought was a necklace for my wife. The lady who gave it to me laughed and said, "No, it's not a necklace—it's a prayer given to us by the Blessed Mother." She then gave me a small book that explained how to pray the rosary.

It didn't take long for the lady and others who were familiar with Medjugorje to corner me into attending a Catholic service, which was due to begin in a few minutes. "Oh, come on," the lady laughed, I promise you it won't hurt you!"

Following the "Mass" as I learned what Catholics called their service, we were standing on the steps in front of the church discussing Medjugorje when the pastor came out to say hello. "Oh, Father, Wayne has been to Medjugorje where the Blessed Mother is appearing to six visionaries daily," the lady who had given me the rosary said excitedly.

All of a sudden, the priest turned to me and began waving his hands and said, "No! no! Wayne, don't get mixed up in those things; just keep your eyes on Jesus!"

I was stunned. So were the women. The most surprising part of the rejection was that it came from a Catholic priest. I had simply assumed that every Catholic, including the priests, would fully believe in apparitions of the Blessed Virgin.

I soon learned how to pray the rosary and totally fell in love with it. It had such a powerful an effect on me that I vowed to pray it daily. And I did.

Family and friends alike were surprised at how much I loved the rosary. They cautioned me on speaking about it during my talks since it was the most recognizable symbol of the Catholic faith among non-Catholics. The certainty was it would turn off many Protestants. I really didn't care or worry about it. I was so on fire that the Mother of Jesus had come to the little village of Medjugorje in a Communist country to give the world messages from God.

At this point I was going to the Catholic church for Holy Mass Monday through Friday and usually to my Lutheran church on Sundays. One day I received an invitation to speak at a local Methodist church, which was within a mile of the Catholic Church. I decided I would give the talk and then hurry down the highway for Holy Mass.

The fact that I was a Lutheran speaking about the Blessed Virgin Mary was definitely a curiosity. The organizers had arranged for all of the Sunday school classes to attend the talk and I was given a time allotment of 20 minutes. That was fine with me as it allowed time for me to make it to the Catholic Church for Sunday Mass.

As the saying goes, the best laid plans …The problem was my talk ran overtime due to my holding up my rosary and telling everyone about the power of its prayer. Everyone seemed to want to know more. I literally backed my way to the door offering apologies as I only had five minutes to get to the Catholic Church.

Hurrying down the narrow sidewalk I was suddenly stopped completely in my tracks. I then "felt" a gentle hug as the Blessed Virgin placed a message in my heart: *Thank you for telling them about my rosary!*

Dazedly making my way to my car, I felt as though I could have flown to the church!

obedience and humility

It was the last day of my first pilgrimage to Medjugorje (May 1986). I did not want to go home and leave the indescribable peace and love I felt during those six days of pilgrimage. I knew that we were called to this unbelievable place and were to return home to live and spread the messages. Still, I did not want to go.

The source of my reluctance to leave the village was discovery of Jesus in the Eucharist. Here again was a special spiritual grace being given to me that far exceeded in awe the grace of the Blessed Virgin Mary speaking to my heart. How could I leave the place after receiving the real presence of the body of Christ?

I did not know what Catholics believed concerning what we called communion in my Lutheran church. I had never even heard of the word *Eucharist* before coming to Medjugorje. Yet, when I first received completely by accident, I *knew immediately* it was the true flesh of Jesus. I was completely overcome. This incredulous moment filled me to the point of knowing I had to receive it as often as possible for the rest of my life.

There was a second sacrament of the Catholic Church I learned about before having to return home. Throughout the pilgrimage I watched the long lines of people going through another beautiful Catholic ritual, that of confession. Talking to many in my group of the positive results, it seemed to be the final piece of their pilgrimage; I wanted to experience it as well.

It was during that unexpected occurrence in the confessional (as related in an earlier chapter) that I heard myself saying to the priest with some uncertainty that I wanted to become . . . Catholic.

Never in the eight months since first receiving the interior message from the Blessed Virgin Mary had I considered converting to the Catholic faith. My understanding was the messages were for all faiths; conversion meant turning to God, and not necessarily to Catholic doctrine. But in this wondrous week, a week in which I literally fell in love with Jesus through receiving Him in the Holy Eucharist, I had never experienced such an intimate closeness to Him.

Even though Our Lady's message was an all-faiths message, I knew it was no accident that she chose this predominantly Catholic village as a place to bring renewal of the gospel message of her Son. This was a place of deep personal faith that served as the centerpiece for everyday life.

On returning home from that first pilgrimage, I prayed to the Blessed Virgin for guidance to do what her Son wanted. I was going to daily Mass at the Catholic Church to receive the Eucharist – and also going to my Lutheran church on Sundays. One day as I went forward to receive the Eucharist, the priest whispered to me: "See me after Mass!" I knew I was in trouble!

The priest bluntly made me aware that I should not be receiving the Holy Eucharist. I was devastated. What was I to do—I could not imagine not receiving Jesus in the Eucharist. All I could do was to pray—the major lesson learned at Medjugorje. I prayed to the Holy Spirit for discernment.

That afternoon I went to see a priest ten miles away in North Myrtle Beach. Father Mike was the pastor and he believed in the apparitions. I had even given a couple of talks in his parish. Explaining what had happened, Father Mike paused and then said, "Well, Wayne, everybody knows you're not Catholic yet you receive the Eucharist." I began to fear that he would back the local priest. "However," he continued, "If you insist, you can come here and I will allow you to receive."

I knew exactly how to answer: Looking intensely at him, I said, "Father Mike, I have prayed about this and I realize I should not be receiving as a non-Catholic. So . . . I will not receive again until I become a Catholic in name. Now tell me what I need to do to join the Church!"

Father Mike laughed, reached over and hugged me and said, "Wonderful, that is exactly what I hoped you would say!"

In that instant, I had full discernment that obedience and humility are the foundation stones of the Roman Catholic faith, as well as necessary qualifications for pure belief and surrender to God.

I began to depend on Father Mike as my unofficial spiritual guide, asking him to help me enter into the Catholic faith. He quickly pointed out that because of my divorce it might not be possible, and that it would take considerable time. "How long?" I asked.

"Anywhere from six months to a year or more."

"Please, Father, make it six months!" I couldn't imagine waiting longer than that.

Several evenings later as I was praying in thanksgiving for the developments to this point, I suddenly felt the Madonna speaking to my heart again; incredibly, she was saying that I was not to become Catholic *at this time* . . .

Shock and alarm filled my heart as I said out loud: "Why not, dear Mother, why not?"

There was no answer.

I immediately rationalized Our Lady's words to be because of my divorce, and that it would have to be clarified by the Catholic Church Tribunal process before proceeding. That meant going through a trial process to determine if there were grounds for a Church-recognized annulment of my first marriage. There was no guarantee it would be positive.

In spite of this startling message from the Blessed Virgin and the uncertain chances of success, I was determined to continue the process. I would be obedient; I would accept it with humility regardless of the outcome.

It turned out to be a powerful lesson in obedience and humility.

Pope John Paul II: **"If I were not Pope, I would be in Medjugorje today listening to confessions!"**

when, lord?

Long after my decision to become a Catholic, I was dejected; the mission had grown to a global outreach. Just about every talk included praying the rosary and then Holy Mass. I would watch everyone go forward to receive Jesus in the Eucharist and my heart would ache. The needed paperwork had been done; there was nothing left but to wait.

The waiting for word from the diocese had reached more than two years. I felt deserted at times and in real agony of not being able to receive Jesus in the Holy Eucharist. It reached a painful point during a speaking tour in Italy. On the plus side, Medjugorje visionary Marija and her fiancé Paolo and his family were with me, as was another mutual friend, Margaret who was from Scotland.

We took a break from the intense speaking itinerary to visit a little village in the countryside where Paolo's family owned a small vacation cabin.

Marija, Margaret and I were attending Holy Mass in a tiny church just a short few steps from the cabin. As the priest began the consecration of the gifts for Communion, I was suddenly flooded with emotion and fell to my knees, struggling to regain composure. I did not want to break down in front of Marija and Margaret, but the agony of not being able to receive the Holy Eucharist, mixed with a strange sensation of overwhelming joy and peace, finally won out. The tears came in streams and soon became sobs.

I remembered little except for Margaret's arm around my shoulders as I opened my eyes. The Mass was over. The church was empty. The only people there were the three of us, still kneeling. Marija turned to me, smiling and said, "Our Lady came to me in apparition during the consecration of the gifts!"

It was the most beautiful of all the experiences of being present during an apparition of Our Lady – even though I did not realize she was present! Marija explained that Our Lady appeared as she usually does in a brilliance of light, standing near the priest and saying nothing, just smiling and blessing us as she looked over the small gathering of celebrants. Now I understood the holiness felt in this diminutive chapel despite the haste of the priest in celebrating Holy Mass. Gospa was there and as always, wrapping us in her mantle of love.

I came into the Church two years later on December 8, 1991, the Feast Day of the Immaculate Conception. Once again, I was reminded that there are no coincidences with God. Later, on a return to Medjugorje, now a legitimate member of the Church founded by Jesus, Marija reminded me of that day in in the countryside, telling me how sorry she felt for me at that time. I simply smiled and gave her a quick hug, deeply touched that she remembered those times of suffering in not being able to receive the Eucharist.

Slowly over time it began to dawn on me why the Blessed Mother had said *"Not yet"* in her message to me concerning my coming into the Church. Who would have listened to a new convert to the Catholic Church besides other Catholics? However, Catholics *and* Protestants alike would listen to a somewhat eccentric person of a Protestant faith telling everyone to pray the holy rosary! I was a curiosity, a freak! And people listened.

I soon realized the long five years of waiting to receive my Jesus in the Eucharist had a multi-purpose. First, it was a stringent test of obedience and humility. Second, it was a time of learning that would be so vital in establishing my mission.

Still, the agony of waiting was painful. To put it into perspective, the five years waiting to enter the Church were worse than the years I endured of traumatic suffering as a small child.

In the final analysis, it was worth every agonizing day to finally become a member of the Church Jesus established on earth more than 2,000 years ago.

Pope John Paul II, when asked about the faithful going to Medjugorje: **"Let them go—they're going there to pray. When you get there, you pray for me. Sometimes the people follow the bishops. Sometimes the bishops follow the people"**

ultimate grace

As stated earlier, spiritual graces can come unexpectedly without warning. They can also occur in different degrees of intensity and affect. Regardless of timing or size or impact, graces are always given for a specific purpose. I discovered that during my second trip to Medjugorje.

I had returned to Medjugorje in July 1986 at the request of Franciscan Father Svetozar Kraljevac in order to help him translate a new book into English. Unfortunately, Fr. Svet unexpectedly had to leave Medjugorje for two weeks. He had asked me if I would wait for him to return. Reluctantly, I agreed not knowing what I would do with myself since there were virtually no other English-speaking people there at the time.

As is always the case, things happen for a reason—and those reasons are as God wishes when we respond to His call. For the next 10 days, I was on a crash-course of learning more about Medjugorje, more on the importance of meditation and prayer time and most importantly, how to personally adapt to the ways of God on an everyday basis. Being in Medjugorje where everyone prayed and attended Mass made it easier. All of these elements would eventually help me in fulfilling my mission.

There was an extraordinary mystical experience that happened to me during my first trip to Medjugorje. It was now happening in far greater frequency and detail on this second pilgrimage to the village. As I would pray with my eyes closed, especially during the consecration of the gifts in Mass, I would see faces of people from all cultures of the world. There were men, women and children of all sizes, colors and ages; all of them displayed a sense of urgency as they seemed to be looking at me with great anxiety, as though begging me to pray for them. Somehow, I understood this and accepted it even though it was a bit frightening.

Keeping busy by learning all I could, I was relieved when at last an English-speaking pilgrimage group arrived in the village. It was the Boston Center for Peace, the same organization I was a part of on my first pilgrimage to Medjugorje. Oh, how good it was to hear and speak English with others again! We all joined together for a wonderful dinner that evening and made plans for the week of pilgrimage ahead. I was asked to join the group in all of their activities, which pleased me to no end as Father Svet would not return for several days.

We met the following afternoon at the request of the group leader, Sister Margaret Sims who had extended an invitation to the group for anyone wanting to receive a "baptism in the Holy Spirit." Sister Margaret was "charismatic" although I didn't fully know what that term meant. I did know about speaking in tongues from my experience with Father

Scottie in the early days. So, I decided to "go with the flow" and accept this as another learning experience.

Those of us who had never received baptism of the Holy Spirit lined up inside and up front in Saint James Church with the experienced members directly behind us and placing their hands on our shoulders. Sister Margaret instructed us to just relax, close our eyes and simply focus on what was happening. Prayers than began with many praying in tongues.

I relaxed as much as I could, though wondering if all of this was occurring too soon for me to digest. Suddenly I saw in my mind in brilliant color the clear image of a rather short and slightly stout woman with hands folded in prayer and a huge smile on her face. She looked directly at me while nodding and bowing in the affirmative. The vision lasted for several seconds, long enough for me to get a good look at her as well. Was this just more of what had been happening to me since my first pilgrimage?

The session was soon over and everyone behind us was clapping and shouting amen. The image of the woman was still in my mind's eye, leaving me thinking it was the most dramatic of all the previous visions of what I learned may be souls of Purgatory.

I didn't really feel any different after receiving the baptism of the Holy Spirit. All I could think of was the image of the woman, but soon that thought faded and things seemed back to normal. Yet, the event and the face of the woman would pop up occasionally, leading me to believe it had something to do with my mission. I could only be patient and wait for further confirmation.

Visionary Ivan: **"The world has decided to go into the future without God."**

the JOY *of* MEDJUGORJE

It had been a very interesting and informative stay in Medjugorje on this second trip. The learning was in line with my early days of discovering the graces of the village of apparitions.

I read everything I could get my hands on about the Virgin Mary, pushing it to the limit as any good journalist would do. That included several heavy-reading volumes of works penned by saints and mystics on the life of Jesus and His mother Mary. I discovered the works of 19th century German mystic Blessed Anne Catherine Emmerich, followed by Venerable Mary of Agreda (Spain in 17th century). Both sets of works were fascinating. It seemed to bring an even closer relationship to Jesus and His mother Mary.

Several months later, I was on a speaking tour in the northeast ending with a talk in Providence, Rhode Island. After the talk, I was introduced to Archbishop George Pearce, now retired and very much interested in Medjugorje. He had requested our meeting stating that he had a special present for me.

We settled in the small living room of Archbishop Pearce's apartment and he immediately began telling me about an Italian mystic, named Maria Valtorta (1897-1961), who had also written volumes on the life of Jesus and Mary as dictated to her by them. It was basically the same type of charisma similar to Mary of Agreda and Anne Catherine Emmerich. He then produced from a nearby table two copies of Maria Valtorta's writings telling me they were copies of the first edition in English.

"It's a wonderful gift and I am very grateful for the opportunity to learn more about her writings," I told the archbishop.

"Oh, but there's more to come," Archbishop Pearce answered. "This is just the first volume of five that are now being translated into English!"

While working at my desk a few days after returning home, I casually picked up one of the volumes of Maria Valtorta's works that Archbishop Pearce had given me. There was a curiosity to see if it was as informative as the works of Anne Catherine Emmerich and Mary of Agreda.

I suddenly stopped on one of the opening pages, literally doing a double-take as my heart leapt. On the page was an old black and white picture of Maria Valtorta. It was the *same* woman I had seen in my mind while being prayed over to receive the baptism of the Holy Spirit in Medjugorje!

It didn't take long to comprehend that the vision of the smiling woman I had received in Medjugorje was an expression of joy in that I was being asked to become the main distributors of Poem of the Man God in the United States. We began the "mission within the mission" as soon as all of the volumes had been translated into English.

Over the years, we have distributed more than 5,000 sets of Maria Valtorta's Poem of the Man God, now titled, The Gospel As Revealed to Me.

Mystic Maria Simma: **"A poor soul from Purgatory told me Medjugorje was true…With Medjugorje there is only one great danger, and it is that the world does not take it into account."**

holy love

I found Maria Valtorta's works were far more modern than Blessed Ann Catherine Emmerich and Venerable Mary of Agreda, having been composed starting in April 1943 through parts of 1951. In 1920 at the age of 23, while walking on a street with her mother, a delinquent youth struck Maria in the back with an iron bar for no apparent reason. In 1934 the injury eventually confined her to bed for the remaining 28 years of her life. It is there that she produced over 15,000 handwritten pages in 122 notebooks, mostly detailing the life of Jesus as an extension of the gospels. The works now titled, "Gospel As Revealed to Me."

The writing of this mystical Italian woman was incredible, if somewhat effusive. It was as if her dictations from Jesus and Mary were putting flesh on the bones of Scripture. We began to sell all of the volumes through our web site. The books were a huge success even though quite expensive.

There was so much to learn by reading the works of Maria Valtorta. Passages and stories of Scripture came alive with far more detail. I couldn't get enough of reading and rereading each volume, while learning and understanding far more than from reading Holy Scripture alone. That is not to say the writings of Maria Valtorta are equal to or take the place of Holy Scripture, but that they give more depth to each passage.

One passage in particular touched my heart. Jesus and His disciples are traveling on a long journey on a dusty road. The disciples begin debating between themselves as to who of them loves Jesus the most. The debate continues and at times borders on argument. Each disciple relates a story or moment, which proves their love for the Master. Jesus stops for a moment and asks His disciples why they are arguing about love. John then comes to Him and says, "Master, I love you and he then lays his head on the chest of Jesus. Jesus looks at the others and softly tells them, "This is the purest way to show me your love."

I was so deeply touched as I read this passage that I softly said aloud: "Oh, Jesus, I want to love you like John—I just want to lay my head on your chest and tell you how much I love you!"

All of a sudden, *I felt Jesus lay His precious head on my chest!* It was so real that I actually gasped and flinched. And then my Savior said to me: *This is how much I love you!*

My steps have held fast to thy paths, my feet have not slipped. I call upon thee, for thou wilt answer me, O God; incline thy ear to me, hear my words.

—Psalms 17:5-6.

PART THREE:

the good fruits

Dear children! I am calling you to a complete surrender to God. I am calling you to great joy and peace, which only God can give. I am with you and I intercede for you every day before God. I call you, little children, to listen to me and to live the messages that I am giving you. Already for years you are invited to holiness but you are still far away. I am blessing you. Thank you for having responded to my call.

—Message of March 25, 1989.

12

Jaime and the children of the sewers

The incredible story of Jaime Jaramillo and the "children of the sewers" as I later named them, is easily one of the most soul-touching experiences of my mission. His story epitomizes what all of us are asked to do by Jesus, which is to love our neighbors not just with words but with actions. What greater response to this commandment can there be than to act as Jaime did against a horrific injustice?

The injustice was an inhumane act by police of an abandoned child on the streets of the sprawling city of Bogota in Colombia, South America. Jaime was sickened with disgust as he watched the police commit a deliberate and cruel act of intentional murder of a young street girl. She had been doused with gasoline and cruelly set afire and left to die on the street. The child was a victim of a heartless new police policy of making examples of children caught stealing from the merchants.

Even more cruel were crowds of people ignoring the little girl who was screaming in pain. People simply walked around her continuing on their way. But Jaime, only 19 years old at the time, was deeply shaken by the cruelty of the police and the apathy of the people. He quickly grabbed a blanket from his car and doused the flames. The young man

193

then wrapped the little girl in the blanket and took her to a hospital emergency room for treatment.

Jaime, who was studying to be a petroleum engineer, took time out from his school work for the next week to visit the little girl. Days later he paid the hospital bill, picked her up and asked where she lived. The child led him to an affluent neighborhood, then to a manhole in the street and pointing to it said, "This is where I live – down there!"

It was then that Jaime Jaramillo took it upon himself to begin a one-man outreach program to care for these abandoned children who were actually living in the sewers of the city.

At first, Jaime was mocked and laughed at; why would he bother about these children who were a serious nuisance to the merchants and the tourist industry? His continued work with them caused rejection by friends and family members alike. The police also disliked him because he protected the street children. Over the ensuing years, the general public viewed him as an eccentric. But like other "eccentrics," such as St. Francis of the past, and recently named Saint Teresa of Calcutta of the near present, Jaime continued his mission.

I met Jaime during a speaking tour through Colombia in the spring of 1991. The lady who had arranged the tour to Colombia, Lillian Gorman, as native Colombian who could not stop talking about him, assured me several times that arrangements would be made for me to meet him. Admittedly, I really didn't care if we met as the schedule was jammed and I didn't know how we could fit in another meeting.

As it turned out Lillian and I were unintentionally seated next to each other for the flight to Bogota. Lillian was brimming with joy. "I am so happy you are finally coming to my country to speak about Medjugorje!"

I knew from the outset the tour through the drug-infested country of Colombia was going to be a powerful trip. Lillian had been trying to get me to commit to the trip for several months—repeatedly telling me about this man who rescued children from the sewers of the city of Bogota. My focus was on the opportunity to speak in the three major cities that were home to the drug cartels. If the meeting with Jaime could be arranged, fine. Only later would I realize just how powerful meeting Jaime Jaramillo would be and how much it would affect the entire mission.

During the flight, Lillian explained that Colombia was a very traditional and conservative Catholic country, and Marian apparitions without approval of the Church were definitely not a part of their devotions. Knowledge about Medjugorje was virtually non-existent.

Lillian had a niece now living there who had lived in Memphis for a long time. The young woman named Leila, had gone to Medjugorje with Lillian and was the only source of help in arranging the tour. She began working on it and eventually a small prayer group of dedicated volunteers was formed. Now, a full schedule of talks had been arranged in Bogota, Medellin, and Cali, the three largest cities in Colombia.

"Liela has done a good job and a young man from Memphis whom she has been dating is there now as well, so you won't be the only American," Lillian concluded.

The thought suddenly popped into my mind. "Lillian, has Jaime Jaramillo been to Medjugorje?" I asked.

"No, but I hope we can arrange for the two of you to meet some time during your stay in Bogota and maybe you can arrange a trip to Medjugorje with him."

There it was again—Lillian's desire that I meet this man. With three cities in only eight days, I didn't hold much hope for a meeting. "Maybe he'll come to one of the talks and we'll have a few minutes," I said, hoping this would satisfy her.

We were met at the Bogota airport by a sizeable delegation of tour volunteers. Leila was an engaging young woman filled with excitement now that the tour was starting. "There is a reception at my home, with some good Colombian food, and you can meet the other volunteers," she told me, "then we'll take you to your hotel for a good night's rest."

Leila then introduced me to Roy Peters, her American boyfriend from Memphis.

"I certainly hope you have time to meet Jaime Jaramillo," Roy said in a quiet voice as we walked to the cars, "Maybe even visit one of his safe houses he has established to help these kids."

Once again, I explained that meeting Jaime was dependent on the timing of the talks. On the car ride to Leila's home, he told me about Jaime coming to Memphis. "From the time I met him, I knew he was special. I wanted to help so we convinced him to come to Memphis for some talks to help raise funds. He told me this week that upon his return home, he received many phone calls from Memphis parents, thanking him for what he said about family and values. He also said that during his time in Memphis and since, no child had died in the sewers, and no one was hurt. That is highly unusual."

Slowly, my interest in Jaime grew. The more I heard about him, the more I wanted to meet him. I sensed Our Lady had something special planned for the two of us.

"We hope people come to the talks, especially the first one in the morning," Leila said. "I've been worried because it is at a very large church on a military base. The talk is at 10 AM, and it is on a work and school day."

Those concerns became secondary on arrival at Leila's home. One of the volunteers informed her that a call had come from the archbishop's office in effect canceling all of the talks, saying they could not be held in the churches. "But who was calling?" Leila asked plaintively. The volunteer did not know. There was suddenly mass confusion.

I looked around the large living room at the somber faces. "Wait a minute, let's not panic!" I said, but inside, I was dying. Had I traveled thousands of miles here just to have everything canceled? "Our Lady's message at Medjugorje is to pray, fast and do penance," I plowed on, "I suggest we begin this tour by praying the rosary. The rest will be up to Our Lady's intercession!"

And with that, everyone dropped to their knees as I led them in an intense prayer of the rosary. I didn't eat much of the "good Colombian food." I was anxious to go to the hotel and sleep, hoping everything would work out by morning.

And it did – well beyond expectations! We left for the first site, not sure if anyone would be there or if the church would be open, hoping that news of the cancellation was a mistake. As we approached the base, there was an abnormally slow movement of automobiles on the road. "It's probably an accident," Leila said, "or maybe it's a special event."

My talk was the special event! The church was open and literally hundreds of people were pouring into the streets and surrounding parking lots. Included in the crowd were many priests and nuns, and busloads of school children. "Would you look at this!" Leila squealed with delight.

I let out a long sigh of relief – and happiness. "I didn't think Our Lady would bring me this far and have no one to listen to her messages." People were standing elbow-to-elbow, even in the choir loft. The entire assembly prayed the rosary with a fervor and the talk lasted more than two hours.

Word spread like wild fire and that evening was more of the same. Thousands crammed into a large church, which again, was open. "I have received no word of any prohibition," the priest responded upon our arrival. We had asked to assure we were not being disobedient to orders from the archbishop.

But the next morning, we found the church closed, the priest not sure about allowing the talk. With another turnout of thousands, a makeshift stage was hastily put together and a microphone set up. The prayer group had preplanned, in the event of a lockout and before it was over, thousands more had come from nearby apartment buildings. Again, this was a fervent praying of the rosary and consecration to Our Lady. Afterwards, it became a huge block party with people filling the streets, singing, dancing and clapping their hands.

As we dined in a small restaurant, one of the volunteers entered and informed Leila that the afternoon session had been cancelled, "But tonight is okay."

In light of what had already occurred, we felt fortunate it was the only cancellation. "One good thing is we can spend more time with Jaime," Roy said. On learning about the cancellation, he had managed to arrange a short meeting with Jaime at one of his safe houses. "It will give you the time to see his facilities and speak to the kids."

I had learned about the street children from conversations with members of the group. The street children had taken to their underground world because it became too dangerous to sleep outside at night. Army and police forces had militarized the city as a result of car bombings and shootings, direct byproducts of the multi-billion-dollar cocaine trade that had become the major export and worldwide symbol of Colombia.

The children were constantly attacked by paramilitary personnel; to eat they would rob, and when they became involved in a life of crime, they eventually got into drugs and other criminal activities. Merchants, fearing the loss of revenue and angered at the thievery and peskiness of the children, hired criminal hit men to rid the sewers of them as though they were an epidemic of rats. They viewed Jaime as a cause, and thus, targeted him as well.

Jaime's reputation grew by quantum leaps. In the last several years, Jaime, now 33 years old, had been kidnapped twice by gangs that prey on the affluent for ransoms. Each time they let him go unharmed when they discovered who he was. I shook my head as I read the last brochure. I began to understand their push for me to meet Jaime as I muttered to Roy, "This guy is something else!"

"Yes, he is," Roy said. "Last year he was nominated for the Nobel Peace Prize, but he never completed the papers necessary to place his name among the candidates. He said he didn't have time."

meeting jaime

Finally, I was face to face with Jaime Jaramillo, whom I had learned so much about in so short a time. He was about my height and weight, with striking features and eyes filled with kindness. Jaime looked at me, smiling. "So, you are the one speaking about this place in Yugoslavia where the Blessed Mother is appearing?"

"Yes," I countered, "and you are the one living her messages by assisting these children."

There was immediate friendship and respect between us. "Come," Jaime said, "I will give you a tour so that you can see and meet some of my children."

As we entered the main building, a toddler came down the hallway toward us, followed by a small teenage girl who quickly scooped him up in her arms. Jaime told me the child had been born in the sewers. The mother was only sixteen years old; she also had a six-month-old baby, both children fathered by an eighteen-year-old boy she had met in the sewers. "They have been together in the sewers for three years and only last month was I able to convince them to leave and come here. Jaime smiled. "Would you like to see the baby?" I followed Jaime into one of the small side rooms to find the little baby asleep on a lower bunk bed, the father napping on the upper bunk.

It was all deeply touching. On completion of the tour, I turned to Jaime. "Can I see you outside—alone, for a moment?"

Jaime followed me into the front area of the complex. I had felt the familiar inner urging of Our Lady again. She was asking me to go into the sewers, to see for myself this horror of abandoned children. My heart leapt. *Really?* I thought, *you want me to go down into the sewers with him?* I wasn't overly enthused—and somewhat afraid. But I asked, sure that is what Our Lady wanted. "Jaime, would you take me into the sewers to see these children?"

Jaime was only mildly surprised – and pleased that I wanted to go. Looking directly at me he said, "But it is dangerous. Many of these children have become hardened criminals and drug addicts. They have killed."

Fear filled my stomach but it was too late to back out. "I understand, but I need to go. I think the Blessed Mother wants me to go there with you."

Jaime slowly shook his head. "You could become very ill." He told me how members of the CBS television crew of the 20/20 program who had come to film his story had become so sick that many of them were hospitalized.

I didn't hesitate. "Jaime, *I've got to go down there with you!*"

It was settled. We arranged to meet at my hotel after the talk, which would be around 11 PM. Throughout the evening, I was edgy, wondering what was in store. It was amazing knowing that even though Our Lady was doing the asking, I was inundated with doubt and fear.

After the talk, I waited at the hotel dressed in jeans, a shirt and one of my favorite sweaters. I was glad I had brought it as it was drizzling rain with temperatures in the low fifties. I waited until midnight but no Jaime. At one o clock, still no Jaime. That surprised me as he had a car phone and always kept in touch with family and others during his excursions into the sewers. At last, and with great relief, I went to bed thinking, *it wasn't meant to be. Maybe I hadn't really heard Our Lady asking me to go . . .*

I was awakened at 5:15 AM by the shrill ring of the telephone. It was Jaime. "Wayne, I am sorry that I was unable to come last night." His voice was heavy with fatigue and emotion.

"That's okay, I understand your schedule..."

"No, it wasn't that. A terrible thing happened; I was trapped in the sewers all night with two little children and couldn't get out to call you."

Jaime had gone into the sewers to prepare the children for my coming. He told how a large drainage pipe that he and the children were in, had become blocked with refuse, suddenly ruptured, filled with raging water and swept the boy away. "I went down early to clear the way for you to come so that you would not be harmed, and found these two little ones. The water caught us and swept the little boy from my grip, but I was able to hang onto the little girl. We were trapped until just a few minutes ago."

I didn't know what to say, numbed by the events he had just described. After a long silence Jaime asked, "Do you still want to come down with me?"

My fear was gone, replaced with a mixture of awe for what Jaime was doing with these children and sadness for the little boy who drowned. "Yes, I'll be ready in a few minutes." The decision to go with him wasn't bravery, or foolishness – or sense of adventure. I now had to go!

Hastily dressing, I met Jaime a few minutes later in front of the hotel. We set out at breakneck speed through the steady rain, routinely running red lights along the still-quiet streets. "Aren't you afraid the police will stop us?" I queried, hoping he would take the hint and slow down.

"My friend, you do not stop on the streets if possible," he answered with a sardonic smile. "It is too dangerous, especially in this area!" Suddenly wheeling around a corner, Jaime came to a stop on a narrow side street. "We will stop here for food to take to the children. Please bring the bags."

I grabbed the large sacks lying on the car floor and hurried after Jaime into a small grocery store. It was immediately discernible that the people knew him. Taking the bags from me, Jaime began pointing out items to the clerks who raced to fill the order, while the customers stared in mild curiosity.

Thoroughly soaked and shivering, a man in ragged pants and shirt was standing just outside the wide opening of the store, hungrily watching the loading of the food sacks. Jaime motioned for him to come into the store and instructed the clerk to give him anything he wanted to eat. The man rushed to the counter, thanking Jaime profusely as the clerk and customers stared at him with disdain. A boy of about 10, seeing what had transpired rushed up to Jaime, speaking rapidly in Spanish. Jaime tousled his long, wet hair and told the clerk to take care of him as well.

"The two of them live on the streets. I try to help them also," he explained as the beggars gulped down sandwiches and hot coffee.

As we prepared to leave with the sacks of food, a man in a stylish long leather coat suddenly stopped Jaime, speaking in a hushed tone and then handing him a small card. He thanked the stranger and we headed for his car with the two street people insisting on helping us. "That man," Jaime said, motioning to the man in the leather coat leaving the grocery, "he is a famous football star here in Colombia. He has promised to help me with a donation."

"Do you receive much help locally?"

Jaime shrugged. "Yes, we have many problems in our country with the drug cartels, but there are also some good people. The government also helps some because it is good for their public image. But you see these two," he said motioning toward the two beggars busily loading the food bags into the rear of the car, "there are thousands like them that receive no aid."

Just before leaving, I gave each of them a Medjugorje medal, and as we drove away, they screamed thank you's at us and made the sign of the cross.

in the sewers

Ten minutes later, I was carefully following Jaime across a small lot in the now-increasing rain, clutching a bag of food and trying to keep from slipping. This was it—we were actually going down into the sewers. The entrance was a large drainpipe with a putrid, torrent of cloudy water roaring along the bottom. Within seconds, my white running shoes were covered with mud as I struggled to keep from falling into the water. The stench was overwhelming. Jaime, wearing waist high boots and a slicker, trudged through the torrent toward the dim entrance.

Once inside the tunnel, he let out a series of loud shouts. Bodies suddenly began emerging out of crevices, and from the darkness of the backstretches of the sewer. The children were of all ages and sizes. Glancing only briefly at me, they eagerly turned full attention to Jaime and the food bags. It was an incredible sight.

Fifteen minutes later, as we made our way out of the tunnel and back toward the car, several of the children followed to get more food for others deeper inside the maze of pipes. "Will they actually take the food to the others or will they keep it for themselves for later?" I asked Jaime.

"They will give it to the ones who are sick or hiding inside the lines. There is a bond of honor between them no matter what they may have done."

I suddenly felt sick – not from the water or stench, but from the impossibility of it all. Getting into the car to escape the cold and rain, I wondered what would the children do if there was no one like Jaime to care for them?

One boy, about eighteen, stood near the car, shivering in a cutoff shirt, thin pants and no shoes. I got back out of the car and took off my sweater, handing it to him in silence. He took it with a slight nod of his head.

I wanted to return to the hotel. I had seen enough. But Jaime wasn't through. "We have one more stop. There is a girl with a baby I want to see about coming to the home."

It was a solid fifteen minutes away and traffic was beginning to pick up. I glanced at my watch noting that I had approximately an hour and a half to clean up and get to the airport for my flight to Medellin. "Do not worry. We will make it," Jaime said. Somehow, I didn't believe him.

We pulled up under a busy overpass onto a muddy field close to the culvert where the woman and the baby were supposed to be. Again, about seven or eight children appeared as Jaime approached with the last bag of food. But within minutes, a police van also arrived. After a brief, heated discussion with Jaime, several policemen began herding the children toward the van with Jaime in close pursuit, bargaining with them. The police wanted to take us all to the precinct and sort it out there. But Jaime persevered.

Once again, Jaime's reputation saved us. He convinced them to let him take the children away from the culvert. We quickly loaded all of them into his car, and with the help of several of the officers, managed to get the car out of the mud and onto the road. It was now a foregone conclusion that I would miss my flight.

Jaime drove the children to the home of one of his volunteers who would see that they got to one of the safe houses. "Don't worry about your connection. I will get you another," he said, picking up his car phone and calling his office. Within minutes, he had me booked on a later flight.

Pulling up to the entrance of the hotel, I was suddenly in no hurry to leave this man. "I'm going to help you Jaime, I promise you," I said, my voice quivering with emotion. I'm going to help raise funds for your safe houses."

Jaime smiled. "You have already helped just by coming with me. Say a prayer for the little ones I found in the sewers last night, and for all my children."

Hugging him, I vowed I would pray for them every day. "I'll see you again, don't worry!"

I hurried into the hotel and rushed to get ready as I only had half an hour to get to the airport for the later flight. But at the moment, I didn't care. All I could think about was the children living in the sewers. What would they do without Jaime there to save them?

Commentary: As I reflect back on that incredible tour in Colombia, South America, I realize the meeting of Jaime Jaramillo and learning about his work with the abandoned children greatly affected me. I strongly related what these little ones went through in comparison to my traumatic years of childhood. I was absolutely driven to do all that I could to help raise funds for Jaime with his foundation.

The plan to raise funds for Jaime's foundation was simple and direct; near the end of my talks as I continued to spread the messages of Medjugorje, I would tell the audiences about the "Children of the Sewers" as I had named them and how Jaime's Foundation was continuing to rescue abandoned children. I would then ask for donations to assist the work of the Foundation, emphasizing that I was not asking for a collection at that time, but for them to be sent to our office.

Amazingly, we began receiving thousands of dollars as the majority of the audiences complied and sent donations directly to the office. There was no marketing plan or special promotion—just a 10-15-minute pitch near the end of my regular talks and establishing a special nonprofit bank account, which we named "Children of the Sewers."

Still, people would give me donations for the Foundation at the talks. One such donation will never be forgotten. A man approached me and asked if he could speak to me in private. We moved to a quiet corner and after telling me that he had just received a sizeable settlement from a car accident, he pulled a check from his pocket and said, "I want to make a donation to help that man!" (meaning Jaime). With that he handed me a check for $3,000. It was the largest single donation we had received since starting the charity and I could not thank the man enough, adding that I was sure the Blessed Mother was pleased with his generosity.

Fifteen minutes later, the man returned, pulled me aside again and said, "Look, I'm kind of embarrassed. When you said that Our Lady was pleased with me, I felt I should do more; so, please tear up my first check and accept this one." He handed me the new check made out for $10,000!

Over the years, our non-profit business, Weible Columns, has raised more than three million dollars for Children of the Sewers. Kind donors from my talks and readers of my monthly newsletter have been very generous. Imagine this with no organized effort, no marketing or promotion; just the intercession of the Blessed Virgin Mary.

Several years would pass before I would see Jaime again. This time, it would be in Medjugorje. It took Jaime sitting in an embassy close to 12 hours in order to receive a visa for his travel to the village of apparitions. He was determined to come to the land where the Mother of God was still appearing daily to four of the six visionaries. Within a matter of hours, Jaime was overwhelmed—and as he would say later, very much spiritually changed.

As we reminisced about the morning I went into the sewers with Jaime, he said, "Do you remember the police coming and me telling you they wanted to take us to the station?"

"Of course I remember—I was sure we were going to be late and I would miss my flight."

Jaime paused, smiled slightly and then said, "Well, the truth is, they were going to take all of us and kill us, and then dump our bodies somewhere in the country side."

"Are you serious?" I felt the fear of that morning as though it had just happened. "Why didn't you tell me?"

Jaime shrugged. "I didn't want to scare you."

Learning of the real danger of that stupendous morning, I just shook my head. I realized that Jaime faced such danger every time he ventured into the sewers to save a child.

Today, there are no longer abandoned children living in the sewers of Bogota. Jaime is a legend and now receives financial assistance from the government and other charitable sources. The Foundation has expanded and now has a formidable program that trains the children for a normal life of skilled work.

Jaime continues to live the message of Medjugorje through the work of his Foundation.

And this is love, that we follow his commandments; this is the commandment, as you have heard from the beginning, that you follow love.

—2 John 1:6.

...You cannot imagine what is going to happen nor what the Eternal Father will send to earth. That is why you must be converted! Renounce everything. Do penance. Express my thanks to all my children who have prayed and fasted. I carry all this to my Divine Son in order to obtain an alleviation of His justice against the sins of mankind. I thank the people who have prayed and fasted. Persevere and help me to convert the world.

—Excerpt from the message of June 24, 1983

🌸 13 🌸

to russia with love

In the early days of involvement in the Medjugorje apparitions, I read everything I could about past apparitions of the Blessed Virgin Mary. Her appearances at Fatima, Portugal in 1917 to three small children stood out from the rest. Adding to its stature, the Blessed Virgin stated in an early message that her apparitions at Medjugorje are the *fulfillment* and the *continuation* of what she started at Fatima.

One particular statement made by the Blessed Mother to the little seers especially peaked my interest: She had asked that the Pope and all the bishops of the Church pray for the conversion of Russia to Christianity, and that it would one day be a great glory to God.

Russia's conversion to Christianity would indeed be a major event given the long-standing Cold War relationship with most of the western world. Even today, it continues and seems to be at a high level of concern, regardless of the fulfillment of the request by the Blessed Mother.

The request by the Virgin to pray for the conversion of Russia deeply touched me. I wanted to go there and bring the Medjugorje message to its people; I wanted to be part of the conversion of Russia! Of course, a speaking tour would provide the platform to allow me to fulfill that desire, if only on a tiny level.

I returned to Medjugorje in the early fall of 1991 with a pilgrimage group, and after everyone was settled in their quarters for the evening, I left for visionary Marija's home where I would be staying. It was after 10:00PM; still, Marija insisted on preparing a small meal. I knew better than to resist. Besides, it afforded me the opportunity to sit around for two more hours catching up on the latest happenings in Medjugorje. Sleep could come later.

"I have just returned from a trip to Czechoslovakia and Russia," Marija said casually as we settled in her small living room. That caught me off guard.

"You were actually able to speak to the Russian people about Our Lady's apparitions?"

"Yes, also in Czechoslovakia. The people knew about Gospa's apparitions in Medjugorje. We would stop at a church to prepare for the apparition and one hour later, the church would be filled with people!"

I listened in awe as Marija enthusiastically talked about her trip. "People want to know everything about Our Lady and her messages," Marija said with a happy glow of remembrance. Even in the heart of Moscow, the city that housed the feared Communist government power that had wreaked social havoc for so long, thousands came to see and hear her.

As I lay in bed in the still of the night, I realized again where I was and the absolute grace of being a part of this incredible apparition. In my opinion Medjugorje was the greatest of them all. I rehashed the conversation with Marija about her trip to Russia. Someday I would take the message there, I was convinced of that. "I guess you'll send me when its time, Blessed Mother," I muttered sleepily as the fatigue of the day finally won out.

It was Sunday, December 8, 1991, the Feast of the Immaculate Conception and the final day of the New Orleans (Louisiana) Marian Conference. I was a guest speaker for the event and my family was with me. Something special was about to occur and no one among the nearly 6,000 people in attendance for the closing of the conference with Holy Mass knew about it. This was the day, at last, that we would formally become members of the Roman Catholic Church.

I waited for Mass to begin, during which at some point we would officially be brought into the Church. Of course, it was no coincidence that this was happening on Our Lady's feast day and at three o'clock in the afternoon—and, on a Sunday! Five long years of waiting; and now, it was about to occur.

The entire event had been planned within a week's time when the letter of approval arrived from the diocese allowing us to formally become Roman Catholics. When the conference organizers discovered it, they asked if I would consider coming into the Church at the conference during the closing Mass. I happily agreed. And, in order to keep it in perspective, it would not be announced to the conference attendees until just before the start of the closing Mass.

As we sat together on the front row of seats in the cathedral, a diminutive woman timidly approached me. "I apologize if I am bothering you," she said with a trace of an accent, "but I need to ask you something important."

"It's all right, how can I help you?"

Her face brightened. "I am Zofia Sordyl and I am from Poland but I have been living in the United States twenty-seven years. I know you went to my homeland but gave only two talks. Would you return to Poland if I can arrange a tour for you to go to many other places?"

I didn't hesitate. "Yes, if that's possible, I would be honored to go back." And then out of nowhere, I quickly added: "Listen, could you also arrange the tour to include Russia?"

She looked at me puzzled, seemingly caught off guard. "I don't know but I will be happy to try." With that we exchanged addresses and telephone numbers, briefly discussing details. She said she would contact me when all was arranged.

It took a few moments for what just happened to register with me. Could it get any better than to finally be able to join the Church and possibly get an invitation to speak in Russia, all at the same time? As soon as Sofia left, I thought: *Oh, wow, I'm going to be part of the conversion of Russia!*

Several months passed and no word came from Zofia Sordyl. She reminded me of a little sparrow and I wondered how could she possibly arrange such a trip that demanded so much specific detail. Thoughts whirled in my mind: *Maybe you scared her away with the idea of adding Russia to the Poland tour. . .*

Sometime later, Christina, my secretary knocked on my office door and said, "There's a lady on the telephone who wants to talk to you about going to Russia. She says she has called several times. Do you want to speak to her or shall I take a message?"

I jumped to my feet: "Put the call through!" I knew immediately it was Zofia Sordyl, I was completely unaware of her previous attempts to reach me. Only later would it become clear that the missed calls was the beginning of Satan's plan to do all he could to ruin my opportunity to be part of the conversion of Russia.

After greeting Zofia, I started to ask about Russia, but she beat me to the punch: "Yes, we can get you to Russia. "I am leaving in three weeks for St. Petersburg, where I will be staying for the next five months.

If you can give me a date you can come, I will arrange everything for a tour of Russia and Poland."

I was ecstatic! Fifteen minutes later, I had committed to three weeks for tour starting in late October. "I'm going to Russia! I'm finally going to Russia!" I told Christina. Somewhere in the excitement of the moment, I suddenly wondered *How could this little woman arrange all that?*

The thought passed quickly as I was awed at the prospect of playing a role in the conversion of Russia. It was constantly in my thoughts. One day as I was driving home from the office, the thought struck me that in a few days I would leave for the beginning of a five-country tour of Eastern Europe. It was so overwhelming I had to pull to the side of the road for a few minutes to regain composure.

st. petersburg

There was a lump in my throat, mixed with the excitement of a new adventure, as I boarded the plane for the long, international flight to St. Petersburg, Russia where the tour would begin. I was very much aware of the significance of the departure date: October 25—the anniversary day of Medjugorje.

As the plane descended toward the airport outside of St. Petersburg, there was just enough evening light left to see a rather desolate landscape. There were thin patches of early snow in little gullies where the sun was unable to penetrate. Structures and roadways were sparse until we passed over the city. Even then, the lights were dim and traffic only a trickle. It was surprising considering this city was home to six million Russians.

There was more surprise on entering a shabby, dingy building that was customs. The entry process was swift and nonchalant. *This is Russia? I thought, this is the big bad bear of the cold war?*

It was hard to imagine this was the country we feared for so long during the Cold War years. Exiting the building to stinging cold, I saw Zofia, faintly remembering her from our brief meeting in New Orleans; but she recognized me.

"So now, you are finally in Russia," she said, shaking my hand lightly. "Welcome! Here, let Stepan carry one of your bags." She shoved a bag at her Russian driver and grabbed the other over my protests, following Stepan to a small, dilapidated automobile. It was immediately evident there was a strong determination housed in the frail frame of this little sparrow of a Polish woman.

We journeyed into the city in near darkness. The headlights of Stepan's ancient automobile were barely bright enough to see the road. It was an intensely dark night with no moon, adding a pale of uncertainty as I asked Zofia details of the tour. She looked away for a moment and paused. "Well, we have many problems now at the last minute," she began hesitantly.

"Problems? What kind of problems?" Suddenly, thoughts of being "part of the conversion of Russia" were dimmed.

Zofia sighed. "I have been here for five months now. I did not know anyone when I came and I did not speak the language. Now, I have traveled everywhere by train arranging each conference. The telephones do not work very well and it takes hours to call contacts in the different countries. Each time details for a talk were arranged; they would call and tell me it was changed. It has been very difficult."

Zofia continued the bleak news. The group that was going to assist her, backed out at the last minute. "I only have Stepan and his wife Helena who live here, and some youth from the church." She paused and sighed deeply again. "Now, I am not sure we will have many people for your two talks on Sunday here in St. Petersburg. Many of the young people I paid to distribute the posters and flyers announcing your talk threw them away or just did not put them out."

"Don't worry, Zofia. Whoever is meant to be there will come." Even as I said it, I sank into a feeling of doom. Maybe I made a mistake in coming.

"But don't *you* worry," she said, mustering up what little optimism was left. "Poland is all set and I think the other stops will be fine." And then adding proudly: "And I have learned the Russian language!"

"That's nice," I said weakly.

As always, things looked better after a night's rest, despite a cold, overcast morning. It had also been a night of a little soul-searching. What was I thinking when I was so obsessed with being a part of the conversion of this country? *Self-glory,* I thought, *you've let your ego over shadow your common sense, not to mention the real purpose of travel to any country.* I uttered a weak "I'm sorry" to Mary and vowed to focus more on just doing what she was asking of me.

The next morning, Stepan and Helena took us on a tour of the city and for a little shopping. St. Petersburg was at one time a beautiful city. Now, it was grimy. Every building seemed in need of repair and painting, while the roads were filled with potholes and huge cracks. It reminded me of a once-beautiful lady that had fallen on hard times.

Shopping like everything else was complicated. Items purchased had to be paid for at a central cashier before they could be wrapped and received from the original section of the stores. Prices were extremely high on some items and too low on others; the entire system made little sense.

We returned to Zofia's small apartment for a long conversation over coffee and sandwiches. I knew little about this woman who had single-handedly set up the tour. After some coaxing, she told me of wanting to become a nun as a teenager growing up in Poland, and being told by a priest that her calling was in the world. She married, came to the States, and for twenty-seven years had lived in a suburb of Detroit, Michigan. Planning retirement soon from work as an operating room nurse, the future became unsure when her husband, who worked for the U.S. government, died suddenly of a heart attack in April 1991.

"But I accepted that as God's will," Zofia continued. "It is strange that you requested of me to also arrange a tour in Russia when I first asked you to return to Poland. My plans had always been to come here one day to work as a missionary for the Catholic Church by distributing literature and materials. When my husband died, I was prepared to do that."

It was incredible what she had accomplished in the five months she had been here. Cold, sleepless train journeys of 20 to 30 hours were common with little or no food and drink. There had been no one to assist her. Yet in addition to Russia, she had arranged venues in Latvia, Lithuania, and the Ukraine; then on to Poland, for a tour in the eastern half of the country, including returns to Krakow and Warsaw.

I marveled as she laid out our travel plans. "Zofia, what you have accomplished is unbelievable. But why didn't you call me and just cancel the tour when you discovered you had no help?"

"That is another story," she said with a mysterious smile.

I returned her smile. "Well, we have all day!"

"After my husband died, I resigned from my work and began planning to come to Russia. That is when my best friend, Veronica, told me that you were going to be speaking at a conference in New Orleans, and she felt something important was going to happen. Both of us heard you speak before in Detroit. We began to follow your work, and we read your books and listened to your tapes.

"So you decided to come to the New Orleans conference?"

"Yes – at the last minute." Zofia folded and unfolded her hands nervously. "You have to understand that I have never experienced anything like what happened next. Saturday morning of the conference, when I was waking up, I heard Our Lady speaking to me, saying, *Bring Wayne to Poland, as a birthday gift for me.*

I was not surprised at Zofia receiving such a message, but puzzled at the last part. "A birthday gift? But her birthday is in September."

"Yes, I know," Zofia nodded. "But, you must understand that it was Our Lady and that is what she said! Well, I tried to see you Saturday afternoon but there were too many people around you. I asked one of the conference people if they would arrange for me to see you. He told me to come to the front of the auditorium just before the start of Mass on Sunday, and of course, that is what I did. And then right after our meeting, I find out you are entering the Church during the Mass! So, right away Veronica and I knew that was the important thing that was going to happen." Sitting back in her chair, she added, "And now, you are here. So, even if we do not have many people tomorrow for your two talks, you are meant to be here – and so am I."

I could hardly argue with that reasoning. It again reminded me that perhaps my ego was leading me to think about being part of the conversion of Russia.

That evening, another Polish friend of Zofia's came by the apartment. His name was Marian Radwan and he knew of my work and would be meeting us later in Lublin, Poland, where he lived. He talked of working for the church for fifteen years by secretly training seminarians from throughout the former Soviet Union in Lublin, and then returning them to their native countries as underground priests. I was still feeling the effects of jet-lag, and only after Zofia called him "Father" in Polish several times did I ask, "Wait a minute. Are you a priest?"

Father Marian Radwan smiled at me and said, "Yes, of course I am."

"But you're dressed in a suit and tie."

Father Marian nodded. "Yes, I can understand now why you did not know. You see, my assignment is directly from the Vatican. I have worked quietly during these years because of the political conditions."

Suddenly, I was wide awake – and feeling a little sheepish at expecting so much on this tour. After listening to his stories of the underground church for the next hour, I asked him, "Father Marian, would you hear my confession?"

Preparing for bed after Father Marian Radwan had left, I prayed to be able to accept whatever God wanted of me in this land. My being a glorious part of the conversion of Russia no longer mattered. If only a handful of Russians attended the talks, so be it.

Sunday, after early Mass in a tiny room serving as one of only three Roman Catholic Churches in St. Petersburg, I waited at Zofia's apartment for Stepan to come for me. I had packed my bags, as we would be leaving late that night for Latvia by train. Zofia and Helena had gone to the conference hall immediately after church to oversee preparations.

There would be two talks – one in the early afternoon, and one in the evening. Prior to the talks, a video titled, "Marian Apparitions of the 20th Century" would be shown. It had been dubbed in Russian and would serve as an introduction to the events in Medjugorje.

The quiet time was a blessing. I prayed my rosary, praying for success throughout the tour, success based on conversions to Jesus, not on numbers of people present. I marveled at the work Zofia had accomplished in such a short tenure. Not only had she arranged the entire tour, but had managed to have 50,000 copies of my original articles printed in Russian, having already distributed thousands in St. Petersburg. She was just one little woman, and not nearly as frail as I had imagined. A strong mixture of determination and stubbornness had allowed her to accomplish her goals.

Thus, as I rode to the site of the first talk, recalling that Zofia said this would be the first Christian event held in this famous concert hall since the beginning of the Revolution, I prepared myself for the worst.

Although Stepan spoke no English, I clearly understood his excitement as we approached the concert hall. There was a line of people at least five wide, running from the entrance to around the corner and down the entire block! Somehow, word had spread and Zofia's estimation of only one or two hundred people had swelled to thousands.

Entering at the rear of the concert hall, I found Zofia engaged in intense conversation with a swarthy Russian man. "Zofia, have you seen the line of people coming in? It's incredible! There are thousands!"

"Yes, but this man refuses to turn on the microphones or the lights unless I pay him additional money."

I was incredulous. The crowd size did not faze her, only the last-minute bribe demands of the theater manager. "But Zofia, look at the people coming in. This is wonderful!"

There was a near-riot as copies of my articles ran out, followed shortly by all 3,000 rosaries, which were supposed to be distributed throughout the tour. And the concert hall was filled to standing room only, with more than 2,000 Russians. It was repeated in the evening with a total of more than 4,500 people learning of the miracle of Medjugorje. No matter what occurred during the rest of the tour, this made the entire trip worth it.

I ended the evening talk in a highly animated state, practically shouting at the audience, "Do you realize that you, the Russian people, through your total conversion, will be the greatest glory of God? That is what the mother of Jesus said at Fatima, and now again at Medjugorje!" The crowd rose to their feet and cheered for more than a full minute, sending chills throughout my body.

The mood was euphoric as we drove toward the train station for an overnight journey to Riga, Latvia. I felt sheepish and uplifted at the same time. Regardless of what lay ahead on the tour, this first stop made it all worthwhile. Suddenly, Zofia exclaimed, "Oh, I wanted you to ride on the metro (subway) system before we leave. It is a very good system."

I gave her a light hug. "Don't worry about that, this has been a tremendous evening!"

"But you must see this system!" And with that she spoke to our driver. "Stepan will drop us at the next station where we can ride the metro for several blocks." She turned to me and smiled, "He will pick us up at the next station."

"Whatever you say," I answered, happily resigned to allowing her this extra little pleasure.

We dashed down marble steps for a good five hundred feet to a clean, well-lighted platform. It was a stark paradox to the poor conditions of the city streets. Within minutes our metro arrived, and we grabbed seats near the door for the short ride.

Casually glancing around, I did a double take as a young man sitting next to me was reading a copy of my articles in Russian! It was one of the copies Zofia had printed for the tour. "Zofia, look at this," I whispered, motioning to the young man sitting next to me.

I couldn't contain myself. I tapped the young man on the shoulder reaching over and turning the tabloid to my picture on the front page, pointing to it and then to myself. He was perplexed for a moment and then it registered. Just then, we arrived at our station stop and got off, waving to the young man who kept staring at the tabloid and then at us, as the metro car pulled away!

Shaking my head in wonder, I asked Zofia, "What are the chances of us randomly deciding to ride the metro in the middle of St. Petersburg, only to sit next to this young man reading my articles about Medjugorje?"

We both knew it was a special sign that the message of Medjugorje had arrived in Russia.

Another surprise awaited us at the train station; Father Marian was there. "I wanted to make sure everything was all right," he explained as we made our way down the long platform. I was glad for his presence and the opportunity to see him again. He pulled me aside and said, "I must tell you that this evening was wonderful. I never thought that I would hear the word of God being preached here in this city."

I was deeply touched. "Thank you Father for your kind words…"

"Wait, I have more to say," Father Marian said with seriousness as he put his hand on my shoulder. "I have worked for the Vatican for fifteen years, directly for Pope John Paul, and I have never asked for any favors. But now, I am going to ask the Pope for a favor. I know you are going to Italy for a tour soon; so, I will ask him to allow you to be present with him at Holy Mass in his private quarters."

I didn't know what to say. Tears gleaned in my eyes. I had been a Catholic for just a few months and I would be attending Mass with the Pope? "Father Marian, I am deeply touched. "Just keep doing your mission, you deserve this little treat." Father Marian said as he smiled and hugged me.

"This is my car," Zofia said as we reached the midpoint of the long train, "I have arranged a first-class sleeper for you. Father Marian will assist you. I will meet you in the morning when we arrive." I began to protest. "It is no use, everything has been arranged," she said, disappearing into her car.

"Ah, here is your car." Father Marian hoisted my bags into the doorway and we made our way to the proper compartment. I opened the door and was taken aback by the sight of a woman who would be my traveling companion. She was in her mid-thirties and already settled in the lower of the two bunks in the cramped, narrow compartment. Father Marian, after speaking to the woman, stated, "I told her you were an American and asked her to assist you if necessary." He seemed totally unconcerned that I would have to share the compartment for the night's journey with a woman. We hastily said our goodbyes. I knew I would never forget this great priest for his work and for the so-called "little favor" of arranging Mass with the Holy Father.

The only thing "first class" about the compartment was the name! I struggled to load my luggage on one end of the upper bunk, the only place available. I was still dressed in my suit and determined to stay so for the duration of the night.

The cramped quarters and presence of the woman made sleep near impossible. Finally, I had had enough. Slipping down from the bunk, I motioned to the woman that I would be just outside the compartment. Shaking her head vigorously, she indicated I should stay, but I couldn't stand it any longer; I had to get out and stretch my legs.

The clickity-clack of the wheels and the dark, eerie landscape barely visible through the train windows presented a setting straight out of an old Russian spy movie. I stood there for nearly half an hour, until two men squeezed by me, staring and looking as unsavory as any casting director could ask for. I immediately returned to my cramped bunk, sensing it wasn't too safe in the corridor.

And finally, I dozed off – only to be suddenly awakened a short while later by hard banging on the compartment door and shouts in Russian. The woman responded and then quickly opened the door. Two Russian soldiers burst in, loudly demanding our passports. After several seconds of staring at my passport and visa papers, one of them frowned at me and mumbled, "Problem!"

I was petrified. The woman began arguing with the soldiers who finally tossed my passport on the bunk but kept the visa. "Wait a minute, I need the visa!" But with a cold glare, they left slamming the door. Immediately, the woman locked it and placed the safety chain in its slot.

Again, I lay there trying to calm down when suddenly, the door opened quietly, stopped only by the chain lock. Someone was attempting to enter our compartment – and it wasn't soldiers! The woman yelled something sharp in Russian, and the door slowly closed without a sound from outside. My heart began to pound as I realized someone was trying to rob me, in all probability the two men who passed me earlier in the corridor.

After several hours, exhaustion from the night's ordeal brought a fitful sleep, again harshly interrupted with knocking on the door. But this time, they were Latvian soldiers, and it was daylight; right behind them was Zofia. "Oh, wow, am I glad to see you! What a night!" After relating the events of the evening, I took Zofia by the shoulders. "Look, we're not going to separate again. I don't know what would have happened if it hadn't been for this woman!"

"This is the only train trip. We will not be separated again." And with that, she opened a bag containing juice, bread sticks and home-made Polish dried sausages, which we promptly shared with the woman. Only then did I realize that we had been on the train for fourteen hours without food or drink. Enjoying the food as much as I would an expensive gourmet meal, I felt a renewed respect for the travails Zofia undertook to arrange this tour.

riga, latvia

Riga, Latvia was a welcome sight. We departed the train to bright sunshine, offsetting the biting cold. Immediately, several people from the group that arranged the talk welcomed us. I was taken to my hotel, free until the evening talk.

Literally as well as figuratively, the dark Russian night was replaced by the bright daylight of Latvia, which was beautiful. Old but well-kept buildings and bustling traffic of vehicles and people replaced empty, unrepaired streets and unpainted buildings. The stores were busy and loaded with food and merchandise.

A major difference, explaining the stark contrast to Russia, is that the people of the Baltic States never lost their faith in God. Even though discouraged and harassed by the Russians, they continued to live their faith, often in secrecy. Thus, today, with newfound freedom, they were prospering, while the Russians, without God, had floundered.

At the talk, there were as many Lutherans present as Catholics, as the two religions dominated the republic. And again, the people did not want the evening to end. I discovered later they had never seen or heard of a layperson speaking about the Gospel. A lone man approached as we prepared to leave the church. After speaking to him, my translator replied, "This man is a Lutheran."

"That's wonderful. Tell him I was Lutheran for many years."

"But you do not understand – he is a Lutheran pastor!"

I prepared for debate, thinking that is why he approached us. "He tells me that he has been seeking a relationship with the Virgin Mary all of his life, but has had difficulty due to his church theology, his congregation and his family. But something strange happened tonight."

The stranger continued talking, his voice quavering. It took my translator a moment to digest the man's statement. "Well, this is beautiful. He says that tonight, he came home and was preparing for a quiet evening when he heard a voice inside telling him to come to this church; it was so strong, he immediately came. He did not know anything about a talk being held here this evening, or about Medjugorje, or you. But after listening, he feels at last that closeness to the Virgin Mary."

I was deeply touched, and promised to leave him a picture of the statue of Our Lady from the church in Tihaljina. I would also include a medal blessed during the time of an apparition. He could pick them up at the hotel desk in the morning.

From there, we traveled to Vilnius, Lithuania, the last stop in the former Soviet Union, before journeying on to Poland. The church again was full and the talk, extended by people not wanting to leave.

It was a Sunday, November 1, All Saints Day, when we arrived at a beautiful church for early morning Mass, and an impromptu talk afterwards. The day before, we had visited the church at the urging of our translator. "This is one of the most beautiful churches in all of Lithuania You really should see it," he had related.

While there, he introduced us to the young associate priest, who immediately began asking questions about Medjugorje. After a while, he asked, "I wonder, if I can arrange it, would it be possible for you to speak after the early Mass tomorrow?"

Zofia looked at me with a look I was beginning to recognize, a plea to say yes to anything these people requested for the sake of conversion. This time, it was easy. "I'll be happy to speak, Father. We have to attend Mass and this is a wonderful place."

And arrange it, he did! On a bitterly cold morning, the church was filled. We entered the sacristy, looking for the associate, but instead, found the pastor. He was not pleased. As soon as Zofia told him who we were, he exploded in a tirade of words. The translator listened attentively and then said. "I am very sorry, but he says it is impossible to have a talk because of the time."

Just then the associate arrived and once again the pastor began an angry tirade. "Please accept my apologies," the young priest explained, noticeably embarrassed, "but yesterday, he gave his permission to have the talk. Now, for some unexplained reason, he says he cannot allow it."

When the associate announced that there would be no talk, a rumble ran through the crowd. An angry rumble! Many had arisen in the very early hours to endure long, freezing rides on public transportation to come.

Following Mass, there was a rush of people into the sacristy engulfing the pastor. It didn't take a translator to know they were extremely angry and did not hesitate to let the pastor know it. I felt sorry for him, but knew that his denial of the talk was done out of pride, and this was Our Lady's way of letting him know he had made a mistake.

We left that afternoon for Poland, having completed what I felt was a triumphant tour of Russia and the other countries of the former Soviet Union. I was sure I would return sometime in the near future. There was still much work of conversion to accomplish.

After our tour of Poland was complete, it was extremely difficult and emotional saying goodbye to Zofia, who would remain in Poland for a time before joining a friend for a pilgrimage to Medjugorje. There was no way to properly thank her for she had done in arranging the tours of the two countries. "I can only ask Our Lady to give you a much-needed rest in Medjugorje."

"Well, I have one more thing to ask you," she responded, giving me that pleading look again. I felt like I knew what that "one more thing" was before she asked.

Smiling, I returned her look with one of mock consternation. "Okay, what is it now?"

"There is still so much to be done in these countries. Will you come back next year if I can arrange it?"

I hugged her tightly. "You can count on it!"

But you, beloved, build yourselves up on your most holy faith; pray in the Holy Spirit; keep yourselves in the love of God; wait for the mercy of our Lord Jesus Christ unto eternal life.

—Jude 1: 20-21.

If you would abandon yourselves to me, you will not even feel the passage from this life to the next life. You will begin to live the life of Heaven on earth.

—From a message given to Jelena's prayer group 1986

🌺 14 🌺

return to russia

Zofia greeted me at the doorway of the small arrival terminal at St. Petersburg Airport, wondering why the Russian customs officials had delayed me. "At last, they let you in! What was the problem?"

"Just the usual annoyances! Since the airline changed the schedule for my flight and I'm arriving a day earlier than originally planned, the visa, which had already been processed is not official until tomorrow, which is in three hours," I said, looking at my watch. "The customs official wanted me to wait until midnight, but after a lengthy discussion they reluctantly decided to let me in."

"And everything has gone wrong here in these last days." Zofia shook her head. "There is a fuel shortage for airplanes and your schedule is centered around the dates I could get airline tickets. And I have had little help . . ."

"Wait a minute," I laughed, I've heard this story before!"

I refused to be discouraged with this return trip. I was sure that it would be a triumphant continuation of the last one. I now knew in my heart that our work in Russia would indeed be part of the conversion of this vast region.

Despite steady rain, the following day brought nothing to discourage my optimism. A young television journalist from Odessa, where we would end the tour, had traveled to St. Petersburg, to film the entire tour for a documentary to be shown in the future. We did some filming for him, plus a short radio interview. Overall, it was a quiet restful day.

There was another good sign; the first talk was on the 25th of the month, just as it was last time in St. Petersburg.

I carried an air of expectant confidence - until we arrived at the auditorium.

a different scene

There were less than 700 people present, a far cry from the 4,000 in attendance last year. While the majority of those present were enthusiastic, there was actually some heckling and the questions after the talk were less than friendly. It didn't bother me. I knew where it was coming from. Satan would be crushed with the conversion of Russia and the captive countries that made up the old Soviet Union. He would do everything possible to ruin this tour and we knew it. In many ways, tiny steps of spiritual conversion were already happening. I found the faith strong and devout in all of the satellite countries, while Russia struggled with the new order of things.

Zofia though, was disappointed. "I am sorry, but I told you, there have been many problems. Cults of all faiths have come into all of these countries, causing great confusion among the people. There is even one lady from Ukraine, who claims to be the reincarnation of both Jesus and the Blessed Mother, and she has many followers. Some people think our tour is part of her cult. It is terrible!"

I had seen the posters of this woman. They were everywhere, placed high on buildings and light poles, making it difficult to remove them.

Additionally, there was a priest of questionable credentials, who did everything possible to discourage his parishioners from attending my talks. "I still do not believe he is an authentic priest," Zofia said. "It is known that he worked with the KGB."

"Well, I'm sure the talk in Moscow will be better." That was our next stop, the one I looked forward to the most, not having been able to speak there on the last tour.

But it wasn't. We arrived at the airport in Moscow to the usual mass confusion that seems part of the flying experience in Russia. It was worse now due to the acute fuel shortage. A man approached us. "This is Vladislav," Zofia said, introducing us. "He will be our driver and assistant while we are here."

Vladislav spoke in halting English, but was well educated. He was a devout Christian who had become interested in Medjugorje, and was part of a Moscow prayer group. His wife taught English and thus, he had also learned, adding, "But since I do not have opportunities to use it, I am not very good."

As we journeyed to the hotel in his small car, I asked him about the present attitude of the people, pointing out the differences from last year. "Yes, at that time, we were experiencing freedom for the first time. Everyone thought life would become better right away but it did not happen. There have been food shortages and much unemployment, and now this shortage of gasoline, which makes it difficult to find gasoline for our automobiles."

Vladislav worked as an engineer after completing his studies at the university, but only earned the equivalent of thirty dollars a month. "And, I have a wife and new baby, so it is very hard."

It was another hard piece of evidence of how Russia was struggling during its transition. Here was an engineer making far less than a janitor in the United States.

When asked about the political, social and spiritual life in Russia, he was pessimistic. The government was in total confusion with infighting between the president and the parliament. No one seemed to be in charge - except a new Russian Mafia, a criminal element that had swiftly taken control. They controlled everything sold; even the small stands and kiosks that had sprung up everywhere. There was also corruption at all levels of government, he added.

As though to prove the point, we were suddenly stopped on the highway by a policeman, who fined Vladislav three thousand rubles (about three dollars) for having a dent in the rear fender of his car. "Now this policeman will put the money in his pocket," Vladislav wryly pointed out. "That is the way the system works with everything these days."

My hotel was a huge structure that had been used by Olympic athletes at one time. As we pulled to the front, Zofia gave Vladislav the amount of the fine, insisting he take it as he was transporting us at the time. "Yes, please accept it," I urged him. "Also, I would very much like to see Red Square on the way to the talk if you can take us."

"But you only have time to check in and have dinner before the conference," Vladislav said.

"That is alright," Zofia interjected. "We will have to come back through Moscow in four days. I would like to hire you to pick us up and take us to the other airport, and since we have four hours before our flight to Rostov, perhaps then we could visit Red Square and some of the other historic spots of Moscow."

"Yes, of course I will be happy to drive you again." Vladislav then smiled broadly. "And if you would permit me, I would like to take you to my apartment to meet my wife and have coffee with us!"

It was agreed. I checked in, grabbed a quick meal and we were off to the talk, which had a turnout of only 300 people. Back in the lobby of the hotel, I went over a large map of Russia, trying to pinpoint exactly where we were going. "After three days in the Ukraine, we go there, to Rostov," Zofia said, pointing to a distant city on the coast of the Black Sea. "And then on to Minsk, in Belarus, and finally to Odessa."

"But why go way over there?" I asked, pointing to Rostov. For some reason, I had an uneasy feeling about going there.

"Oh, but they are wonderful people and they need you there. The priest is so excited that you are coming!"

I could only utter a weak "okay." But the ominous feeling remained.

There was one exceptionally good experience on this trip to Moscow. I had agreed to a radio interview that would occur near noon the next day. A beautiful young woman who spoke near-perfect English met us in the lobby. She would be conducting the interview.

It was a professional and thorough interview. I wanted to know more about this young lady and how she seemed to be the exception to what we had encountered in journalists up to this point. Would she join us for a quick cup of coffee, I asked? "Of course, I would be delighted and I also want to know more about how you became involved in this project."

We talked for more than an hour, exchanging personal stories. I discovered that she was a devout Christian, which explained the aura of goodness that seemed to surround her. I then asked her, "Which church do you attend?"

"Oh, no, I'm sorry but I do not attend any church yet. I am trying to decide which one will bring me closer to Jesus."

I was surprised, having assumed she was Catholic. "Then, how did you become a believer?"

The young lady smiled. "I found a bible that a group of Christians from the United States had brought to our country. I began to read it and the more I read, the more I believed. It was exciting and wonderful to know that God existed."

I wanted to make a push for the Catholic Church but left well enough alone. She was a Christian and that was enough. We departed, promising to pray for each other.

As we left the next morning for Kiev, Ukraine, I wondered if maybe we had planned the return to Russia to occur too soon. This was a far cry from what I had expected after the first trip. Possibly it was the wrong time of year. The political unrest didn't help. Adding to the confusion of the people, every religious cult possible was invading the country, creating a religious war for converts.

Something outside of all the changes in this tour compared to the first nagged at me. It wasn't just small crowds and inconveniences of travel. Inside, I felt an uneasiness that I had experienced only a few times in the past six years; it was a feeling of evil.

"Yes, but you cannot get discouraged," Zofia stated as we discussed the first days of disappointments. "We are here for Our Lady and she will take care of us!" I smiled and patted her hand, saying nothing. Zofia had that solid, blind faith that many have found through Medjugorje. She had worked hard only to watch plans crumble beyond her control. "These people need our help," she continued. "You have seen their churches and the need for repairs."

I truly hoped Kiev's talks would be better—for her sake. It was Sunday and we attended Mass in a once-beautiful church that was under almost total reconstruction. In fact, it was the Cathedral of Kiev. Mass was held amid scaffolding and work tools. Everything was covered with dust. In spite of the surroundings, it was a beautiful service.

This church and others I had seen created a graphic picture of the faith in Russia and the former Soviet Union. The rebuilding appeared to be an almost impossible task. St. Petersburg only had three Catholic churches for more than a million Catholics. There were only a few more in Kiev, a onetime Catholic stronghold. I had to wonder how Russia and the former Soviet Union could ever be converted without churches. But then, our God was the God of the impossible.

The talk in Kiev was the lowest point yet. Two churches had feuded over which location would host the talk. The result was a boycott by the loser, and less than a hundred people in attendance. I returned to the hotel in a steady drizzle of rain that continued throughout the night and into the next day.

We were scheduled to go to Zhitomir next, about a two hour's drive from Kiev. It had been the highlight of the tour last year and I looked forward to returning. I sat in the lobby of the hotel dressed and waiting for Zofia and the driver. The minute she walked in the door, I knew something was wrong.

"I am so sorry! The materials advertising your talk never arrived in Zhitomir and there has been no publicity . . . we had to cancel the talk."

I was crushed. Surely, this was the nadir of the entire tour. "How?" I asked, totally frustrated and losing the confidence I had arrived with. "How could the materials not reach the city? I mean after last year..." I stopped in mid-sentence and began pacing. Turning to Zofia, I took her by the hand and led her to the small couch in a corner of the lobby. "Listen, I know you've worked hard, but this is not accomplishing much. Maybe we should just cancel the remainder of the tour."

"Oh, no, please!" She gripped my hand. "Please, we must complete this! The people in Zinnetsa and Rostov and Odessa—they are so excited! It will be fine; I know it. If just one soul is touched . . ."

The magic words again. "Okay, okay. It's just that Rostov is so far and with this fuel shortage and all; but we'll tough it out to the bitter end." I smiled and gave her a reassuring hug.

The next day, things seemed to get back on track as we journeyed to Zinnetsa. Franciscan priests were in charge and it was an entirely different setting. A joyous, enthusiastic, assemblage of villagers sang beautiful hymns with great gusto, reminding me of Medjugorje itself. I spoke for two hours and took another two hours to answer questions. The priests insisted we stay for dinner, which we gladly accepted, realizing we had eaten little during the day of travel. We arrived at the hotel after midnight, but it didn't matter to me, or to Zofia. The day had been a success!

As if to signal things were better, we were unexpectedly placed in business class on a new Russian airline, called Transeara, as we left for the four-hour layover and change of airports in Moscow before flying to Rostov. "This is not what I purchased," Zofia whispered as we settled into roomy seats at the front of the plane.

"I'm not complaining," I grinned.

Zofia was beaming. "See how Our Lady is taking care of us. This is a good sign for the rest of the tour!" Little did we know it would be the only point of light in a day that would turn into almost total darkness.

We enjoyed a nice breakfast and a relaxing flight to Moscow, happy to see Vladislav awaiting us as we entered the Moscow terminal. "There is just one little problem," he stated, loading our bags into the small trunk of his car. "I was not able to buy gasoline this morning, so we will have to wait in the line. It should not take long."

But it did; we waited in line for almost two hours before Vladislav was able to purchase a spare tank from someone in the front of the line.

It was enough to take care of the day's driving as we headed for the city, but our time before the connecting flight at the other airport was now less than two and a half hours. "Maybe we better skip the sightseeing visit and go directly to the airport," I suggested to Vladislav.

"Please, we go to my home for only ten minutes. My wife has prepared some fresh pastries for you." Reluctantly, we agreed; it was a mistake. We suddenly found ourselves in a horrible traffic jam in the middle of Moscow, something rare according to Vladislav. As time ticked away, I urged him to go directly to the airport. "Please," he pleaded. "Just five minutes. We are close!"

On arrival at his apartment building, there was less than an hour before our flight. "Vladislav, tell your wife to come with us. We don't have time for coffee—hurry!"

We waited an excruciating ten minutes, with no sign of our driver. Zofia began to panic. "We must go now! Why isn't he here?" Finally, he came, without his wife as the baby was sleeping and she could not leave. "Hurry! Hurry!" Zofia was fairly yelling at him.

Reentering the traffic clog, it became worse. Zofia kept yelling at Vladislav, telling him not to let anyone in front of him and to drive fast. It was impossible and I soon knew we were not going to make it. I gently eased Zofia back into the seat. "Zofia, please, sit back and calm down. There's nothing he can do now. I think it's too late and we're going to miss the flight." Strangely, I felt a great calm that this was confirmation we were not supposed to go to Rostov at all.

"But we must make it! These people are counting on you." She then added bitterly, "You didn't want to go there and now see what has happened!" I had never seen her upset. "Oh, no," she moaned, "Satan is having a good laugh at us. He is responsible for this horrible traffic!"

I placed my hand firmly on her arm. "Zofia, listen! Maybe this isn't Satan. Maybe *it's Our Lady*! I told you I haven't felt comfortable about going to Rostov from the beginning. It's not a matter of not wanting to go, but because of these inner feelings."

Resigned that we were in all probability going to miss our flight, Zofia sunk into the seat. "I'm sorry, it's just that these people need you."

"I know, but possibly this isn't the right time. Besides, you know how Aeroflot Airlines is. They might be late with the flight. If so, that's a sign we're meant to go."

The minute we arrived at the terminal, Zofia jumped out and ran for the building, calling out to us, "I will check quickly to see if we can make the flight."

"We'll meet you at the entrance of the terminal," I yelled back, hoping she heard me. We unloaded the baggage and entered into pure chaos as people were everywhere; there was hardly room to stand next to our baggage, and the noise was deafening. We waited an hour and a half, with no sign of Zofia. After Vladislav had made several excursions through the melee of people looking for her, I suddenly sighted her near one of the ticket counters. "Zofia! Over here!"

The look on her face and the tears that began running down her face as she came running over, said it all. "I thought you would follow me to the counter," she said. "When you were nowhere to be found, I thought you had been kidnapped!"

I gently hugged her. "It's okay. Everything's fine now. We'll just go on to Minsk. At least we'll be there early and there will be time to rest."

Vladislav interjected quickly, "But you can catch the next flight to Rostov and..."

"No, Vladislav, take us back to the other airport so we can go to Minsk." There was no way we were going on to Rostov now. Zofia worried we would not be able to change our tickets. I assured her that even if we didn't fly to Minsk tonight, we could stay in the airport and make arrangements for the next day.

It was a shock when we arrived at a different terminal building from where we had arrived that morning. This terminal was new, clean and sparse in the number of passengers, a far cry from the chaotic crowds of the other airport. "This is a special place where visiting dignitaries and business leaders arrive," Vladislav told us.

The stress of the day was finally over and a calm, like that which follows huge storms, set in. We were able to get tickets for a 10:30 PM flight to Minsk. Vladislav departed for his home only after being assured we would call if anything went wrong.

I spotted a small coffee shop at the far end of the terminal, with several tables in the front. "Zofia, let's go and have a nice cup of coffee and see if we can find something to eat."

Through the rush of the day, we had not eaten since the small meal on our early morning flight. Zofia, always prepared, had some Polish sausages and a few stale pretzels. "And," she added, "I have this little bottle of wine they gave me in business class this morning."

It was the finest meal of the entire tour! I couldn't believe how good stale pretzels and cold sausage could taste when the stomach was empty!

True to the form of the day, we almost missed our flight to Minsk as Zofia was on the telephone trying to get in touch with our contacts to inform them we were arriving early. Late into the night, we landed at a beautiful— and empty—airport, where Zofia was finally able to reach our contacts. They came an hour later, immediately telling Zofia they had been trying to contact us for several days to tell us *not to go to Rostov,* because there were no flights back from there!

The bottom line was we would have been stranded in Rostov for an unknown number of days. Once again, Our Lady had rescued us.

I slept until noon, having informed Zofia to please leave me in peace until the next day. After a wonderful meal, I strolled through the streets of Minsk, unable to find a Catholic church for Mass, but relieved and happy to have quiet time. On returning to the hotel late in the afternoon, I passed an unusual sight, a crowd of mostly senior citizens kneeling on the sidewalk in front of a large building, praying the rosary. Close by was a small kiosk with many religious articles in the windows, including copies of my articles in Russian!

Later when Zofia telephoned my room, I agreed to have lunch with one of the priests the next day. "He wishes to show you his church which is still not open for holy Mass yet. We will pick you up at noon."

Saint John Paul the Great: **"Medjugorje is the hope for the entire world!"**

the promise

Everywhere we had been on the tour I witnessed the church buildings in shambles and undergoing extensive refurbishment. This latest visit was no different. Weaving our way through construction and scaffolding, we entered a long room, which served as kitchen, conference room, and sanctuary for Mass. "It is the only part of the church we can use right now," the priest explained through the interpreter.

Inquiring about the people I had seen praying on the sidewalk the day before, the priest told me that they were part of his parish, and they were praying in front of a building that was once their cathedral. "Now, it is a sport palace for youth," he explained. "Every morning and evening, we conduct Mass on the sidewalk, and the young people come out and insult and push the worshipers around, but they continue to come. They have vowed to worship and pray the rosary there daily until the government returns the building to the Church."

"You actually conduct Mass there twice a day?"

"Yes, and I invite you to join us this evening before your talk at the auditorium," he added.

That floored me as we sat down to a light meal of hard bread and borsht soup. Here, in a city of three million people with a third of them Catholic, there were literally no Catholic churches; the only Mass conducted was on the sidewalk in front of the old cathedral building and here in this tiny room! It was all so - hopeless. I wondered again what I was doing here.

Suddenly, as I stared into my cup of coffee, I felt Our Lady's presence as her words filled my heart: *My dear son, you are here not just to spread my messages given at Medjugorje, but to see the condition of the Church in Russia; to see and feel and experience how these children of mine live everyday of their lives. I am asking you to help them to build their churches so they can find my Son . . ."*

It all became immediately clear. "Zofia, please tell the translator I have something important to tell the priest," and with that, I related what had just been given to me by Our Lady, adding, "Father, when I return to the United States, I am going to raise funds to help your church, and also the churches in Moscow, Kiev and Zinnetsa. I promise, you will soon have help for your churches!"

There was a loud, happy cheer from the twenty or so people in the room as the message was repeated for them. Zofia was beside herself, "The instant you began telling this, I felt confirmation in my heart that this is why you were sent here!"

The priest suddenly asked, "And will you return again to speak in our new churches?"

I hadn't counted on that. I didn't want to ever see this country again after these past days; but I heard myself answering that I would indeed return in the future.

Even though there was peace in now knowing the reason for the tour, the struggles were not over. Satan had not finished sifting us. However, I had just made a promise I had to keep.

That evening I joined the people praying the rosary in front of the cathedral that was now a youth hall. The Mass was the most difficult I had ever attended, with the disruptions of the young people and the constant shouting. Afterwards, the priest announced my presence and that I would be giving a talk in an auditorium just down the street. Suddenly my translator repeated the words of the priest: "And now I am going to ask him to say a few words to us, so please welcome our guest from the United States!"

I turned to Zofia with a look of alarm. "Did you know about this? What can I say to them?" Zofia assured me she did not know the priest was going to ask me to speak and then added, "Just do what you always do and speak from your heart."

I immediately calmed down and through a translator spoke of the courage of the people to continue to come and pray the rosary and attend Holy Mass. "Prayer works with full belief," I stated and then inexplicably I added, "and with faith, I am going to pray for you to have your cathedral returned to you—I promise you, it will happen!" even as I said this and my translator was wide-eyed, I was thinking: *Are you crazy! You can't make such a promise!* Yet, somehow, I knew it would happen.

odessa: the trip from hell

We returned to Minsk airport where we took a flight to Kiev to meet the driver who would take us to Odessa, the last stop on the tour. It would be a grueling nine-hour automobile ride over extremely rough and dangerous roads. The man had attached five spare tires to the top of his car and within an hour, I understood why as we had our first flat tire. Two more would follow before our arrival.

We prayed the rosary with fervor nearly the entire way, arriving just before the talk. I was starving since we had nothing to eat since breakfast. Zofia asked the priest if there might be a restaurant or café nearby where I could get something to eat. The priest sent a young man to see what he could find. "Just a sandwich would be fine," I added.

Within a few minutes the boy returned with a plate containing a chicken leg and some small potatoes. The chicken was nearly raw. Thus, we would be on an "involuntary fast" until after the talk!

Again, the crowd was limited and restless as the young man who was serving as translator and who had spoken nearly perfect English with me before the talk, simply could not translate. "I have been to Chicago and I even know all of your slang words," he had boasted. Yet, he would hesitate and on several occasions, simply did not translate the proper words. After a short while, a large man stood up in the middle of the crowd and shouted at my translator as he started toward us: "You, young man, that is enough! Give me the microphone and I will translate!" amazingly, the man did a far superior job to the young man! I just shook my head at another bizarre incident on this tour.

"Well, at least you will be able to fly back to Kiev in the morning for your flight to Poland," our contact told me. "And, we have a room for you at the best hotel in Odessa."

I was ushered into an old, dilapidated "famous" hotel, and shown to my room. The bed was swayed in the middle and as the door closed, a cockroach scurried across the warped floor boards. A small television sat on a rickety table in a corner, but it did not work. Laughing, I said out loud, "Okay, Blessed Mary, you want me to continue doing penance!" With that I got undressed, grabbed my rosary and sank into the narrow bed and fell asleep, praying the Glorious mysteries!

And of course, the flight was canceled on arrival at the airport the next morning; thus, another tortuous drive back to Kiev. Along the way, we had three more flat tires, nearly wrecking on the first, as the driver was traveling at over seventy-five miles per hour. Hitting the outskirts of Kiev with the last of the spare tires shredding we hailed a passing taxi. It was in worse mechanical shape than the car we had just left, and got us to the airport barely in time for our flight to Warsaw, Poland.

It was difficult saying goodbye to Zofia at the airport the following morning as I left for Milan, Italy. She would remain in Warsaw for a few days before returning to St. Petersburg. "There is still a lot of material to be distributed," she said. "And when I return to my home in Michigan, we will arrange for your return trip here."

I grimaced, giving her a skeptical look. She quickly reminded me: "Remember, you promised to the priest you would return!"

I laughed and waved as I passed through customs. "Yes, Zofia, I'll come back—but not right away!"

Saint Maximilian Kolbe: **"Never be afraid of loving the Blessed Virgin too much. You can never love her more than Jesus did."**

the third time's a charm!

The third trip to Russia took place in May 1994. As I had promised, I was able to raise nearly ninety-thousand dollars to assist in the refurbishing and construction of churches in Russia and its surrounding nations. I carried the cash taped to my body with fervent prayer that I would be able to get through customs and not get robbed by someone during my travels.

Zofia had preceded me again to arrange the schedule. We were able to take the donations directly to the priests and bishops of no less than thirteen individual churches, far above the original estimate of helping only five churches. Also, we were able to fund a strong prayer group, which established a Medjugorje center in Minsk. From that center, Zofia would continue her mission of distributing materials, now having a base and group to assist in these projects. Medjugorje's message would continue to renew the Gospel of Jesus to these special children of Mary.

Highlights of the return were twofold; in Kiev, where work on the cathedral had stopped due to exhaustion of funds, our donations enabled the priest to complete the work in time for a special celebration. Holy Mass was now to be celebrated in the refurbished sanctuary, rather than the small, cramped sacristy as it had for years.

Even greater, the old cathedral in Minsk, which the Communists had taken and made into a sport hall for youth, was *unexpectedly returned* to the Church shortly after my visit in August 1993 - a grace attributed to our prayers, according to the bishop. There was no explanation by the Communists as to why they were returning the cathedral. The story made headlines throughout Eastern Europe.

Then came another of those very special moments that will never be forgotten. We had a light meal with the bishop. Afterward, I turned to him and said, "Bishop, I am so happy for your returned cathedral and I know there is a lot of cleaning and repairs that are needed. On behalf of the generous American people who donated to rebuild churches here, I am pleased to give you $13,000 to assist you in this work."

I watched the tears stream down the bishop's face, mixed with sincere surprise and gratitude. He immediately got up and began running around his apartment, looking for something to give me in return. "Really Bishop, that's not necessary."

Finally, the bishop came to me with a small, ornamentally carved box in his hands. "My dear friend, this is all I have to give you to thank you, but it is precious to me and I have had it for many years. Please, accept it with my humble gratitude."

Of course, I agreed. The rest of the evening before the talk was filled with plans to refurbish the cathedral. Suddenly, the bishop said, "Excuse me, but may I ask a special favor?"

"Yes, of course, Bishop, what can I do for you?"

"Well, we have a wonderful choir group here. It is possible I could use part of the donation to buy a small organ?"

"It is your money Bishop, use it as you wish!"

The people of Minsk simply rejoiced by participating fervently in the Holy Mass now held *inside* the building. For years, they had come every morning and evening to attend Mass and pray the rosary on the sidewalk in front of the building, no matter the weather.

That evening, I spoke in the returned Cathedral of Minsk to an overflow crowd that spilled onto the very sidewalk that had served as their only sanctuary for years.

The tours to Russia and the countries that formerly made up the Soviet Union were the most dramatic of my entire mission. The first tour was filled with great expectations; the second was akin to passing through the eye of a needle; and the third - simply triumph. I knew I would return in the future.

And, I did.

I want you to know, brethren, that I have often intended to come to you, in order that I may reap some harvest among you as

well as among the rest of the Gentiles. I am under obligation both to Greeks and to barbarians, both to the wise and to the foolish:

—Romans 1:13-14.

...In my messages, I recommend to everyone, and to the Holy Father in particular, to spread the message which I have received from my Son here at Medjugorje. I wish to entrust to the Pope, the word with which I came here: 'MIR' (peace), which he must spread everywhere...

—Excerpt from message of September 16, 1983.

15

meeting a saint

Of all the graces, gifts and special moments received during this mission, none can top the honor of attending Holy Mass with Pope John Paul II in his private quarters at the Vatican. Ironically, it came about during what I now consider to be the second greatest grace of the mission: that is, bringing the message of Medjugorje to Russia.

It was while in Russia on my first trip that I met Father Marian Radwan, who worked secretly for Pope John Paul for more than 20 years recruiting seminarians in Russia and the countries of the Soviet Union. He would bring them to the seminary in Lublin, Poland for training and then covertly place them back in their countries of origin to serve in the underground church. Such work is what kept the Church alive during the reign of Communism in all of the countries forced to be part of the former Soviet Union.

Father Marian told me after my first talk in St. Petersburg, Russia that he had never asked any special or personal favors during his service to the Pope. Now, he would. He would ask the Pope if I might be invited to private Mass at the Vatican. Father Marian was prompted to do this due to our bringing the mission to Russia. He will always be remembered in connection with this holy honor.

I was in Monza, Italy, enjoying dinner with Medjugorje visionary Marija and her fiancée, Paolo and his parents. She had come for a short visit. I was there for the start of a fifteen-day book promotion and speaking tour, traveling from the northern part of Italy, to the south and back to Naples. I was anxious to relate to the Italian people that Medjugorje and its message was alive and well.

Paolo had started the translation of "Medjugorje: The Message" and his father Dino had finished it. Now a major publishing house in Italy had published it.

Paolo and Dino had done a masterful job, working with prayer groups throughout the country and coordinating venues with the book publishers. "Paolo will drive you to most meetings and serve as translator," Dino commented as we went over logistics for the tour. "And of course, all of us will be with you for the talks here and in nearby cities."

That meant Marija would be in the audience, which made me a little nervous. "No, no, I am on holiday," she said smiling and shaking her head when I suggested she might want to share speaking duties, "But I will be listening carefully and taking notes!"

It was a relaxing evening, amply spiced with light teasing and laughter. Never had I seen Paolo and Marija so happy and at ease together. All concerns were now past; they were simply two people in love and had announced their engagement. While a date had not been set, they would likely marry within the year.

"That's great news," I responded, when told of their plans. "And I also have some potential good news." I related the promise of my Polish priest-friend, Father Marian Radwan, to attempt arranging our attendance at a private Mass with Pope John Paul II. "He has given me the name and number of a Father Stephano, at the Vatican, and I'm supposed to fax him tomorrow." Hesitating, I added, "I'm going to ask him if he will include all of you as well!"

"That is wonderful," Dino said softly, "It would be a great gift. But please, do not lose the opportunity yourself if we cannot be included."

I assured him it could probably be worked out as I had already asked Father Marian to include them if possible.

Paolo shrugged and smiled. "Well, we will pray and see what happens!"

The next morning, Ash Wednesday, I typed a fax to Father Stephano: "I know this is the beginning of Lent and a time of sacrifice," I wrote while praying silently, "I pray this request will be approved for all of us."

I promised to pray more, fast more and be completely open to the workings of the Holy Spirit throughout the tour. To actually be able to not only meet the Pope but also have Holy Mass with him was beyond my imagination.

That evening, I made the call that had been on my mind the entire tour; I called Father Stephano at the Vatican, checking on the availability of space for us at the private Mass with the Pope. "I am very sorry, but I still am unable to give you a response. Please telephone me again tomorrow morning." My hopes began to fade. I called again Saturday morning; still no news, he related; please call again this evening.

The final stop of the tour was Naples, with a Friday evening talk in a small community on the outskirts of the city, followed by an early Saturday evening talk in the inner city; we would then leave Sunday evening for Rome, where Dino and Paolo would drop me at the same hotel where I had stayed before. I was to fly home Tuesday morning and they would return to Monza.

Telephoning Father Stephano at the Vatican again Saturday, just before the talk, nothing had changed. "Well, that's it," I thought, "It isn't going to happen."

Surprisingly, I was at peace. It had been a tremendous tour and we had been able to speak to thousands about the message of Medjugorje. The response had been exceptional, causing me to develop a new respect for the Italian people. Their indefatigable energy, acceptance and resulting participation in the spreading of the Medjugorje message was something special. Maybe there would be other opportunities in the future to meet the Holy Father.

Sunday morning as we prepared to leave for Mass, Dino approached me. "Our hosts want to ask you if you would consider stopping at the home of a young man who is dying of cancer. They want you to pray over him. His parents were at your talk last night and asked you if you might consider doing this."

I readily agreed, no longer fearing such encounters. In fact, I was grateful for the opportunity.

Arriving at the home of the young man, named Genaro, I discovered he and his parents spoke fluent English. He was at peace with his disease and able to talk about it freely. Thin and jaundiced, Genaro's deep brown eyes shone as he spoke softly of his belief and trust. "Of course I want to live," he said, "But it is up to God and I accept that."

Suddenly, his mother interrupted. " But why does this have to happen to my son?" she wailed, breaking into tears. "He has always been a good boy, never in trouble and always in Church each week. He is a good Christian. Why does God do this to us?"

She covered her face with her hands. "Oh, I am sorry to be so angry with God but what can I do? I cannot seem to pray anymore!"

I went to the distraught woman. It was evident it was she, not her son, who needed prayer. Our meeting had been planned for only a few minutes, but it stretched into an hour. Words flowed effortlessly, just as they did in the talks. We talked about redemptive suffering and how fortunate they were to have a son like Genaro.

It was gift to have had the opportunity to meet this family and to pray over their son. Arriving at the Mass just as the priest was coming up the aisle, I prayed fervently, dedicating the Mass to Genaro and his entire family, asking specifically for his healing. I felt a warmth and knew the opportunity to use the healing gifts of the Holy Spirit was probably the greatest grace I could have received during this tour. Mass with the Holy Father no longer seemed important.

Just before lunch, Paolo, who had telephoned home to talk to Marija, rushed into the room. He paused, smiling widely and hardly able to contain himself. "Listen! I have very good news! Father Stephano telephoned our home a little while ago. It has been arranged *for all three of us* to attend holy Mass with the Pope on Monday morning!"

My heart was about to burst! I knew instantly this was pure gift from Our Lady. "Bravo!" Dino roared, clapping his hands as Paolo and I embraced in celebration. I hardly remembered eating lunch!

Of course, such a tremendous honor topping off such a successful tour of spreading God's messages through the apparitions of Medjugorje, could not be overlooked by Satan. As we departed for Rome after the talk, a drive of about two and a half hours, Paolo was driving when suddenly he said, "I don't know where we are. I've driven here before and know these roads but I don't recognize this area."

It seemed as though we were driving in circles, returning several times to the same spot from where we started. "Here, let me drive. I know this part of town well," Dino said. Paolo turned the driving over to him. The results were the same. We were lost.

Panic began setting in. *Wait a minute,* I thought, *we are not going to miss having Mass with the Pope!* With that, I began to pray with intensity.

"Oh, now I see our mistake," Dino exclaimed, "we were missing the exit road to Rome and I am sure it is the next left turn!"

And it was. Finally, we were on the road to Rome for Holy Mass with the Pope.

Monday at 6:45 AM, we stood shivering outside the huge doors of the Vatican, leading to the living quarters of the Pope. None of us had really slept, having arrived in Rome after midnight. We were so high with excitement that we decided to go out and celebrate with a late-night dinner, finding a quaint all-night restaurant near our hotel.

My heart raced as the Swiss Guard opened the doors a little past six o clock in the morning and ushered us inside, leading us to the small private chapel where the leader of the Church celebrated Mass each morning. Pope John Paul II was seated in a large chair in the middle of the chapel deep in meditation. Approximately twenty-five other people were there, including a Gregorian choir from Austria, which was singing a low, steady chant, adding to the drama of the moment.

I sat just a few feet away, awed at being so close to John Paul II. And yet, I felt very much as though I was attending a regular morning daily Mass. I joined my prayers to his, praying also for my family, for the entire Medjugorje family –and especially for Genaro's healing.

After a long meditative silence, the Pope arose and slowly approached the altar. He then turned to the group and said, "This morning I will be the main celebrant—and the Mass will be in English."

There was a slight stir among the gathering. The Gregorian choir from Austria made up the bulk of the group with the rest Italian, except for three of us from the United States. I felt a warmth within me as Our Lady placed the words in my heart: *This is a special grace for you.*

The Holy Mass began and soon I was lost in the liturgy. Only when we were moving forward to receive Jesus in Holy Eucharist, did it register that I would be receiving Communion directly from the hand of Christ's vicar on earth. *Please, Blessed Mary,* I prayed silently as I stood in front of the Pope; *Let my eyes remain on Jesus! Let him be just another priest . . .*

As we sat in meditation another thirty minutes after Mass, I realized that my prayer had been answered. Yes, he was the pope, but at that moment of receiving the Eucharist, he was simply another priest during these precious moments, giving us the greatest gift of all: the body and blood of our Lord, Jesus. To a degree, it was like every Mass; no more holy—no less holy.

We were then led into a large reception area to meet with Pope John Paul for a few minutes. I had brought two copies of "Medjugorje: The Message," one in Polish and the other in Italian, to present to him. Suddenly, he was standing in front of me. "Holy Father, I would like to present my book to you..." There was so much more I wanted to say, but the words wouldn't come.

"Ah, Medjugorje!" the Pope said slowly, smiling. "Have you been there recently?"

I relaxed immediately, feeling completely at ease. "Yes, Holy Father, I have."

"But have you been there during the war?"

"Yes, Holy Father. I was there in January, just two months ago."

He smiled again. "Good. That is good!" And he moved on to Paolo, who was next in line.

It was over so fast. So very fast. As we crossed St. Peter's Square after leaving the living quarters, I felt a momentary letdown as the huge doors shut behind us. But just as quickly, the realization of the grace we had been given to be with the Pope filled me with gratitude. Now, we were once again part of the throng of people walking through the square.

The memory of the nearly two hours shared with my hero Pope John Paul II, hand-picked by Our Lady for these times, would last forever. It was a crowning moment of the entire mission.

Commentary: The impact of meeting Pope John Paul, this man who is now a public saint, would affect me for the rest of my life. Of course, I had to share the experience during my talks.

At one such venue, a Marian conference in Lowell, Massachusetts, I related the story of having the honor to not only attend Holy Mass with Pope John Paul II in his private chapel, but to also receive the Holy Eucharist from his hands. I emphasized with deep feelings that I wanted to see the Pope as just another priest giving out the Holy Eucharist.

Father Slavko, who was so instrumental in establishing the daily program for Medjugorje, was also in attendance as he had been a speaker at the conference. As I came off the stage, he approached me shaking his finger at me, but with a smile on his face. "I was going to give you a good scolding," he said as he reached me. "But when you said you saw the Holy Father as just another priest, I changed my mind!"

With that, Fr. Slavko gave me a big hug.

The point was this very holy priest thought I was bragging about my experience with the Pope, and then realized his error when I said he was just another priest. However, the phrase "Just another priest" really does not do justice to these men who give their life to Jesus to serve as His special servants in the priesthood.

Even a priest who becomes lost in the humanity of the world is still a priest. We should always treat them with respect and dignity.

. . . **and you will be hated by all for my name's sake. But he who endures to the end will be saved.**
—Matthew 10: 22.

Dear children! Love, pray and witness my presence to all those who are far away. By your witness and example, you can draw closer the hearts that are far from God and His grace. I am with you and intercede for each of you so that, with love and resoluteness, you may witness and encourage all those who are far from my Immaculate Heart. Thank you for having responded to my call.

—Message of April 25, 2017.

16

africa: the challenge

From the outdoor elevated wooden platform, I stared silently at the massive crowd of approximately 12,000 people as their welcoming applause came to an end. There was a collected sense of eagerness as they waited to hear what I had traveled so far to share with them about the Blessed Mother in Medjugorje.

Yet, I said nothing for several seconds. Then, taking my rosary in hand and holding it high above my head, I quietly walked back and forth across the platform. Slowly, the crowd caught on and they started holding their rosaries up as well. Suddenly, the crowd erupted into a loud and continuous cheer.

"I have come to Uganda to tell you about the apparitions of the Blessed Virgin Mary in the village of Medjugorje," I began as silence replaced the cheering, "In one of her messages, Our Lady has asked us to take our rosaries in our hands and let Satan know we belong to her!"

Joyful bedlam erupted. My heart raced and I felt as though I was floating. For the next hour, I spoke of the messages of Medjugorje and how they were transforming millions throughout the world. The massive crowd hung on every word, interrupting many times with applause. Clearly, it was an event dominated by the Holy Spirit.

Prior to my talk, a famous local healing priest known for his powerful gift had revved the crowd into frenzy, with many claimed healings among them. It was as though the flames of Pentecost were being generously distributed to everyone present. The reaction at the four following talks in Uganda was the same.

The tour of this openly corrupt and exploited African nation came about from meeting a man named Stephen during a Medjugorje pilgrimage several months earlier. He had asked me at that time if I would come to Uganda on a speaking tour. Of course, I said yes if it could be arranged. He would do that, he assured me, and would contact our office when ready.

Truthfully, I had forgotten about the offer to come to Uganda until months later when Stephen contacted our office and declared he was ready and had organized a tour.

It did not take long to realize that this unexpected 2014 trip to the African nations of Uganda and Rwanda—and a return with renowned fellow author and good friend Immaculee Ilibagiza to Rwanda in 2015 with 45 pilgrims—would become one of the greatest experiences of my mission. It would also be a tremendous challenge in Uganda to assist the overwhelmingly poorest of the poor I had ever encountered with desperately needed spiritual food as well as daily bread and clean water.

The African continent was not new territory for my mission; I had toured South Africa in the late nineties for more than 30 days giving dozens of talks. We are also able to set up a national charity to help severely physically sick children brought on by near starvation. However, I quickly discovered the trip to Uganda and Rwanda would become an even larger part of my mission.

Shortly after Stephen contacted us, we began to make travel arrangements for the speaking tour. My wife Judi quickly realized this trip needed to do more for the people of Uganda than just bring a message of conversion. We needed to bring practical help to these people who live in such poverty. We decided to not only bring much-needed gifts like clothes, toys and sandals, etc. Most importantly, we would also bring love. As such, we opened the trip to our monthly newsletter readers with an invitation to join us and soon we had 16 enthusiastic missionaries joining us, each with an extra suitcase full of provisions.

Judi mentioned to her friend, Immaculee Ilibagiza, who is from the country of Rwanda, that we would soon be leading a mission trip to Uganda. Immaculee casually suggested, "Well, you should add Rwanda and visit the apparition site of Kibeho, where Our Lady appeared. Rwanda is right next to Uganda."

Judi quickly accepted the suggestion as a no brainer, why come all that way to Africa and not visit an apparition site?

Having been a travel operator for ten years it was no problem for Judi to arrange and she soon had a two-week itinerary organized with one week in Uganda followed by a week in Rwanda. As an added bonus, about one month prior to departure, Immaculee and her husband Paul decided to join our venture for the week in Rwanda.

Of course, in life the best-laid plans can easily be disrupted. With everything organized and Judi in charge of all the group's travel plans with what I can only describe as an extremely complicated itinerary, Judi had a terrible golf cart accident and broke her neck! Despite this dramatic setback, she was still intent on joining us, but as the departure date came closer, reality set in and she decided she shouldn't come. I was left with the overwhelming responsibility of leading a mission trip through Africa while doing a speaking tour. Reluctantly, Judi would have to stay home with her mother, trusting the Holy Spirit would guide this trip for me!

uganda

Little did I know that after I departed for Uganda, Immaculee was texting Judi and encouraging her to fly directly to Rwanda to join her and Paul, who had already arrived in Kigali. "Wayne will be so surprised," she added. And of course, the "power of persuasion" worked and Judi left for two ten-hour flights, traveling alone and with a broken neck!

Meanwhile, in Uganda, everywhere our mission group visited, the various communities were thrilled to hear about Medjugorje. Many people were familiar with the apparitions at Kibeho and already had a strong love for Our Lady and the Holy Rosary. Despite having very little in the form of possessions, the people exuded a happiness that I can only put down to being filled with the Holy Spirit.

In one particular village we visited, the people lined the red, dusty road as we arrived, dancing and singing and filled with joy. We brought with us clothes and shoes for the children and rosaries. We had pre-arranged and paid for a feast to be cooked for the entire village of several hundred. This day will remain as one of the sweetest memories of my mission reminding me that this mission would take me to the far corners of the world and into the most remote locations.

However in Uganda, the worshippers taught me a powerful message as well. They showed me the real meaning of faith: the ability to have such intense trust in God, joy, happiness, love and gratitude to be alive, despite living in the worst of circumstances. These people remain in my heart long after I left.

Next stop Rwanda. We arrived in the early afternoon. As planned, our guide, driver and bus were awaiting us at the airport. Once loaded on the bus, we headed to a priest's retreat house in the capital city of Kigali for our one night stay before heading the next day to the apparition site of Kibeho.

As we disembarked the bus, grabbed our luggage and headed towards the retreat house, I saw something that I could not understand. Judi was with Immaculee and Paul, who suddenly appeared from behind a small wall and came to greet us. I was totally shocked! Surely, this was my mind playing tricks on me! But it wasn't; my wife was actually standing before me in the city of Kigali in Rwanda, Africa, complete with her huge, plastic hospital neck brace.

We finally settled down, after a highly emotional greeting, to a wonderful lunch and to catch up on our adventures. Immaculee then announced to the group that we had all been invited to a dinner dance in Kigali that evening and Jeannette Kagame, the First Lady of Rwanda, would also be there. What a treat it was for us on our first night in what we would soon discover to be a remarkable country filled with incredibly resilient and friendly people.

The next morning, we packed our belongings once again and headed to Kibeho. I observed during our four-hour drive how different the landscape was to that of Uganda. Rwanda is green and lush, filled with mountains and lakes. It is truly beautiful and a complete contrast to Uganda's flat, dry environment. The streets are cleaner in Rwanda and although one still sees signs of poverty, it is not like the abject poverty seen in Uganda.

The main difference affecting the lives of the people in the two countries is their leadership. Uganda suffers from a selfish and uncaring dictatorship and Rwanda has a wonderful, Christian president named Paul Kagame, who was the Tutsi leader who led his country to peace and ended the 1994 genocide. After being overwhelmingly elected as president, he declared that there would no longer be tribes of Hutus and Tutsies, all people were Rwandans from that moment on. As a result of this brilliant but dangerous policy, Rwanda is now one of the most progressive and peaceful countries in Africa.

at the shrine of kibeho

Our accommodations in the tiny community of Kibeho were somewhat similar to that of Kigali. We stayed with priests at a large retreat house. Dining together, we discussed the amazing apparitions of Our Lady that preceded the genocide in an effort by Heaven to prevent it. The Virgin, known as "Mother of the Word" in Kibeho, brought messages to teach the people to pray, forgive and live in peace. Sadly, they did not listen and act on Heaven's advice and Our Lady's prediction to one of the Kibeho visionaries came true. She said that *"a river of blood"* would flow across Rwanda unless the Rwandan people stopped harboring hatred and animosity for each other, and instead would need to turn their hearts with love and brotherly charity towards one another.

Not surprising, I had the same emotionally charged feelings for this shrine as I did for Medjugorje. They seemed to be a reflection of each other, with the apparitions of Medjugorje dating from June 1981 and Kibeho in late November 1981. The all-powerful underlying message echoing from both apparition sites is that God exists and that He loves us so much as to send His mother to rescue us from ourselves.

However, one major difference between Kibeho and other apparition sites I had studied is that Our Lady seemed to be more personal with the Kibeho visionaries, dancing and singing with them at times. The visionaries often referred to Our Lady as "darling" and other equally familiar names.

My greatest time in Kibeho was sitting in front of the location of the former platform where most of the apparitions occurred. I spent hours there praying; feeling the powerful presence of the Blessed Virgin surrounding me.

During our visit, the group got to spend time with Nathalie Mkamazimpaka, one of the Kibeho visionaries. Now a nun, she has remained at the Kibeho shrine since the beginning of the apparitions, leaving only during the genocide at the bishop's request. Our Lady had invited her to stay there and pray. Nathalie took the time to share her experiences with us. A very quiet and shy lady, I found Nathalie's whole demeanor towards being a visionary very similar to that of the Medjugorje visionaries.

We returned to Kigali a couple of nights before our flight home. Making the best of our final few days in Rwanda, we finally left the country with melancholy, knowing we would soon return.

The following November, about one year after our first visit, we did return to celebrate the feast of our Lady of Kibeho! As our bus slowly chugged along towards Kibeho, we saw hundreds of people walking down the sides of the road towards the tiny community. They were carrying with them bags of rice and huge yellow water containers. Immaculee explained that many of these people walked from all over Rwanda and also from Uganda, Burundi, Kenya, Congo and Tanzania for the feast, sometimes taking several weeks to arrive. Each evening they would cook rice to eat and sleep on the side of the road.

On the day of the feast, we arrived at the shrine to see tens of thousands of people sitting in groups all around us. A touch of guilt seeped in as we arrived on a comfortable bus knowing so many of these people had walked miles to be here. More guilt came as the organizers had arranged seats at the front of the outdoor sanctuary for our group while everybody else had to sit on the ground or stand.

The four-hour mass was truly outstanding! With the bishop as the main celebrant and about 35 priests concelebrating, this was truly a mass of celebration. With singing and dancing at every opportunity, the joy was contagious. The gifts brought to the altar, consisted of bananas and potatoes, baskets and flowers, etc. People brought what they had to give. I had never seen such a display of giving during a mass.

Upon arriving home after these visits to Africa, it was difficult to adjust to life back in the United States. The feelings of helplessness flowed close to the surface after seeing such poverty in Uganda and Rwanda. Our desire to do something more to help the people of Uganda was soon quenched. While on Facebook one morning, Judi, saw a post by a Ugandan acquaintance of one of our missionaries who had traveled with us. The post was made by Kasozi Moses, a man I had briefly met while in Uganda.

Moses works for Life Teen, an international youth ministry within the Catholic Church. The post he shared was written by Moses' friend, a priest who described people dying of starvation in the far northeastern corner of Uganda in the region of Karamoja where he was stationed. The area had not seen rain in a year and many of the priest's parishioners were slowly dying of hunger, literally dropping like flies.

We immediately established contact with Moses and promised him we would do all we could to feed these desperate people. We opened a new charity titled, "Feed My Children," and began pleading for donations. Very soon we were steadily sending money for the local priest to buy food and feed the people. Within a short time period, we were feeding several thousand people a day. It did not take long for us to realize we were the only charitable organization assisting these people—no government or International Red Cross or any other group—just us!

In July 2017, we bought materials and services to construct our first water well in the community of Apetao, which serves about 400 families and their livestock. In August 2017, we received enough donations to being constructing a second well. With the continued help of kind donors, we hope to build another three wells over the next couple of years while continuing our food program.

In addition to this work, we have gone on to head up a charity for Immaculee to rebuild the "Mere du Verbe" school in Kibeho, where Our Lady first appeared. The 640 girls who board at the school live in very poor conditions as the school is in a state of disrepair. With the student's parent's barely able to afford their child's schooling, the children's medical needs, food and clothes are almost non-existent. The children live well below healthy living standards. Immaculee, along with our charity, "Servants of Our Lady of Kibeho," has now raised enough money for the school to be completely rebuilt, which in August 2017 has just begun. Now, we are raising money to sponsor the children who board at the school and various other schools in Rwanda through our charity titled, "Immaculee's Student Sponsorship Program."

God places people and situations in front of us and as Christians it is up to us to say "Yes" and help. We are the hands and feet of Christ on earth and with prayer and some determination it is amazing what we can accomplish.

The charities we have discussed changed people's lives and in some cases, saved their lives. They came into existence from saying "yes", to visiting the African countries of Uganda and Rwanda—and from Judi's close friendship with Immaculee. We could never have foreseen this wonderful grace. Each of us is given gifts to work in God's army. What an incredible joy it has been to open and use these gifts.

Pope Francis: **"Nothing is impossible if we turn to God in prayer. Everyone can be an artisan of peace!**

Commentary: We learn over time as followers of Christ that God offers us what we need in the way of Holy Spirit gifts to successfully carry out His plans of our personal spiritual mission. I was very much reminded of this fact with our travel to Uganda and Rwanda in Africa.

We all have a mission to fulfill during our time on earth. Some missions are huge while others may be small and essentially viewed as less important. Nothing could be further from the truth. It is God alone who decides the level of mission accomplishment for each of us. The bottom line of all missions is reaching the reward of eternal life.

It is through true humility and obedience, that I feel each mission is measured by God. The difficult part is properly discerning the what, when and where of receiving and using the gifts to accomplish our personal mission. There are so many memories of Medjugorje pilgrims asking on their return home in a most sincere way: "Just what is it that God wants from me? Where do I start? When and what is it that I am supposed to do to accomplish His mission?" The general answer to these questions can most easily be explained by our own personal spiritual conversion experiences.

I knew in the early days of my personal mission that I was to travel the world spreading the Medjugorje messages. But there was more. After much difficulty in attempting to understand, I was also given the Holy Spirit gift of healing prayer as I wrote about in an earlier chapter. There is no way to describe how I knew I had it; it was just there, within me.

Therefore, the bottom line is this: Don't waste your precious time on earth wondering about what you are to do to accomplish your Godly mission. Seek your mission through prayer and then just do it with the applications of humility and obedience. I have since marveled over the nearly 33 years of my mission on how God uses us despite our struggles to live daily life according to His general plan of salvation.

But if anyone has the world's goods and sees his brother in need, yet closes his heart against him, how does God's love abide in him? Little children, let us not love in word or speech but in deed and in truth. By this we shall know that we are of the truth, and reassure our hearts before him.

—1 John 3: 17-19.

Dear children! In this time of grace, I am calling all of you to conversion. Little children, you love little and pray even less. You are lost and do not know what your goal is. Take the cross, look at Jesus and follow Him. He gives Himself to you to the death on the cross, because He loves you. Little children, I am calling you: return to prayer with the heart so as to find hope and the meaning of your existence, in prayer. I am with you and am praying for you. Thank you for having responded to my call.

—February 25, 2016.

17

lessons from the mother

An important fact we should all keep in mind concerning the Blessed Virgin Mary and her apparitions over the centuries is that she is a human mother chosen before time to be our spiritual mother; as so, she is always teaching us lessons on how to become good children of God.

The lessons of the mother are constant. If the individual striving to be a child of God wishes to accomplish the goal, then he or she needs to be attuned to every word she gives us through the public monthly messages given through the visionaries Marija and Mirjana. The messages received by Marija on the 25th day of each month are for all of humanity. Those directed to Mirjana on the second day of the month are primarily but not exclusively for those who have not yet discovered the love of God. The bottom line is all of the messages given by the Blessed Virgin are lessons from the Mother!

The primary example of Our Lady's human motherhood starts with the lessons to the Medjugorje visionaries in the early weeks of the apparitions. She always came in radiant happiness. She was quick to compliment the visionaries for following her teachings, but she was just as quick to point out areas that needed improvement! Visionary Marija is a good example. She is quiet, kind and always willing to help others. Yet, the Blessed Mother gently chastised her on more than one occasion for talking in church during Holy Mass and not paying attention.

My "initial" lesson from the Mother came shortly after she had placed the original message in my heart. It has stayed with me throughout the years of travel. It was simply about making a choice, as you will see in the following story.

the choice . . .

Sitting comfortably in my office a few days after the completion of the sale of my four newspapers, I began thinking about what I could do to keep myself in the business world. The building was near empty now that the newspapers had been sold. All we had left was the printing business and that would be gone as soon as we could find a buyer. Thus, the only employees left was my secretary and two crewmen who ran the printing press.

It was approximately eight months after the Blessed Virgin Mary had spoken to my heart, asking me to spread her Medjugorje messages throughout the world. *Of course, I will do what the Blessed Virgin is asking of me,* I thought, *but I could also serve as a business consultant or open an advertising agency . . .*

The possibilities were endless. I was certain I could do both. One thing was for sure, I wanted to continue writing. I actually added a clause in the sales contract of my newspapers that I would write a weekly column for the papers. The buyer agreed and we set a fee of $25 for each column I wrote. Obviously, it wasn't about the money; it was about pure ego to stay in the public eye.

As I sat there thinking of all the possibilities, I suddenly felt the Blessed Virgin's presence in my heart. She spoke gently but firmly as she said: *My son, if you do not want to do this* (mission), *someone else will!*

I sat there for a few moments somewhat in shock. Then, the meaning of her words registered and I jumped to my feet and nearly shouted: "Yes, dear Mother, yes, I want to do this!"

There was no further response from the Blessed Virgin. Suddenly, I felt embarrassed. What was I thinking? There would not be future involvement in the business world for me; the mission would take all of my time from that moment on.

I later realized that in order to serve Jesus in His Mother, it would definitely be a full-time job. It was a lesson from the Mother I would never forget.

Visionary Ivanka: **"This feeling** [of seeing the Blessed Virgin daily] **cannot possibly be put in words, for there are no words to describe it. It is something special, a special peace, satisfaction, a joy that cannot be experienced with any man, but only with Our Lady."**

"how can you say no?"

I was up in time to pack for a six-hour automobile journey to a city called Turon, our first stop in Poland. We would be there for an hour-long radio show on a station called Radio Maria.

Exhausted and suffering a mild letdown after riding the high of the Russian tour, I was grateful the radio show was the only venue scheduled for the day and then hoped for time alone at the hotel. I asked again anyway. "Are you sure the radio show is all that we have to do tonight?"

"Yes, and then you will be free to rest until the next day." Zofia had taken note of my mood and chose to agree to the quiet time I needed to rejuvenate the mind and spirit. The pensive mood of the journey was broken only by prayers of the rosary.

We arrived in Turon, but after searching and asking directions, we could not locate the building that housed the radio station. Irritation was beginning to set in. Zofia glanced at her watch. "Don't worry, we will find it; we still have a little time before the show."

After several more inquiries, we arrived at a small wooden building. "This is the radio station?" I asked, expecting something more professional.

We were greeted by an ebullient, bouncy, happy priest who was the founder of Radio Maria. He escorted us, along with a local translator, to a small kitchen in the basement of the building, seating us at a table covered with sandwiches and drinks. "Zofia, I really don't want to eat now so if you could explain to the priest that I was hoping for a good meal in peace at the hotel after the radio show."

Zofia gave me the "look". "Please, they are so excited about you being here, can you eat just a little?"

Reluctantly, I took a sandwich. While we ate, the priest quickly told the history of the station, how he felt called to start it at the request of Our Lady. "And you know," Zofia interjected, "the station went on the air December 8, 1991, the same day you entered the church, and the same day I asked you to come back to Poland as a birthday gift for Our Blessed Mother . . ."

I nodded in acknowledgement with a wane smile. Zofia was doing all she could to change my dour mood.

The show began as I briefly told my story of learning about Medjugorje, and then details of her messages to the world. That was followed by call-in questions. From the beginning, my impatience grew as the translator was slow and unsure of himself. During a short break, I whispered to Zofia, "Listen, this guy doesn't know how to translate; why don't you take over, or at least jump in and help?"

Zofia paused, sighed and turned to me. There was that look again. "He will do okay. He just needs a little more time to adjust."

But time didn't help and soon Zofia was forced to assist him. The show was finally over. "Thank goodness, that's done," I said shaking my head. "I can't wait to get to the hotel and just relax."

Again, Zofia gave me her look, this time with some apprehension. "I know you are tired, but Father insists we accompany him to Mass. They are going to broadcast it live and there are thousands who will be listening. Please, just be patient and say yes."

"No way, Zofia! Tell him thank you for asking but we went to Mass this morning and I am very tired after the long day."

"But the listeners are expecting you to make a few comments about Medjugorje after the Mass. It has already been announced. And . . . he has made plans to take us to dinner afterwards."

I struggled to restrain my anger, knowing this priest would not give up. "Okay, okay. Tell him I'll go to Mass and do the broadcast—but no dinner!"

Zofia was almost afraid to continue. With a nervous little laugh, she added, "Oh, my, I know this is difficult for you but he wants you to return after dinner to the station to take caller's questions for two hours." The last words become slower and quieter as she turned her hands up in resignation at being caught in the middle.

I begin shaking my head furiously. "No, no! Can't you tell him I need the rest?"

Zofia looked up. "Please—for Our Lady?"

That did me in. Slumping in the chair and staring at the wall, I let out a deep, tired sigh. "Alright Zofia, I give up. But I'm only coming back for half an hour of questions—no more!"

Zofia smiled lightly and gave me a reassuring pat as she related my words to the priest. He clapped his hands excitedly and hustled everyone off to the waiting automobiles.

I excused myself to recompose in the washroom. The second I closed the door, I heard Our Lady's voice, clearly and resonantly: *How can you say no, when you know it is I who is asking?*

Startled and filled with discernment that I was saying no to her "birthday gift," I dropped to my knees. "Oh Blessed Mary, I'm sorry . . ."

Sliding in the back seat next to Zofia, I mumbled, "I'm sorry for being so rude. Please tell the priest I'll do whatever he wishes." Later, I told her of Our Lady's message in the washroom.

Of course, it was a spirit-filled evening. The Mass was magnificent, the talk uniquely inspired. And the dinner was delicious. We returned to Radio Maria for more than two hours of questions.

At a little past midnight, I sank into my hotel bed, spent-and happily humbled.

Our Lady to the six visionaries in June 1981: *I invite you. I need you. I chose you. You are important!*

he is my brother

Traveling to Medjugorje had changed after the publication of my first book, "Medjugorje: The Message." I was no longer an anonymous pilgrim.

Everywhere I went people wanted to stop me and tell their conversion stories and how the book had brought them to conversion. It took me back to an earlier pilgrimage to the village after the articles I had written on the apparitions were published in an eight-page tabloid. I was surprised to have been recognized and approached by a small group of pilgrims from California. "Are you Wayne Weible, the Protestant who wrote about the apparitions?" one of the group asked.

Yes, I had responded and then quickly excused myself and hastily entered Saint James Church and made my way to the beautiful statue of the Blessed Virgin in the far-right corner. *Blessed Mother, I don't want all of this attention!* I prayed silently. I then asked a rather strange question of her: *Dear Mother, please help me; maybe if I could just see you for a moment . . .?*

The Virgin's answer was immediate and clear: ***My son, if you wish to see me, go out to the people and do what you promised to do!***

I felt about two inches tall and was totally embarrassed. Quickly composing myself, I left the church and found the California group, apologized for being so abrupt with them and telling them I would be glad to answer any of their questions.

It was another lesson learned—but soon forgotten. Now, on this Medjugorje pilgrimage two years later I just wanted to be a pilgrim—to find a place where I could pray in peace. That evening I found it. The outside altar area was just in the beginning stages of construction. The altar was in place but the installing of seating was just underway. I went to the last row of newly installed benches and took a seat thinking *this is the perfect spot!*

There was no one in the area with the exception of four people seated in the very front row. I noticed immediately that one of the four, a young man, was ill and the others were tending to him. As I settled in and joined the praying of the rosary, I suddenly felt the presence of the Blessed Mother in my heart as she said, ***You should go and pray over that young man.***

Incredibly, I closed my eyes tightly so as not to see the little group and responded: *I'll just pray for him right here.* The second I thought it, I knew it was the wrong answer. I tried hard to concentrate on the rosary, ignoring the feeling of the presence of Our Lady. Suddenly, I felt a tap on my shoulder. I opened my eyes and saw that it was one of the women who was with the sick man. "Excuse me for bothering you and interrupting your prayer," she began, "but are you Wayne Weible?

I flinched and felt the words of the Blessed Virgin as though they were suddenly branded on my soul. I knew in advance what the lady would ask me. "Yes, I am, how can I help you?"

"Well, that's my brother up there and he's very sick." She then broke into tears. "He has AIDS and my mother and I brought him and his partner here hoping for a healing. Would you come and pray over him?"

At this point, there was definitely no Holy Spirit healing power within me. "Look, I'm terribly sorry but I can't pray over him tonight for reasons I can't explain. But if you come here tomorrow evening at the same time, I will be glad to pray over him."

The young woman smiled through her tears and agreed they would return the next evening, thanking me profusely as she left. I felt ashamed. "Blessed Mother, I am so sorry; please forgive me for being so selfish . . ."

The following evening, I met the other members of the group. We talked for a long time. I explained to the two men who had been together for 17 years the need for a full confession. It was then I learned the man who was sick, Sean, was a Catholic while his partner, Jim, was Protestant and had no idea about confession (not real names). He simply was there hoping for a healing for his partner. I then placed my arms around them and prayed for total healing for both of them.

As a new year began, I was off on my first mission trip of the year. Just before leaving the house I had grabbed a stack of mail that had been accumulating over the holidays. I planned to go through them during the flight to see which ones to answer directly. After reading several letters I picked up the next one and began reading it. It started out:

"Dear Mr. Weible, this is Sean's mother and you prayed over him along with his partner in Medjugorje last August. I wanted to tell you that Sean passed away in September. He died in great peace having received the last rites at our church. We plan to take Jim into our home and take care of him as he is also now getting sick . . ."

I said a prayer for the repose of Sean's soul and then turned the envelope over to copy the address so that I could respond to Sean's mother. I was shocked to see that they lived in Little River, South Carolina, a small community about 17 miles from my home.

God had brought us together 4,700 miles from our homes for me to pray over Sean and his partner Jim. It was another lesson never to be forgotten.

God is good.

Visionary Marija: **"Our Lady always asks us to live her messages. She doesn't want us to depend on them, but she calls us to be joyful bearers of her words and to be good Christians."**

baptists and catholics

By the time I arrived in Greenville, Mississippi, I was as ill as I had been in years. It was a combination of traveling from hot to cold climates—and mental exhaustion.

The sickness was so overwhelming that I stayed in bed all day, too weak to do anything that required moving. I would get up only to prepare for the evening's talk. All other attached events scheduled for the daytime had to be cancelled. Strangely, while hardly able to even kneel for the rosary before each evening's talk, I would suddenly feel fine, give the talk and within half an hour be sick again.

On the last day of the tour, I had had it. I was ready to cancel the last talk and head home. One of the ladies who had arranged the Mississippi schedule of talks was a nurse and had been taking excellent care of me. I couldn't help but wonder if Our Lady had arranged this knowing that I would be ill.

I told her of my desire to just cancel the talk for this evening. "Well, she replied, we understand if you have to cancel tonight's talk, but it's a real shame because you were to speak in the largest Baptist church in Greenville, Mississippi, which is the only place big enough to hold the expected crowd."

That did it—and I think she knew it would work! I slowly shook my head. "Speaking to Baptists and Catholics in the same place? I can't pass that up! We've stuck it out this long; just give me something to get me though the day!"

Once again, the minute we arrived at the Baptist church, I felt my strength return. There was no way we could have missed this opportunity. It was an enormous structure that stood out in size alone, while indicating the predominance of the Baptist faith in this area. In hindsight, it was the perfect place to again stress to the crowd that the mother of Jesus came to Medjugorje for all of us.

The evening was a huge success. Catholics mingled with Baptists and everyone in attendance seemed to be sincerely touched. As we prepared to leave, I thanked the Baptist minister for opening his church to the message of Medjugorje. The look on his face indicated he wasn't quite sure about what had transpired in his church, but shaking his head he said, "This, of course is all new to me, but I certainly am impressed with your sincerity and the response of the people, especially those of our Baptist congregation."

I returned to the motel room and within minutes, the illness was back! Smiling through the misery I softly said: "Dear Mother, forgive me for wanting to cancel this evening's talk." The lesson was clear as to who was in charge, regardless of how her chosen "son" felt.

Cardinal Christoph Schoenborn: **"If I was an opponent of Medjugorje, I'd have to close down my seminary since almost all of the candidates have received their call to the priesthood through Medjugorje!"**

another lesson from the mother

In the late nineties, I was working on getting the pastor of our local church to join me on pilgrimage to Medjugorje but I was making little progress. Every year this priest would lead a group to Rome, which was a good source of extra income.

One day as I again made my pitch for him to join us on a pilgrimage, he countered with a compromise: If I would join his annual trip to Rome, he would consider coming to Medjugorje with me. Reluctantly, I accepted. My reluctance was due to having been to Rome many times—plus the exorbitant cost of my pastor's tour. However, if it would get him to Medjugorje...

I found myself in Rome with my pastor's group, a wonderful collection of what I would call devout Catholics, many of whom I knew personally. However, I was not at peace, nor was I enjoying this holy city as I had so many times in the past.

For a number of years, I would come directly to Rome after leading a pilgrimage to Medjugorje. It was a good place to unwind by spending hours in the Vatican, attending Mass and wandering around the center of the Catholic Faith. Being an avid runner, I would run the streets surrounding the Vatican and along the river in the early mornings and late afternoons. I had also visited just about every important site there; so, for me, this very expensive excursion was without real purpose or inspiration.

The time spent in the evenings with the others was the best part of the trip. And then came a special grace. My pastor announced at dinner just two days before our departure for home that we had received tickets to a limited special tour. We would take what is known as the Scavi Tour, which is a visit to the necropolis (Tomb of the dead) underneath the Basilica, where the tomb of St. Peter is located.

Tickets for this exclusive tour are more difficult to obtain than those of a top rock star, and getting through the Vatican bureaucracy took a Houdini act.

Suddenly I was excited to be in Rome. It wasn't the exclusivity of the Scavi tour that had me excited; it was the opportunity to visit Saint Peter's tomb. I suddenly knew deep within my soul that this event is why I was on this tour. It was another reminder that with God there are no coincidences; everything in our life is by plan and design.

The next day we assembled in groups of 12, which was the limit of people allowed in each tour below because of the oxygen effect on the ancient tombs. A trained guide, who made it clear from the beginning that no pictures could be taken, accompanied each group. The tour itself would take about one and a half hours.

Our tour guide explained to us during the tour that the tomb of the first Pontiff had been discovered along with the catacombs beneath St. Peter's Basilica in the 1940s (around the time of World War II) when the Vatican commissioned excavations to be carried out there before Pope Pius IX was set to be buried in the space. While there was speculation over the centuries that it was the final resting place of St. Peter, it was countered by skeptics that there wasn't much down there. What archaeologists found however, was a burial ground dating all the way back to the fourth century. They found sketches of the temple of Emperor Constantine who had ruled at that time and a spot of ancient graffiti that translated as *Peter is here.*

It was one of the most awe-inspiring tours I have ever taken anywhere, well worth the entire cost of the trip. Amazingly, in our little group of twelve there were three of us who were converts through the apparitions at Medjugorje. At each stop where the guide would explain what we were seeing, all three of us were like New York City tourists gaping up at each high-rise building-except we were seeing Church history. We were all filled with deep emotion when we arrived near the end of the tour at the tomb of Saint Peter. As we stood approximately ten feet away from Saint Peter's burial plot, all three of us who were converts to Catholicism broke into tears—I mean sobbing tears.

The others in our group just stared at us, dry-eyed and wondering what had set us off. Later, we explained to them that for us, this was pure Shangri-La. This was the burial site of the first pope, the leader of the disciples, the rock on which Jesus would build His Church. To top it off, our guide had explained that the tomb of St. Peter was directly below the main altar of the Basilica.

Again, with God there are no coincidences.

Pope John Paul II to Mirjana during a private meeting: **"Take good care of Medjugorje, Mirjana. Medjugorje is the hope of the world!"**

the obnoxious priest

The following year, as I prepared to return to Medjugorje, I still had only one remaining problem: I did not have a Catholic priest to go with our pilgrimage as a spiritual guide. An opportunity to solve this concern was presented a few days later when I received a telephone call from a Medjugorje friend who lived in Wilmington, North Carolina. Karen Stoffel had been to Medjugorje, and her mission on returning was to try to get the priests in Wilmington involved.

Karen was determined to "convert" these priests to belief in the apparitions. She was calling to ask me a favor: would I be willing to come to a luncheon at her home to speak to these priests about my experiences? "They're very reluctant when I try to tell them about my trip, but you being a Protestant, I think they'll listen!"

Karen was ecstatic when I said I would come with the hope that possibly one or more of them would accept my invitation to join our October pilgrimage. "That would be incredible," she gushed, "if one of them actually went there, I know it would influence the rest!"

A few days later I was sitting in Karen's home assessing the possibilities of which of the five priests she had invited would actually accept the invitation to come with me to Medjugorje. "There is only one that I'm absolutely sure won't accept," she added as we finished discussing each priest. "That's Father Jim Watters. He's into some strange things—New Age things, and he doesn't believe in Medjugorje. The only reason he's coming to the luncheon is because I assist him at his church periodically—plus it's a free lunch!"

Soon there was a knock at the door; Karen, busy in the kitchen preparing the meal, asked if I would answer it. I opened the door to see a huge man standing there. He was at least six feet, four inches and close to 270 pounds. "Hey, how are ya?" he said in a fast-talking New York accent as he mangled my hand. "You must be the guy involved in the apparition thing. Gotta tell ya right off—I don't believe!" With that he clapped me on the back, let out a loud laugh and yelled, "Okay Karen, I'm here, where's the food!"

Karen's right, I thought, *Priest or no priest, this guy's definitely not going!*

After the others arrived, I uttered a silent prayer to Our Lady asking that one of them might say yes. Any of them, that is, except Father Jim Watters!

As we sat over coffee following the lunch, I began speaking about Medjugorje and answering their few questions. After a noticeable hesitancy, I decided to make my move. "I understand your caution concerning such things as apparitions," I began, "but I will be leading a pilgrimage to Medjugorje in several weeks. It might be more acceptable if one or more of you actually came with me to see for yourself. Then you could relate your feelings and findings to the others."

"So" I hesitated a moment and smiled, "I'm inviting each of you to come with me on this pilgrimage as a spiritual guide."

There was silence before one of the priests thanked me for the "generous offer" but politely declined, citing a busy schedule. Soon the rest chimed in with similar excuses.

And then Father Watters: "Well, hey, that's a great offer! I tell you what—I'll go! It should be interesting!"

Karen and the other priests were as stunned as I was. Later, as he was leaving, Father Watters pulled me aside. "Look, since the others declined to go, how about taking a priest-friend of mine from Florida? He's a monsignor; just tell us what we need and where to be and I'll take care of the rest!"

My answer was slow in coming. *How did this happen?* I wondered. "That's fine Father, just give me the details and I'll work it out."

I drove home in a stupor. This was *not* at all what I had expected. I was stuck with this odd priest and now his friend as well! "That's great," I muttered as I pulled onto the highway heading home, "it's going to be some trip—we have a Lutheran pastor, a Baptist preacher—and now the most obnoxious priest I've ever met!"

Several weeks later, the majority of the people making up our pilgrimage gathered at O Hare International Airport in Chicago. Father Jim Watters strode over to where I was and ignoring the two men I was talking to, grabbed my arm, pulling me to where a white-haired, older priest was waiting. "This is my friend from Florida, Monsignor Carter."

I was mildly surprised. The monsignor was an elderly man who spoke in a humble, quiet manner just the opposite of Father Watters. Within minutes, Father Watters interrupted, "Look, I need a few favors; how 'bout getting me a seat in the front of the plane with some legroom? And could you arrange a private room for us in Medjugorje?"

The list of requests continued. My only consolation was that at least he was wearing his priest's collar, which turned out to be my saving grace. Before I could answer his requests a woman from our group came over and grabbed *him* by the arm. "Father, I have to talk to you—now!"

Try as he might, Father Jim could not persuade the woman to wait until we arrived in Medjugorje. She wanted him to hear her confession before we left. Just as we began boarding, Father Jim returned, shaken and pale. "That's the most difficult—and beautiful—confession I have ever heard!" There was a noticeable change in his demeanor. Hours after takeoff, I saw Father Jim sitting next to the Monsignor, his long legs cramped against the seat. He was unusually quiet, remaining that way throughout the flight.

As is the case so many times concerning Medjugorje, conversion began to slowly occur within Father Jim Watters. I was surprised the next day to see Father Jim on the altar for the Holy Mass, and was even more surprised when he came to the podium to do the first reading. The often loud and abrasive manner was gone and in its place, I heard a soft reverent voice slowly reading the Scripture.

Later that afternoon as our pilgrimage group was walking across the fields, Father Jim caught up with me. "Hey Wayne, I'm still not sure I believe in these apparitions but one thing is for sure; the Holy Spirit is definitely at work here. It's a special place and—well, I just want to thank you for bringing me here."

I was dumbounded. Suddenly, the most obnoxious priest I had ever met was changing right before my eyes! Once again, I was learning a lesson from the Mother the hard way. Would I ever learn to just trust the plans of Heaven?

Pope John Paul II: **"Let the people go to Medjugorje if they convert, pray, confess, do penance and fast!"**

the "new" father jim

As for Father Watters, he now fully believed Mary was appearing in Medjugorje, he told me by telephone several weeks after our return home. He was "newly born again of the Spirit". Fasting twice a week, he had already lost 15 pounds. He was now hard at work on a return trip to Medjugorje in several months, with a chartered plane containing 165 pilgrims, the bishop from his diocese, and a television news crew.

I received a telephone call from Father Jim shortly after his return from his second trip to Medjugorje asking me to come to his parish in Wilmington to give talks on Medjugorje during the coming weekend Masses. He was sure that my coming would help in recruiting others from his area to go to Medjugorje.

"You mean *this* coming weekend? I asked.

"Yeah, this weekend. I've already announced that you'd probably be here."

"Okay, okay," I laughed, "I guess I'd better come since you've already announced it!" I smiled, shaking my head and thought *some things never change!*

However, my somewhat eccentric priest had very much changed. He had undergone a deeply spiritual conversion through his trip to Medjugorje, but his personality was still the same. The fact that it had not changed brought to mind an important spiritual lesson for people to understand. God gives us a personality, which makes us unique from others. No one else is exactly like us. Our personality is an outward reflection of who we are. Spiritual change does not mean personality change, just a rearrangement of priorities.

It was good to see Father Jim again. He was still losing weight due to his now fasting twice a week. "And I've also cut out almost all TV time," he related as we drove to the rectory. "Boy, I'm glad you agreed to come!"

I smiled at the remarkable change of opinion I had experienced with Father Jim since our first meeting. Looking over at my now good friend I said, "So am I, Father, so am I!"

The lessons from the Mother did not stop as I took my seat on the front pew of the church where I would speak after Mass. I noticed a woman sitting on the opposite end. She was wearing a bright red blouse and shorts, chewing gum and chatting happily with those around her. I shook my head as I knelt for prayers, hoping that maybe my talk this evening might instill in this lady a little more reverence and respect for the Mass.

It was a good evening. Many of the parishioners thanked me for having taken Father Jim to Medjugorje. As we drove to the rectory afterwards I noticed that he was unusually quiet. Trying to break the mood, I said, "You know, your people are really happy with you; there's a strong spiritual wave building here."

"Yeah, it's great, but I have to tell you a fantastic story about one of my former parishioners, whom I hope will be going with us when we return."

Father Jim paused a moment. "This is a really an unbelievable story. I went into a restaurant last week and saw this gal who used to be in my parish a couple of years ago. She was sitting alone in a corner. She had moved away from here and I was surprised to see her after such a long absence.

"Well, we talked for a while catching up on things when suddenly she asks me if I could sit down with her for a few minutes and she begins to tell me about how she's now divorced, lost her job—her whole life's a big mess."

Father Jim paused again and then suddenly pulled the car to a stop at the side of the road. "The thing is," he continued now turning and facing me directly, "She suddenly tells me straight out that she plans to commit suicide! She says it with a real calmness that convinces me she means it."

Father Jim slowly shook his head. "Wayne, I spent the next two hours talking to that woman, telling her about Medjugorje and all and the changes it created in me. I made her promise me she wouldn't do anything drastic until we could talk some more. The bottom line is, we met a couple more times, she started coming to Mass, and she was there tonight to listen to you. She was sitting there on the front row. Isn't that something?"

"Yes, that really is something!" I answered, realizing that Father Jim was talking about the woman in the red blouse and shorts that was chewing gum, laughing and talking to everyone around her. It was the woman I had judged so quickly. The clothes and talking suddenly amounted to nothing in comparison with the fact that if this converted priest hadn't taken the time to talk to her, she might have taken her own life. I felt terribly small because of my quick judgment of her, and told Father Jim of my feeling at the time.

a priest's confession

There was long silence as Father Jim sat there staring at me. "Wayne, I have to tell you something else," he finally said in a low voice. I had never seen him so serious. "Before I went with you to Medjugorje—I had no real faith. Before Medjugorje, I'd never taken the time to talk that long to someone like that woman."

I was stunned. "Father, maybe you ..."

He held up his hand. "No, let me finish; I've been a priest for 22 years. Do you have any idea what it's like to stand at that altar day after day, holding up the gifts of the Blessed Sacrament and not really believing in the real presence of Jesus?"

"Father, maybe your faith had just diminished." I didn't know what else to say, embarrassed by this sudden confession from a priest.

"No!" Fr. Jim shouted, hitting the dash of the car hard with his hand. "I mean *I had no faith!*

We talked long into the night. The next morning, I left for the short drive home, vowing that from now on, I would pray extra hard, every day, for every priest, nun, religious and other clergy and I would work hard not to judge others. I thanked the Blessed Mother for another valuable lesson.

Several months later, Father Jim was in a horrific automobile accident that seriously damaged his brain. He could no longer carry out his priestly duties and sadly did not even remember his life changing pilgrimage to Medjugorje. He died a little more than a year later of apparently choking on a bone in a restaurant.

There is no doubt in my mind that Satan had struck this converted priest who had slipped his grasp. There is also no doubt that Father Jim Watters is a true martyr and a saint.

But the fruit of the Spirit is love, joy, peace, patience, kindness, goodness, faithfulness, gentleness, self-control; against such there is no law. And those who belong to Christ Jesus have crucified the flesh with its passions and desires. If we live by the Spirit, let us also walk by the Spirit.

—Galatians 5: 22-25.

Little children, do not forget that your life is fleeting like a spring flower, which today is wondrously beautiful but tomorrow has vanished.

Therefore, pray in such a way that your prayer, your surrender to God, may become like a road sign. That way, your witness will not only have value for yourselves but for all eternity.

—Message of January 25, 1988.

18

witness

The witness of faith by individuals is the most powerful use of the gifts of the Holy Spirit. We have expressed that in the pages of this book. God offers us the opportunity to accept the gifts and we can accept or reject them based on our free will, which is the greatest of the gifts.

The following witness in this final chapter bears full truth in acceptance of the gifts. It concerns acceptance of the most difficult of crosses, and to do so with humility and obedience—and eventually, joy.

War is the full presence of Satan and the total absence of God. Satan always comes where the Blessed Virgin Mary is sent to bring God's peace and Medjugorje is no exception. He comes to destroy that peace. He came to Bosnia-Hercegovina with the sole intent of destroying the fountain of grace pouring forth from the tiny village of Medjugorje.

Neither ethnic differences nor opposing religions caused the abyss of darkness that was the evil war, which raged throughout former Yugoslavia from August 1991 through the late months of 1995; they were just the tools. Like all wars, this conflict grew from the hell-inspired contest of greed, power and pride. It was simply another chapter in an endless story of evil, intent on destroying God's creation.

Yet, God creates light where there is only darkness. He brings forth good seed from utter desolation and hopelessness. Out of the atrocity-filled conflict comes a bitter account of a young nun who was viciously raped by a Serbian insurgent and became pregnant. She chose to have the child and to raise him even though she knew it might cost her dearly in having to leave the convent.

The witness is given in the words of the nun by way of a letter written to the superior of her convent. It is edited only for clarity and to protect the identity of the nun and her order. It states all that is necessary to describe the full inhumanity of war. It is also the perfect response to the messages of Medjugorje.

The content of the letter so bravely stated by the victim also serves a far greater purpose: It completely obliterates all debate for justifying the horror of abortion. It ends the argument with an honest witness of a *mother* who in the throes of her greatest trial, gives full surrender to the will of God.

Here is the letter as it was written by the victim nun to her mother superior. It completely relates the Supreme Sacrifice of a human mother in imitation of that of Jesus.

Dear Mother,

I am one of the novices who was raped by the militant Serbs. I am writing to you in regard to what happened to my sisters and me.

Permit me not to give you any details. It was an atrocious experience, incommunicable except to God, under whose will I placed myself during my consecration to Him as I made my vows. My tragedy is not only the humiliation I was subjected to as a woman, or the irreparable offense against my choice of existence and to my vocation, but the difficulty of inscribing deep in my faith, an event, which is

certainly part of the mysterious will of the One I still consider to be my Divine Spouse.

Only a few days before, I had read a dialogue of the Carmelites of Bernanos, and the thought had come to me to ask our Lord to let me die a martyr. He took me at my word.

I find myself today in an obscure interior anguish. They have destroyed my life's plan, which I had considered permanent; now, they have traced another, which I have not yet succeeded in unraveling. In my teens, I had written in my private diary: "Nothing is mine; I belong to no one and no one belongs to me." Yet, one night, which I do not want to remember, someone took me and wrested me from myself and made me his.

When I came to, it was daylight. My first thought was of our Lord's agony in the Garden of Olives. A terrible struggle took place within me. On one hand, I asked myself, why did God allow me to be broken to pieces and destroyed precisely where I had placed my reason for living. And, to what new vocation was He leading me on this new path?

I got up, exhausted, while I helped one of my sisters, and then I got dressed. I heard the bell ring at the Monastery next to ours. I made the sign of the cross and mentally recited the liturgical hymn: "At this hour, on Golgotha, the True Pascal Lamb, Christ, pays the ransom for our sins to redeem us."

What then, Mother, is my suffering and the offense endured, in comparison to that of the One to whom I promised a thousand times to give my life? I said slowly, "Your Will be done, especially now that I have no other support but the certainty that You, Lord, are at my side."

I write to you, Mother, not to seek your consolation, but your help in giving thanks to God for letting me join millions of compatriots, offended in their honor, and to accept this maternity not wished for. My humiliation is added to that of the others. I can only offer it in expiation for the sins committed by the unknown rapists, and for peace between two opposed ethnic groups, by accepting the dishonor I endure and then offer to God's mercy.

Do not hold it against me if I ask you to share with me a "grace" which may seem absurd. These past months, I shed all my tears for my two brothers, assassinated by the very ones who terrorize and attack our towns. I did not think my suffering could be worse, or that the pain could reach any greater dimension.

Every day, hundreds of scrawny-looking people, trembling with cold and bearing a look of despair, knock on the door of our convents. A few weeks ago, a young girl of eighteen told me: "You do not know what dishonor is."

I thought hard about what she said and knew that it was a question of my people in pain, and I was almost ashamed of living close to all this suffering. Now, I am one of them. One of my people's many anonymous women whose body is torn to bits and whose soul is ransacked. The Lord has made me penetrate into the mystery of this shame, and also to the religious that I am. He has accorded me the privilege of understanding the diabolical force of evil.

I know that from now on, the words of courage and consolation I will try to speak from my poor heart will be believed, because my story is their story; my resignation, strengthened by faith, will be, if not an example, of some help to confront their moral and emotional reactions. God has chosen me – may He forgive the presumption – to guide these humiliated people toward a dawn of redemption and freedom. They will not doubt the sincerity of my intentions since, like them, I too come from the frontier of abjectness.

I remember that during my studies in Rome, a Slavic professor of literature had read to me this verse by Alesej Mislovic: "You must not die, because you were chosen to be on the side of light." On the night I was raped by the Serbs, I repeated this verse which was like balm on my soul when despair threatened to destroy me. Now, it is all over and it seems as if it were a bad dream.

All is past, Mother, and now all begins. When you called me on the telephone with words of consolation, for which I will always be grateful, you asked me this question: "What will you do with the life placed by force in your womb?"

I felt your voice tremble while asking this question to which there was no immediate answer. Not because I had not thought of the choice I had to make, but because you did not wish to cloud my decision. I have made my decision now. If I become a mother, the child will be mine and no one else's. I could entrust him to others, but he has the right to my motherly love, even though he was neither desired nor wanted.

We cannot separate a plant from its roots. The grain, fallen into the soil, needs to grow where the mysterious Sower scattered it. I ask nothing of my Congregation, which has already given me everything. I thank my sisters for their fraternal support, especially for not asking embarrassing questions. I will leave with my child. I do not know where, but God, who suddenly shattered my greatest joy, will show me which path to take to accomplish His will.

I will be poor. I will don once more the old apron and sabots, which women wear on working days, and I will go with my mother to collect the resin from the pine trees in our forests. I will do everything in my power to break the chain of hatred that destroys our countries.

To the child I am expecting, I will teach only to love. My child, born from violence, will be a testimony that forgiveness is the unique greatness that glorifies a person.

Commentary: Acceptance of a child borne out of the evil of rape is the embodiment of the ultimate sacrifice of obedience to God. It is obedience and humility. The rarity of willingly embracing both is graphic witness to the preciousness of life.

This holy nun's story reveals Satan's bitter hatred of God's chosen ones, the women who have consecrated their lives to God as nuns. Here, in the destruction of a way of life and vocation by the most hateful of crimes against a woman, is found the very essence, reason, and joy of the messages given by the Blessed Virgin at Medjugorje.

It is a seed that will yield more than a thousand-fold.

One last, but extremely important note: By an unprecedented unanimous consent, the religious community of the victim nun chose to allow her to remain a nun and to assist her in raising the child.

God is good.

"My God, my God, why hast thou abandoned me?
—Matthew 27:46.

EPILOGUE

the joy continues

And so, the joy of Medjugorje remains as the Blessed Virgin Mary continues to come daily to the village of Medjugorje as of this writing. The messages continue to come to all of her children throughout the world. They are, in fact, the lessons all of humankind needs to hear and to follow.

The lessons that are given to us through the messages have shifted slightly in these modern times. In the 36-plus years of daily apparitions, the "teacher" now continually implores us to put them to work in our lives. They are still gentle but more direct and blunt in light of the distressing state of the world today.

The overriding theme of the messages is as it has been since its inception: putting God in the first place and living what Our Lady has given us, which comes directly from the throne of God. This, when accepted and acted on, leads to the *joy,* found in spiritual conversion.

And, conversion is the joy of Medjugorje.

To summarize, the lessons she has given us through her messages at Medjugorje is this: We are to first come to the reality of recognizing our sins and then repenting of them, and we are to do so of our own free will. We are to accept the individual mission given to each of us, put on the armor of God as earned through submission, and then engage in the battle of good (God) versus evil (Satan and the world).

As a result of our waging a successful battle we can change hate into love; we can share what we have with our brothers and sisters who do not as yet know the love of God and its power. We can become children of God and carry on the penance of love, which is simply reaching out to those most in need regardless of the hardship or cost to us.

When the time of hope fully arrives within our hearts and souls, we can then ask God to give us His will in place of ours. We are still graced with the gift of free will so it is our choice. Thus, we choose for our will to be His; and for His will to be ours.

There is a common thread in my mission travels. people want to tell me their spiritual conversion story. They express every detail of it and very often, the usual end is, "I should write a book about my life!"

My answer to them generally is, yes, you should, if for no other reason than for yourself and for your family. Every life is a story worth telling. Each one of us is created in a unique way; there is no one else like us. God waits for the moment when we first engage in our mission and the moment when we finish it.

The finality of it all is that we are His joy!

May the peace, love and joy of God be with us!

Therefore, since we have this ministry through the mercy shown us, we are not discouraged. Rather, we have renounced shameful, hidden things; not acting deceitfully or falsifying the word of God,

but by the open declaration of the truth we commend ourselves to everyone's conscience in the sight of God.

—2 Corinthians 4:1-2.

DONATING TO OUR CHARITIES

Feed My Children

Our charity **Feed My Children** focuses on the people of Karamoja, a tiny corner of northeast Uganda. We are able provide this necessary aid due to the kindness of our monthly newsletter readers and those people I have met through Medjugorje. This year we are also building water wells to give the communities access to fresh water. The fresh water is not only used for the individual's drinking water but also helps the people water their animals and their crops and also prevents them from contacting waterborne illnesses.

Make checks payable to **Feed My Children**

Children of the Sewers

This charity supports the abandoned and abused street children of Bogotá, Columbia. It provides a safe home and an education for the children plus caring for their social and spiritual needs. When they are 18 years old they are also given a good job and supported into adulthood.

Make checks payable to **Children of the Sewers**

Immaculee's Student Sponsorship Program

This charity was born out of my visiting Kibeho, Rwanda. Along with author Immaculee Ilibagiza, we receive donations and sponsor selected children for school and university in Rwanda and seminarians within the Gikongoro diocese where Kibeho is located.

Make checks payable to **Immaculee's Student Sponsorship Program**

Weible Columns, Inc., is a 501C3 nonprofit corporation; as such, all donations are tax deductible.

At the end of the year, all donors receive tax donation letters.

Mail all checks to:

Weible Columns, Inc.

P. O. Box 10, Hiawassee GA 30546

Telephone: 1-877-896-6061 Email: info@weiblecolumns.org

Or visit our website www.weiblecolumns.org and click on donate (No website link to Children of the Sewers (checks only)

What does it profit, my brethren, if a man says he has **faith** but has not works? Can his faith save him? If a brother or sister is ill-clad and in lack of daily food, and one of you says to them, "Go in peace, be warmed and filled, without giving them the things needed for the body, what does it profit? So faith by itself, if it has no **works, is dead.**

—James 2: 14-17.

KEEP UP-TO-DATE ON MEDJUGORJE WITH
WAYNE'S MONTHLY NEWSLETTER

Cost: $27 per year/$50 per 2 years
$40 international per 1 year (we no longer accept international checks, cc only)

- Weekly column by Wayne
- Monthly messages from Medjugorje
- Medjugorje latest news
- Latest books, CDs & DVDs
- Books, music by other authors
- Vatican & church news

- Spiritual testimonies
- Monthly scripture
- Prayer of the month
- Prayer list
- Wayne's speaking schedule
- Medjugorje pilgrimages info.

SUBSCRIBER INFORMATION:
Name: _____
Street: _____
Town: _____ State: _____
Zip: _____
Telephone: _____
Email: _____

PAYMENT INFORMATION:
Credit Card Number: _____
CC Expiration: _____
CC Verif. Code: _____

Or mail check to: Weible Columns Inc, P O Box 10, Hiawassee GA 30546

Or sign up through the website www.weiblecolumns.org and go to tabs "Shop" and then "Medjugorje Newsletter"

Tel: 706-896-6061 Fax: 706-896-1467
Email: info@weiblecolumns.org www.weiblecolumns.org